# Engi-Shiki

## PROCEDURES OF THE ENGI ERA
## BOOKS VI–X

A *Monumenta Nipponica*
Monograph

*from*
*The Japan Foundation*

The Heir Apparent and Princess Michiko in Court Dress
of the Heian Period: for their Wedding, 1959.
(Courtesy of Mainichi Graph)

# *Engi-Shiki*

# PROCEDURES
# OF THE ENGI ERA

## BOOKS VI–X

TRANSLATED WITH INTRODUCTIONS
AND NOTES BY
FELICIA GRESSITT BOCK

PUBLISHED BY
SOPHIA UNIVERSITY, TOKYO

PUBLISHED BY

SOPHIA UNIVERSITY

7 KIOI-CHŌ, CHIYODA-KU

TOKYO, 102

PRINTED IN JAPAN

THE KAWATA PRESS, TOKYO

The research for this volume

was made possible in part by a grant from

The American Council of Learned Societies

CORRIGENDA to _Engi-shiki_ VI-X

| PAGE: | | INCORRECT: | CORRECT: |
|---|---|---|---|
| viii, | no. 26 | Envoy Dispatched | Envoy is Dispatched |
| 40, | l. -8 | shallow | large |
| 44, | l. 9 | " | " |
| 47, | l. -2 | " | " |
| 62, | l. 11 | divine chiefs | shrine chiefs |
| 63, | l. 4 | See no. 7 of the rituals. | (See no. 7 of the rituals.) |
| 69, | n.318 | (Should apply to line 7, first instance) | |
| 70, | l. -2 | divine chiefs | shrine chiefs |
| 71, | l. -9 | " | " |
| 74, | n.340 | , and so forth. | . (delete "and so forth") |
| 182, | under Komura | zakan | zukan |

# CONTENTS

# LIST OF ILLUSTRATIONS

# Chapter One

## INTRODUCTION TO BOOK SIX

### THE PRINCESS CONSECRATED TO THE KAMO SHRINES

THE institution which consisted of having a daughter of the sovereign in attendance at religious ceremonies to deities of the Imperial House at shrines located away from the Imperial Palace developed as a part of the movement to strengthen and solidify the role of the Imperial House and the sovereign during the seventh to tenth centuries in Japan. The first example that comes to mind is that of the Saigū, or Itsuki-no-miya. She was the Imperial Princess appointed to participate on behalf of the sovereign at ceremonies to the Sun Goddess at the Grand Shrine of Ise. The second example is the Sai-in, or Itsuki-no-miko, an Imperial Princess similarly appointed to participate in ceremonies at the Kamo Shrines near the capital. We also see fleeting mention of a princess assigned to the Kasuga Shrine in the capital, but that institution did not really take hold or endure. We may at this point dismiss the Kasuga Princess as an unsuccessful attempt of the Fujiwara Uji[1] to enhance the importance and influence of their own shrine in relation to the state cult.

The most important shrine connected with the Imperial House was that which enshrined Amaterasu-ō-mikami, the Sun Goddess, at Watarai in Ise Province. The worship of the Sun Goddess at that location ante-dated the Nara period. But the elevating of this shrine to national status and the rise of the official cult surrounding the divine ancestress and *ujigami*[2] of the Imperial House came about

[abbreviation *E-S* = *Engi-shiki*]

[1] The *uji* 氏 is the lineage group possessing the same surname, translated as 'clan' or as 'family'. *Uji* of the highest nobility were granted a title called *kabane* 姓, of which there were a great many in the pre-Nara age. During the reign of Temmu Tennō (673–86) the ranking system was revised and a total of only eight *kabane* decreed. However, archaic *kabane* titles continued in use even into the Heian period. Thus in this text we find these hereditary *kabane* attached to the surnames of prominent *uji* on whom they had been conferred— *omi, muraji, asomi* (or *ason*), *atae* (or *atai*), *sukune,* and so on. Thus Tomo no *sukune* refers to a member of the Tomo Uji who had been granted *sukune* rank. At the end of Book VI appear the signatures of five compilers of the *E-S*, chief

of whom was Fujiwara Tadahira; he signs with his titles thus: *omi* (meaning 'chief' or noble') Fujiwara *ason* Tadahira.

[2] A particular *uji* worshiped its own clan deities, or *ujigami*, originally in the locality where the family had settled and had its base. During the Nara period some leading families built new shrines to their *ujigami* in and around the capital. Simultaneously, the Imperial House increased the importance and reverence paid to the Shrine of the Great Deity in Ise, who was the principal deity of that House and the Sun Goddess from which it claimed its descent. After the capital was moved to the Heian-kyō new shrines were erected there, festivals increased, and new cults replaced the old ones of Yamato Province. See N. Miyaji, *Jingi-shi taikei*, p. 45.

toward the end of the seventh century. After that time the adjective 'great' or 'grand' came to be used for the Ise Shrines and the number of districts and households designated to support these shrines was vastly increased. The institution of Imperial Princess to serve at the Ise Shrines may have had its origin in the type of gynecocracy that prevailed in parts of Japan prior to the formation of a centralized Yamato state. The rule of women among certain tribes, or their function as high priestess or shaman for the tribe, may have been the remote precedents of the custom of having an imperial virgin presiding over ceremonies to the clan deities of the ruling house. The appointment of a princess to represent the throne at the Ise Shrines was a prominent and long-enduring institution, though no provision for it is written into the law codes that were drawn up in the Taihō and Yōrō eras,[3] since these law codes were based very much upon Chinese models not containing annual requirements for ceremonies to the gods. The actual practices connected with the Ise Shrines were not set down until the Enryaku era, in the *Kōtaijingū-gishiki-chō*, and later in the procedures of the Engi era, the *Engi-shiki*, completed in A.D. 927. Out of the fifty books (*kan*) therein, the longest is devoted to procedures for the Bureau of the Consecrated Princess, the Itsuki-no-miya of Ise, and the third longest to procedures and specifications for the Ise Shrines. The book containing procedures for the Office of Consecrated Princess, the Sai-in, of the Kamo Shrines, is one of the shorter books.

The consecrating of an imperial princess for service to the deities of Kamo appears to have come about in an entirely different manner from that of the one to the Great Deity of Ise. The Consecrated Princess of Kamo is perhaps unique in Japanese history because it is an institution whose beginning and end are fairly accurately known, as well as the names of the individuals who held the office. There are of course superficial resemblances between the Kamo Princess and the Ise Princess. First, both are extra-legal institutions[4] not treated in the Yōrō civil code. Secondly, the method of selection by divination after the accession of a new sovereign, the appointment, the special offerings, the three-year period of preparation, the royal progress when she assumed office, the duration of her term and reasons for termination of office—all are parallel.

However, the custom of appointing a princess to the deities of Kamo did not commence until the beginning of the Heian period. The deities of Kamo are not mentioned in the *Nihongi*, nor is their festival. The first references to the *Kamo* Festival occur in *Shoku-nihongi* in the 2nd year of Mommu Tennō (A.D. 698) and

---

[3] The Taihō codes of law completed A.D. 701–2 were the culmination of a long process of drawing up a framework of law based on Chinese models of Sui and T'ang. Soon afterward these were supplanted by the Yōrō codes of 718, the only complete codes extant. While these were the basis of administration, they did not adapt fully to existing Japanese custom. The codes needed interpretation and extension. For these purposes

the *shiki*, or procedures, were spelled out for the use of officialdom. The lengthy process of drafting and compiling these procedures resulted in the *Engi-shiki* of 927.

[4] Known as *ryōgai* 令外 'outside the codes', the *shiki* for the princess sent to Kamo as well as those for the princess sent to Ise Shrines, and procedures for the shrines themselves, are all supplementary to the *ryō*, or civil code.

the 4th year of Wadō (711), while the deities of Kamo are mentioned in connection with receiving offerings in entries under Taihō, Jinki, Tempyō, Ten'ō, and Enryaku. In the *Nihon-kōki* they came to be referred to as the Great Deities of Kamo, and, in the *Shoku-nihon-kōki* and *Montoku-jitsuroku*, offerings to these deities are specified (in some entries) as being made at the *Amagoi-matsuri* (Festival of Praying for Rain) and also the *Haregoi* (Festival of Praying for Clear Weather). Later entries include records of the reading of important Buddhist sutras at the Kamo Shrines.[5]

The first sovereign to appoint an imperial princess to represent the Imperial House at the Kamo Shrines was Saga Tennō in either the 1st or the 14th year of the Kōnin era (810 or 823). The records say she was Princess Uchiko, either the second or the eighth daughter of Saga Tennō, and that her mother was Queen Kōno.[6] This was the beginning of a succession of 34 imperial princesses who were selected and appointed to serve the deities of the Kamo Shrines, the very last one having been selected in Genkyū 1 (A.D. 1204); this means that the institution lasted nearly four centuries, and it shows the perpetuation of the practice by many a sovereign upon his accession to the throne. The complete record of the princesses who served in this role and the sovereigns whom they represented is found in the *Kamo Saiin-ki*, reproduced below in Appendix I.

The significance of the appointing of a princess to the Kamo Shrines and the regulations surrounding her assignment, her term of office and the participation of the Court and nobility in the *Kamo* Festival, all relate to the high position of the Kamo Shrines and their connection with important clans, notably the Imperial House. Let us look at the historical evidence that is available. The two shrines, Lower Kamo and Upper Kamo, were dedicated to tutelary divinities of the capital. But they were located in Yamashiro Province, into which the capital was removed only in 790, and ascent to the shrines after that time meant crossing the boundary from the capital into the province. They seem to have had little prominence while the capital was still at Nara. However, they trace their history as far back as the 6th year of Temmu Tennō (677), when the worship of the divinities in question was moved from the base of Mt Hiei (where the proto-shrine Mikage Jinja, an auxiliary of Kamo Shrines, still exists) to the base of Mt Kamo. This mountain was situated in the northern part of Yamashiro, an area which was the seat of power of two influential families—the Kamo Uji and the Hata Uji—who were in charge of the worship of these ancestral deities. Other seats of worship for these families in the seventh and eighth centuries were at Matsuno-o in the western part of the province and Inari Shrine in the southeast. After the capital was moved to the Heian-kyō (Kyoto), the Kamo Shrines came under direct influence of the Court. In Enryaku 3 (784) the Court Rank of these ancestral deities had been raised to Junior 2nd Rank, and (after the new capital was established) in 807 they

---

[5] References are cited in *Shoku-nihongi sakuin* and *Rikkokushi sakuin*, vol. 3.

[6] According to the old shrine records, *Kamo*

*Kōtaijingū-ki*, the selection by divination of the first princess to serve the deities of Kamo was in Kōnin 1 (810). See *Kamo chūshin zakki*, p. 40.

were elevated to Senior First Rank. Correspondingly, the lands supporting the shrines were increased. In the Tempyō era (729–69) lands supporting the Upper Kamo Shrine had been greatly augmented: from one *chō* up to 24 sustenance households[7]—14 in Yamashiro and 10 in Tamba Province. An imperial visit to the Upper Shrine was recorded in Enryaku 13 (794) and in Kashō 3 (850) special offerings were made at that shrine upon the accession of the new sovereign, Montoku Tennō. As for Saga Tennō (r. 809–23), R. K. Reischauer says it was his purpose to have his daughter pray to the deities of Kamo to invoke their aid in settling his dispute with Heijō Tennō, the preceding sovereign, who was trying to gain the throne.[8] Whatever the reason, he provided for the capital a close-at-hand cult of ancestral *kami* which flourished thereafter.

Who were these deities of Kamo? The traditions of both Lower and Upper Kamo Shrines hark back to the mythical age. The Lower, or Mioya (august ancestors), Shrine is said to enshrine Tamayori-hime and Taketsunumi-no-mikoto, divine forbears of the legendary first emperor, Jimmu Tennō. Taketsunumi is described as the deity who took the form of a huge crow (the *yatagarasu*) which guided Jimmu Tennō on his eastward path of conquest to Yamato. The Upper Shrine is that of Kamo no Wake-ikazuchi-no-mikoto, divine offspring of Tamayori-hime, who was said to have come to the sacred spot (*miare-sho*) at the foot of the mountain of Kamo to found a holy site there. Both shrines are said to have had buildings erected at their present sites during the reign of Temmu Tennō in the seventh century, and after that time to have enjoyed special reverence from the Imperial House. Although the Hata (an *uji* of Korean origin) and the Kamo families had charge of administering the shrines all along, the Imperial House felt the need to reverence these three deities as ancestral *kami* of its own, and hence gave increasing support to the shrines and to the holding of the festival of these shrines.[9]

Celebration of the *Kamo* Festival is alleged to have been instituted in the reign of Kimmei Tennō in the sixth century! But actually we do not find any mention of it in historical works until the very end of the seventh century in the reign of Mommu Tennō. After the capital was moved to Heian-kyō we find it mentioned as an imperially decreed festival in the reign of Kammu Tennō, in 806; and in the reign of Saga Tennō, in Kōnin 10 (819), it is classified as a 'middle festival'—as it appears in the *Engi-shiki*, Book I.

In the Heian period the festival was celebrated in two different parts: the first was the esoteric festival of *miare*, the second was the colorful public celebration through the streets of the capital. These two elements have been preserved to the

---

[7] Sustenance households, *fuko* or *fugo* 封戸, were those assigned to supply rice and other produce to the Imperial Household, and to high nobility. Those providing sustenance to shrines were *kami fuko* 神封戸, or simply *shinko* 神戸 (also pronounced *kambe*).

[8] R. K. Reischauer, *Early Japanese History*, A, p. 234. This puts the appointment of the prin-

cess in Daidō 4 (809), though the *Kamo Saiin-ki* places the event in 823.

[9] See *Shintō daijiten*, II, 280. The legends concerning the origins of the shrines are found in the *Shaku-nihongi*, quoted from the *Yamashiro fudoki*, the gazetteer of Yamashiro Province written in the Nara period of which only fragments survive. H. Kurita, *Ko-fudoki*, pp. 3–5.

present day. In the secret celebration, the youthful deity Kamo no Wake-ikazuchi-no-mikoto was believed to make his annual return to the sacred spot, the *miare-sho*. *Miare* has been interpreted as 'resurrection'. But in truth it means either 'august birth' or 'august appearance'. This rite is the reappearance or return to earth of a deity from on high. Belief in the return of a *kami* was prevalent, and the evidence for it was the practice in ancient times of having a young maiden await the return of a deity to a spot designated as sacred. She might sit on the shore of the sea or the bank of a river and in the dead of night be waiting to receive the *kami* who came from over the sea, or down from heaven, or from his divine abode on a mountain. The *kami* returns to earth and is greeted by the beautiful maiden, who becomes his bride for a night.

In the case of the Upper Kamo Shrine, the secret *miare-matsuri* is the celebration of the descent of Wake-ikazuchi from heaven to alight on a great rock that is situated on the top of the sacred mountain Kōyama (Kamiyama), the mountain of Kamo at whose base the Upper Shrine is located. Tradition says that priests of the Kamo Uji from time immemorial have sung the following hymn to hail the return of the *kami*:

| | |
|---|---|
| *Hisakata no* | Plying the oars of the |
| *ame no iwabune* | worthy rock-boat |
| *kogi yosete* | from far-away heaven |
| *kamiyo no ura ya* | from the haven of *kami* |
| *ima no miare-sho.* | comes he to the spot of divine revelation. |

To prepare for the divine reappearance, the participating priests were wont to cut two trees (called *miare-gi*), tying cords to them by which to pull the trees after the *kami* had alighted on them. Thus in the dark of night he was to be borne away to the river of Kamo and there the trees were thrown into the water. Hereupon, the Consecrated Princess (Itsuki-no-miko) was to plunge into the river and rescue the *kami*. The priests floated offerings from upstream and the maiden princess became the bride of a night to the god.[10]

The specifications for the Lower Shrine state that there are two *honden* or main sanctuaries: the one on the east for Tamayori-hime-no-mikoto, the one to the west for Taketsunumi-no-mikoto. Likewise, at the Upper Shrine there are two small sanctuaries side by side. Nowadays it is interpreted to mean that there is a spare shrine in reserve. But we see by the *Engi-shiki* text that there were two *shinza* (deity seats), without any explanation given for them, since but a single god, Wake-ikazuchi-no-mikoto, was enshrined there.

Before Saga Tennō set the precedent of sending an imperial princess to be the one to receive the god at Upper Kamo Shrine, what was the essence of the secret ceremony? A possible clue lies in an old term (which survives even today) used for the Sai-in or Consecrated Princess, namely, *miare-otome*, or 'maiden of the

---

[10] N. Tsukushi, *Amaterasu no tanjō*, pp. 31–2. Text of the song, and other songs of praise to the *kami*, are given in *Kamo chūshin zakki*, pp. 8–10.

See also, S. Origuchi, *Kodai kenkyū* (II), pp. 100 ff.

divine reappearance'. The likelihood is that in the local family festival held by the Kamo Uji a member of the Hata or the Kamo was chosen to be the bride of the *kami* and await his mysterious return to earth. Later on, after the capital was moved and the relation of the Court to the shrines was strengthened, it was the sovereign who sent his daughter. This replaced the former custom of having the daughter of one of the local magnates lead the ceremonies of *miare* for Kamo no Wake-ikazuchi-no-mikoto.

The *Kamo* Festival which followed the rite of *miare* was for the participation of the Court and the host of officials who constituted the high nobility. It grew rapidly into a great pageant which displayed the wealth and splendor of the Imperial House for the benefit of all the inhabitants of the capital city. The growth in importance of the Kamo Shrines and their festival may at the same time have been part of the revitalizing of native worship in response to the lavish attention paid to Buddhism by the Court of Nara—against which the very removal of the capital to a new location had been a reaction. The extravagant outlay made by the Imperial Household for the Kamo Princess and the *Kamo* Festival made this festival the greatest public celebration of the year in the new capital.

When the Princess made her progress to the Shrines the procession was a grand parade with mounted ladies in the vanguard and the Princess in a gilded carriage, attended by noble men and women attired in finest silks followed by countless ladies-in-waiting, pages, bearers, and servants—all elaborately costumed for the event. The functionaries of the *Jingi-kan* and priests of the shrines were dressed in ceremonial robes and donned the fresh green leaves of the wild hollyhock (*aoi*) or of the *katsura* tree (the shape of whose leaves resembles the former) at their temples. Eventually, because the leaves of *aoi* became the symbol of this celebration, it came to be called the *Aoi* Festival. The celebration has undergone its vicissitudes since the Heian period, but in the course of a revival of ancient practices, in the 5th year of Meiji (1872), both the secret festival of *miare* and the *Aoi-matsuri* were reinstated. One can attend the *Aoi*, or *Kamo*, Festival on 15 May in the city of Kyoto, while the secret ceremonies of *miare* are conducted on the night of 12 May by the priests of the Upper Kamo Shrine. One priest is charged with the role of receiving the returning god, Wake-ikazuchi, at the sacred site where a *himorogi*[11] is constructed at the base of the sacred mountain above the Upper Shrine. Nowadays a young maiden of a good family is selected to be the Saiō, or consecrated maiden, to re-enact the former role of the imperial princess.

It might be thought that, because this festival occurred in spring in the 4th month and its origin appears to be rooted in the tradition of the return of the youthful god Wake-ikazuchi, it was a spring fertility rite. However, the time of year coincides neither with the planting of the rice nor with its transplanting. The idea of renewal and rebirth is very strong, and the *aoi* and *katsura* leaves used as fillets symbolize new life and rededication. But it is a festival of late spring. The

---

[11] The *himorogi* is a sacred enclosure or area marked off around a sacred object or abode of *kami*. The present-day enclosure is quite large and was photographed by Mr Numabe Harutomo of Kokugakuin Daigaku on a visit to Upper Kamo Shrine at the time of the secret *miare* festival.

connection with agriculture appears to be that the god Wake-ikazuchi is associated with thunder, and it is the proper time of year to pray for deliverance from thunderstorms or rains that would be disastrous to crops. The sporadic references in the national histories to offerings presented to the deities of Kamo at the extraordinary *Amagoi* (Praying for Rain) Festival and *Haregoi* (Praying for Clear Weather) Festival lend weight to the idea that the Kamo was a festival to ensure the safe growth of the crops in the environs of the capital, as well as to propitiate the patron deities of the capital and the Imperial House.

After an imperial princess was selected by divination to serve the deities of Kamo, she dwelt with her retinue in a taboo apartment called Shosai-in somewhere within the Imperial Palace. Here she dwelt until after the middle of the following year, when she moved to a separate palace near the Kamo Shrines and made her first ascent to the shrines. This No-no-miya, or 'Palace-in-the-fields', was her sanctified abode for the rest of her term of office. Her term lasted as long as the sovereign who appointed her was on the throne. Like the princess consecrated to Ise Shrines, she must withdraw from office if the reigning sovereign should become ill, die, or abdicate, or if either of her parents (the sovereign might be her grandfather) became ill, or if she herself was ill or committed an indiscretion. Any of these conditions would constitute a pollution and make her unfit to serve the *kami*.

The government office set up to take charge of all matters relating to this princess was the *Saiin-shi (Itsuki-no-miko no tsukasa)*. The officials of this office were: chief (*kami*), assistant chief (*suke*), third officer (*jō*), and fourth officer (*sōkan*). Besides this hierarchy common to most offices and bureaus under the government ministries, this office also had the *in-no-bettō*—male and female commissioners of her residence, and the retinue of Court nobility who were customarily attendants to a member of the Imperial Family, namely: ladies-in-waiting (*naishi*), ladies who were confidential transmitters of the sovereign's commands (*senjï*), and ladies who personally attended the sovereign and members of his family (the *uneme*), not to mention young girl attendants who were daughters of high-ranking nobility.

The duties of the Kamo Princess were strict religious observance of fasting periods, festivals, and special offerings, culminating in the festival for the Kamo deities held in the 4th month of the lunar calendar. Her first participation in the festival was in the third year after her appointment. The procedures for her period of preparation, abstinence, purification, ritual cleansing in the river, and the exorcising of the buildings in which she and her staff were to reside, are all contained in the sixth book of the *Engi-shiki*, the principal items being as follows:

1. Item on the selection of the Saiō (*Itsuki-no-miko wo sadamaru*)
2. Taboo words (*imikotoba*)
3. Purification and lustration at the river (*kawa no hotori no oharae*)
4. Item on three years' abstinence (*sannen itsuki*)
5. The *Kamo* Festival (*Kamo-matsuri*), including:
   a. Blessing the Princess's Residence (*Ootono-hogai*)
   b. Festival of the Sacred Fire and Deity of the Stove

    c. Lustration in the 4th month and 6th month
    d. Purification on the last day of each month
    e. First day of the year.

It is apparent that this collection of procedures does not follow a chronological sequence throughout, and that it does not cover some events of her tenure at all. Comparing it to the lengthy detailed procedures for the Princess to Ise Shrines in Book V, we find that many things—such as the building of the No-no-miya, for example—are not mentioned. This may indicate that officials simply referred to another source, as the *Jōgan-gishiki*, or the procedures already laid down for the Ise Princess, so it was not considered necessary to give details of procedures which were common to both institutions, the Saigū and the Saiō (Sai-in).

More than half of the book is given over to procedures for the *Kamo* Festival, which grew to be the grandest celebration in the capital, at least in the year when the princess participated. Here we reach the ultimate in a national extravaganza for the enjoyment of the Kamo deities, the Court, and the population of the capital. Very little is written concerning the more sacred and intimate portions of the festival, the secret *miare* festival, or the sacred communion with the deities of Kamo and the frequency of offerings made to them. We do have details on the amounts of offerings to the *kami*, on the ceremonial vessels, foodstuffs, decorations, furnishings, and costumes of all participants, and on the emoluments to be given them. The countless bolts of silk to be hand woven and hand dyed attest to the wealth of the Court and the highly developed textile arts. The treasures of the Kamo shrines and the utensils and paraphernalia listed show the technical advancement of the early Heian period.

Besides the detailed procedures of Book VI, we find that the Kamo Princess and the *Kamo* Festival appear in other books of the *Engi-shiki*. The Kamo Princess is referred to in procedures for the *Dajō-kan*, Bk XI; the *Kamo* Festival is mentioned in Bk I, in Bk XIII in procedures for the Consort's Palace (*Chūgū-shiki*), and in Bk XV under the Bureau of Palace Storehouses (*uchino-kura-ryō*). In Bk XVII under the Bureau of Skilled Artisans, procedures for making furnishings for the No-no-miya are given, and elsewhere there are references to the Office of the Princess under bureaus that are mentioned in Bk VI.

# ENGI-SHIKI, BOOK SIX

*Procedures for the Saiin-shi*

## OFFICE OF THE PRINCESS CONSECRATED
## TO THE KAMO SHRINES

### Translation

AT ALL times, when a Sovereign accedes[12] to the throne he appoints a Consecrated Princess to the Great Deities of Kamo.[13] That is to say, an unmarried Imperial Princess[14] is chosen by means of divination.[15] (If an Imperial Princess is not available, another princess, in order of succession, is chosen by divination.) When the divination is completed an Imperial Messenger is dispatched to her dwelling and announces the fact of her appointment. One official, not lower than a secretary of the *Jingi-kan*,[16] leading the bureaucrats,[17] follows the Imperial Messenger, and together they make the visit. The

---

[12] The event of succeeding to the throne upon the death or abdication of the preceding sovereign is *sokui* 即位, 'accession'. This is discussed in the introduction to Bk VII, below.

[13] The divine parents, *mi-oya*, enshrined in the Lower Kamo (Shimogamo) Shrine were believed to be Tamayori-hime and Taketsunumi-no-mikoto. This is the main shrine, *honsha*. Tamayori-hime appears in the myths as aunt, then later consort, of Hikonagisa-take-u-gaya-fuki-ahezu-no-mikoto, and mother of the 'first emperor', Jimmu. Taketsunumi is identified with the crow sent down by Amaterasu-ō-mikami to guide Jimmu Tennō through the land. Cf. Aston, *Nihongi*, pp. 104, 108, 115-16. The upper shrine (Kamigamo) is erected to Wakeikazuchi-no-kami (or -kami). However, the presence of the *kami* is not indicated in the shrine. Rather, on looking within, the worshiper sees through the shrine to the sacred mountain behind, so that he worships the place to which the *kami* will descend when he does reappear on earth. Tsukushi, op. cit. p. 31. The text of Bk VI tells us that two august seats for *kami* (*go-shinza*) were to be set up in the Wakeikazuchi Shrine, as well as in the Lower Kamo Shrine. Even today there are

duplicate shrines at the upper site. See n. 68 below.

[14] Imperial Princess is *naishinnō* ('inner princess'); she is one not yet given in marriage: '*imada totsugazaru mono* . . .' No age requirement is stated, and often a princess was very young when selected and appointed.

[15] Selection is determined by divination. Here *uranau* (or *boku-su*) is performed by the occupational diviners, *urabe* 卜部, of the *Jingi-kan*. According to the Taihō civil code, the make-up of the *Jingi-kan* included 28 *urabe* diviners, as well as chief diviners, *miyaju* (*miyaji*), and masters of tortoise divination, *urabe chōjō*.

[16] Text says, 'one person, secretary of the *Jingi-kan*, or higher'. The chief of the *Jingi-kan* was the *jingi-haku* or *jingi-no-kami* 神祇伯 (the first officer or *chōkan* 長官), who according to the code must be of 4th Court Rank, Junior Grade. Second official was the senior assistant chief, *taiyū* 大副, who must be of 5th Court Rank. Next came junior assistant, *shōyū* 少副, and the secretaries, *taijō* 大祐 and *shōjō* 少祐 —therefore providing a choice from among five possible officials to lead this procession.

[17] That is, *ryōka* 僚下.

diviners perform exorcism; members of the *kambe*[18] hang bark-cloth[19] upon *sakaki* branches[20] which they set around the four sides of her sleeping-hall as well as inside and outside the gates. (The officials in charge prepare the bark-cloth and *sakaki*; the household prepares the articles for the exorcism.) When these affairs are finished, emoluments are bestowed. Nakatomi, Imbe, and below are differentiated.) After this an Imperial Adviser, or higher, is dispatched to both the Upper and Lower Kamo Shrines. He presents symbolic offerings[21] and announces the selection of the Consecrated Princess. (The Bureau of Palace Storehouses[22] prepares the offerings. One diviner follows this messenger, goes to the riverside, faces the shrines, and performs exorcism.)

At all times, there are taboo words:[23] death is called 'getting well', illness is called 'slumber', weeping is 'shedding salt', blood is called 'sweat', meat is called 'vegetables',[24] to strike is 'to caress', and a tomb is called 'clod of earth'.

At all times, when the selection of the Consecrated Princess has been made, a suitable place within the Palace precinct is determined by divination for the Shosai-in.[25] First she goes to the riverside and performs purification and lustration,[26] after that she enters in.

*Articles for the Purification*
　　4 *shaku* each of 5 colors of pongee,[27] 2 *shō* of salt, 1 *to* each of rice and sake,

---

[18] In the composition of the *Jingi-kan*, according to the *Taihō-ryō*, there were 30 members of the religious group known as *kambe* or *kamutomo* 神部. Most of them were members of the Nakatomi Uji.

[19] Bark-cloth and hemp were the primeval fibres used for clothing and for offerings to the *kami*. Bark-cloth, called *yū* 木綿, was made from the paper-mulberry by stripping, soaking, and pounding the inner bark. Two varieties used were (and are): *kaji* 構 (*Broussonetia kazinoki*), and *kōzo* 楮 (*Broussonetia payrifera*). The hemp used were *asa* 麻 and *kemushi* 枲 (male nettle hemp), which were woven into common cloth, *nuno* or *fu* 布. Other types of fibres commonly used for clothing included ramie, kudzu, wisteria, and tree bark.

[20] *Sakaki* (*Cleyera japonica*) is a tree with shiny dark-green leaves, sacred to the *kami*.

[21] The *mitegura* or *mi-nusa* 幣 were symbolic offerings, usually of cloth, as opposed to food offerings, expiatory offerings, and presentations of tools, weapons, animals, etc. They usually were in the form of strips of cloth, or hangings of bark-cloth and hemp fibres (later silk), or else a branch of the sacred *sakaki* tree (plain, or decorated with streamers of cloth or paper). See n. 438 below.

[22] The *uchinokura-ryō* under the Ministry of Central Affairs, *nakatsukasa-shō*.

[23] A comparatively short list of seven taboo words, *imikotoba* 忌詞, is given here. For the Princess consecrated to Ise Shrines a total of 16 words were tabooed; besides the seven listed here, nine words having to do with Buddhism (hence offensive to the *kami*). See the list given in Bk VII of words likewise tabooed in the presence of the sovereign during the month of abstinence preceding the New Food Festival.

[24] *Shishi* 穴: animal meat, usually deer; *kusabira* 菌: greens or vegetables. T. Torao, *Engi-shiki*, p. 100.

[25] The Shosai-in 初齋院 is the first residence of the princess.

[26] *Harae* or *harai* 祓, lit. 'driving out', is the exorcizing of pollution and defilement. The ritual washing in the river, for the purpose of washing away defilement, is *misogi* 潔 (in the case of the sovereign, *gokei*): lustration.

[27] Pongee, or rough silk, was *ashiginu* 縑. *Goshiki* 五色 may mean 'five kinds' or 'five colors'; it is probably the latter here. The colors were blue, derived from the wild indigo plant (*ai* 藍); red, from fine red-yellow earth; yellow, from seeds of gardenia; white, from bleaching; and black, from dye made of the acorn-like nut of the *tsurubami* 橡 (*Corylus heterophylla*). For values of measurements, see Table of Measurements, p. 173.

3 *kin* each of abalone,[28] bonito, and *wakame*,[29] 1 gourd,[30] 1 palanquin (and carrying-poles for it), 2 *tan* of tax cloth,[31] 2 food-mats, 5 *kin* of yellow-bark,[32] 3 *ryō* of Aki bark-cloth,[33] 1 *kin* each of ordinary bark-cloth and hemp, 2 mattocks,[34] 2 *soku* of rice-in-ear, two porters.

The above, as listed in foregoing item, must be requested from the *Jingi-kan* and used. Two days before the lustration, Controllers of the *Dajō-kan*[35] lead the Commissioner of the Residence[36] and those under them, as well as the Bureau of Divination[37] and the various officials who are to present offerings. They go to the riverbank to determine the exact spot, and they announce it. When the season and day have arrived, the Consecrated Princess rides in a carriage to the spot. [For this] 10 pages on foot,[38] 14 carriage attendants, 10 followers, 10 carriers; one each: Kara chests[39] of adornments and of toilet articles (for porters use servants of the residence),[40] 3 Kara chests of foodstuffs, 2 of various utensils, 2 of clothing, 6 Kara chests of emoluments (for porters and Palace guards); 6 chefs, 2 *toneri*,[41] 10 bearers, 6 escorts from the Sovereign's Private Office,[42] the Lady

[28] The *awabi* 鰒 is sea-ear, or abalone, of which some ten varieties are gathered along the coasts of Japan. Its importance for food and for ceremonial offerings is not outdone by any other item save rice and sake. It was eaten raw, made into broth, or dried and salted. For the varieties, see S. Koyama, 'Kodai awabi sangyō no hattatsu', *Kokushigaku*, No. 81, March 1970, pp. 18–39. Bonito, *katsuo* 堅魚, either fresh or dried, almost always follows abalone in order of presentation.

[29] *Wakame*, or *me*, 海藻, is a common edible seaweed; varieties are *Undaria pinnatifida Sur.* and *Alaria pinnatifida*.

[30] Different sorts of gourds were used as dippers. The character given here is *narihisago* 匏, which Thunberg reports Kaempfer identified as *Cucurbita lagenaria*. Cf. Thunberg, *Miscellaneous papers*. A 'dipper' held 1/10th of a *gō*.

[31] *Yōfu* 庸布 (*chikarashiro-nuno*) signified cloth made of hemp paid in lieu of labor, sometimes translated '*corvée* cloth'. By the time of the *E-S* forced labor had long been outlawed, so we can simply think of it as 'tax cloth'. Cloth unspecified means hempen cloth. See also nn. 71 and 93 below, on tribute stuffs.

[32] Yellow-bark, *kihada* 黄蘗, refers to the inner bark of a kind of oak, *Pterocarpus flavus*, which was used both as medicine and as a dyestuff. The dye is described as 'chrome lemon' (*kihada-iro*). Cf. *Shikimei daijiten*.

[33] Aki Province on the Inland Sea was between Bingo and Suō Provinces, roughly present-day Yamaguchi Prefecture.

[34] The character 鍫 or 鍬 may be read either *kuwa*, mattock or hoe, or *suki*, spade. In either case, these are ceremonial tools related to the cultivation of rice and used as votive offerings to the *kami*.

[35] The *ben* or *benkan* 辨官, of which there were three grades (two each): 'great, middle, and lesser', in the *Dajō-kan* (Great Council of State). See n. 59 below. *Benkan* were assigned, one each, to the various ministries as observers or inspectors.

[36] The *in-no-bettō* 院別當 were commissioners of the princess's residence.

[37] The Bureau of Yin-yang Divination, *on'yō-ryō* (*ommyō-ryō*) 陰陽寮, under the Ministry of Central Affairs (*nakatsukasa-shō*).

[38] *Hashiri-warawa* 走孺: children on foot, probably girls. The carriage attendants are *hito-tamae* or *kuruma-soe* 車副.

[39] The name *kara* 韓 meant either Korean or Chinese in style, in other words, continental or exotic. The *karabitsu* 韓櫃 were large, six-legged wooden chests of Chinese style which were carried hung from a pole by two porters.

[40] *Imaryō* 今良 were menials, sweepers, caretakers—but not slaves.

[41] The *toneri* 舍人 were part of a system made up of youths of the nobility who automatically attained Court Rank at age 21. They were selected from some 100 noble families of the 4th and 5th Rank. They served as personal palace attendants to guard and accompany members of the sovereign's family. Besides *toneri*, the system included 'great toneri' (*ōdoneri*), 'inner toneri' (*utoneri*), and others. The Bureau of Toneri was under the *nakatsukasa-shō*.

[42] That is, *kurōdo-dokoro no baijū* 藏人所陪從. The *kurōdo-dokoro* (not provided for in the codes) was established in Kōnin 1 (810) in order to maintain the strictest confidence with affairs relating to the sovereign. The office continued thenceforth to grow in political importance and influence.

Commissioners of the Residence and those under them, all follow behind her carriage. (Lady Commissioners on down to escorts from the Sovereign's Private Office ride in their own carriages; *uneme*,[43] girl attendants, and below, ride in carriages provided by the Mount Bureau.)[44] One Imperial Messenger who is an Imperial Adviser,[45] one Commissioner of the Residence, four persons of 5th Rank, four of 6th Rank, as well as outriders, two each of Left and Right Inner Palace Guards, Left and Right Military Guards, and Left and Right Gate Guards; ten each of Left and Right Fire Chiefs, all follow. Officials of the Left and Right Offices of the Capital lead the soldiers and officers, who draw up and wait. The governor of Yamashiro Province leads the prefects of the districts and they wait at the road which borders the capital.[46] One controller, one chief ritualist,[47] two scribes, and one office-keeper[48] lead the participating officials to the place of lustration, and the ceremony takes place. The Consecrated Princess reaches the curtain, goes down to the stream, and performs lustration. The Nakatomi of the *Jingi-kan* present the symbolic offerings and the chief diviner[49] recites the ritual of purification.[50] That finished, the food and emoluments are bestowed on all, from Imperial Messenger on down. (The controllers record those in attendance and report this to the commissioners.) The Princess now has returned and has re-entered the Shosai-in. A well for her menage is determined by divination and *sakaki* branches placed around it.

*Requirements for Festival of the Well*

4 *shaku* each of 5 colors of pongee, 1 *hiki* of stiff silk,[51] 1 skein of silk thread, 4 *shaku* of colored hemp-cloth,[52] 1 *ton* of floss silk,[53] 1 *tan* of ordinary cloth, 2 *tan* of tax cloth, 2 mattocks, 2 *kin* of hemp, 1 *kin* of bark-cloth, 4 *kin* each of

[43] The *uneme* 采女 were young women chosen for their beauty from various parts of the country to reside in the Palace and wait upon the sovereign personally. Because they served his food, the derivation of the name is thought to be from *yoneme*, 'rice ladies', but this is not certain. The Office of Uneme was under the Ministry of the Imperial Household (*kunai-shō*).

[44] The *meryō*, or Bureau of the Mount, was divided into Right and Left divisions: *sayū meryō* 左右馬寮.

[45] i.e. an Imperial Adviser, *sangi* 参議, who is chosen to represent the Throne as Imperial Messenger, *chokushi* 勅使, for the occasion.

[46] The Kamo shrines were then in Yamashiro Province, right outside the capital. The governor and the prefects of the districts through which the princess's procession passes come to greet her and her retinue at the point where she crosses the boundary leaving the capital and entering Yamashiro Province.

[47] The term *sōkan* (*sakan*) 主典 (also written 史, as here) means a fourth-class official; in this case, of the Princess's Office, *Saiin-shi*. The first official of an office or bureau was the *kami* or *chōkan*, the second the *suke*, the third the *jō*.

These were the highest four officials, or the four 'classes' of officials.

[48] The scribe is *shishō* 史生; the office-keeper, *kajō* 官掌.

[49] The *miyaju* (*miyaji*) 宮主 of the *Saiin-shi*.

[50] The *harae no kotoba* 祓詞, a ritual of exorcism for this purification ceremony. Presumably this is a shorter and less elaborate ritual than that for the Great Purification, *Ooharae no kotoba*, given in Bk VIII in the collection of *norito*.

[51] This is *katori* or *ken* 絹, a thick silk with nap, used for outer garments. To distinguish it from *hakunokinu* 帛, which is flat and without nap (like modern *habutae*), it is translated 'stiff silk'.

[52] This is *shizu* or *shidori* 倭文, a textile in which the woof was of threads dyed blue, red, and other colors, resulting in a mottled pattern. Usually hemp fibre was used for this, but bark-cloth and ramie might also be woven in this manner.

[53] Floss silk, *men* 綿 or 緜, was used for the wadding or padding of winter garments and quilts. Because of its consistency it was weighed, and the unit of weight was *ton*, or *mochi* 屯, equivalent to 13 ounces or again, according to the *Wamyōshō*, equivalent to 7.8 ounces.

bonito and abalone, 4 *kin* of dried meat,[54] 4 *kin* of *wakame*, 5 *shō* of salt, 1 *to* each of rice and sake, 1 waterbucket, 8 saucers, one gourd, 5 bundles of oak.

The above are requested from the [*Dajō-*]*kan* by the *Jingi-kan*; the chief ritualist is caused to conduct the festival.

At all times, the Consecrated Princess spends three years in abstinence in the Shosai-in. When it is completed, that year in the 4th month she ascends for the first time to the [Kamo] Shrines. Beforehand an auspicious day is chosen and she goes down to the stream for purification and lustration. (Requirements for presentations to the deities are the same as at the first lustration.) The ceremony is that the Princess rides in a palanquin (an official of the Palace Caretakers[55] leading the scribes sets up said palanquin two days before the day of lustration). There are 10 chiefs of the palanquin (wearing yellow tunics); 40 bearers of the palanquin (dressed in dark blue), 12 Outer Palace Guards (two each of Left and Right Inner Palace Guards, Middle Palace Guards, Gate Guards, all wearing blue-printed white tunics of the Guard Headquarters; except that for Gate Guards, if convenient, guards of the Shosai-in may be used); 10 each of Left and Right Fire Chiefs, officials of the capital and the official greeters[56] of Yamashiro Province. And similarly to the time of the first lustration, 16 ladies riding horseback, (2 wet-nurses,[57] 6 members of the Sovereign's Private Office, 4 girl attendants, and 2 young girls), 10 pages on foot; one each: Kara chests for adornments and for toilet articles; 3 Kara chests for foodstuffs and 2 for the utensils, 2 Kara chests of clothing and 6 Kara chests of emoluments; 46 porters (2 servants of the Shosai-in plus 44 Left and Right Guard troops), 6 chefs (in light-purple robes), 2 *toneri* engaged to present food offerings, 10 bearers (all in light-pink robes),[58] 6 escorts from the Sovereign's Private Office (in front of the august carriage), Lady Commissioners and below all riding in carriages (for this see item on the first lustration); as Imperial Messengers, 1 each: Great Counselor and Middle Counselor; 2 Imperial Advisers, 4 each of officials of 4th and 5th Rank, 1 lady-in-waiting, 1 secretary; 1 each: outer secretary and fourth-class official; 1 scribe of the *Dajō-kan*,[59] 2 controllers' scribes, 1 office-keeper, and the participating officials of the *Jingi-kan*, Bureaus of Palace Storehouses, Needlework, and Yin-yang Divination, the Ministries of Treasury and Imperial Household, the Offices of Palace Tables, Carpentry, Palace Kitchens, Palace Caretakers, Housekeeping, Imperial Sake, Water Supply, Left and Right Mount Bureau. When the lustration is finished, the food is bestowed

---

[54] *Kitai* 腊, jerky, or the dried meat of deer or other animals and birds.

[55] The *tonomori* 主殿, an occupational group (*be*) in charge of the care and maintenance of all the palace buildings; they belonged to the *tonomo-ryō*, a bureau under the Ministry of the Imperial Household.

[56] The *shizō* 祇承 were officials in the districts who were in charge of meeting the Imperial Messenger, entertaining him, and making arrangements relating to his travel.

[57] *Menoto* 乳母; nominally engaged to nourish

the royal infants, these women had become over the years bureaucrats of considerable influence in the Court.

[58] Purple is from *ebizome* 葡萄染, a dye yielding a lavender or very light purple. Pink is from *taikozome* (or *tonkō*) 退紅, a pale-pink dyestuff.

[59] The *Dajō-kan* is the Great Council of State, the seat of civil administration, under which were the Eight Ministries of the government. The participation of the highest civil officials as well as those of the *Jingi-kan* was required in this festival.

and emoluments given. (All from Imperial Messenger on down to those of 5th Rank are banqueted by the Bureau of Palace Storehouses; those of 6th Rank and below by the Office of Palace Tables.) When that is done, they all return home. When they stop at the No-no-miya emoluments are again bestowed.[60]

The *Ootono-hogai* (Requirements the same as for the *Ootono-hogai* in the *jingi-shiki*)[61]

This is to be done when she moves to the No-no-miya; the requirements are requested by the *Jingi-kan* and the festival is held beforehand.

At all times, the Consecrated Princess in the 4th month of each year on the middle day of the cock ascends to both the Upper and Lower Shrines. (She goes first to the Lower Shrine and remains a while in the building outside the shrine, where she changes her clothing and dons the pure garments; then she rides in her palanquin; the bearers follow and the chiefs of the palanquin accompany her to the left hall in front of the shrine; when the affair is over she proceeds outside the shrine precinct. She then mounts into an ox-drawn carriage[62] and rides to the Upper Shrine; first stopping beneath the hanging curtain, then proceeding to the right hall in front of the shrine.) The Imperial Messenger and one official of 5th Rank or higher of the Bureau of Palace Storehouses, one of 5th Rank or higher of Inner Palace Guards and the same of the Mount Bureau, all attend her on Left and Right; then 12 running horses (Left and Right Inner Guards take turns leading them); one messenger of 5th Rank or higher from each: the Middle Palace and East Palace; one each: Lady-in-waiting, Palace noblewoman, Sovereign's private secretary, Palace Keeper of the Keys;[63] and one each: noblewoman and private secretary of the Middle Palace. All the rest correspond to the ceremony of the first lustration in 4th month. However, 1 sedan-chair is added, and 4 bearers of the chair (for this see the *Gishiki*).[64]

---

[60] The No-no-miya 野宮 or 'Palace-in-the-Fields' is similar to that occupied by the princess consecrated to Ise Shrines. After the years of practicing abstinence in the temporary Shosai-in (First Residence), the princess moved to a No-no-miya built for her in a secluded place in Yamashiro Province. This is the first mention of the No-no-miya, with no instructions for its location and construction. Perhaps the officials concerned simply consulted Bk V of *E-S*, in which procedures for the No-no-miya for the princess to Ise specify selection of site in the 7th month of the year after she entered the Shosai-in. The No-no-miya was to be completed in the 8th month; the princess then moved in and dwelt there for a year.

[61] The festival of *Ootono-hogai* 大殿祭, the blessing or luck-wishing of a palace, is treated in Bk I of *E-S*, where the requirements are given for conducting this ceremony of exorcising evil and bringing good fortune and blessing to all

parts of the Imperial Palace, the Consort's Palace, and the palace of the Heir Apparent. In the present case, this ceremony is used for the same purpose for the Princess's temporary palace.

[62] A golden carriage, according to the specifications in *E-S*, Bk XVII, which contains procedures for the Bureau of Skilled Artisans (*takumi-ryō*).

[63] An official of the *mikado no tsukasa* 閨司 (one of the 12 offices in the Rear Palace, or Women's Palace: *gogū* 後宮) who was in charge of the keys to all the gates within the Palace precinct.

[64] *Gishiki* 儀式 are procedures for ceremonial. In the *E-S* this term refers to ceremonial procedures given in the *Jōgan-gishiki* 貞觀儀式, 'Ceremonial Procedures of the Jōgan era'. The *gishiki*, like *shiki* (procedures), resulted from a long process of formalizing and setting down in writing the precedents and customary rites for civil, religious, and court ceremonial.

*Requirements for Symbolic Offerings at the Upper and Lower Shrines*
　　4 *jō* each of five colors of pongee (1 *jō* 3 *shaku* 3 *sun* 3 *bu* for each of the three
　　deities).

For the above the office of the residence makes the request to the Bureau of
Palace Storehouses.

*Requirements for Festivals of the Sacred Fire and Deity of the Stove*[65]
　　5 *shaku* each of five colors of pongee, 1 *shaku* of colored hemp-cloth, 1 *tan*
　　of tax cloth, 2 mattocks, 2 *kin* each of bark-cloth and hemp, 1 *kin* each of
　　Azuma[66] abalone, bonito, and *wakame*, 1 *shō* of salt, 2 *shō* each of sake and rice,
　　2 saucers, 1 water-bucket, 2 bundles of oak, 1 gourd.

For the foregoing, the *Jingi-kan* turns the articles directly over to the officials
in charge and causes the chief diviner to conduct the festivals.

*The Regular Lustration in the Fourth Month*
　　For this the requirements for offerings to the deities and the ceremony are all
the same as for the lustration ceremony when she enters the Shosai-in, except that
there is no Imperial Messenger.

*Lustration in the Sixth Month*
　　For this the chief diviner goes to the Shosai-in to initiate the august lustration,
after which men and women officials go down to the riverside and are purified.
However, the articles for lustration and provisions for the feast are all prepared
by the office of the Princess's residence.

*Ainame Festival*[67] (if the Princess is selected by the 7th month this is celebrated
　　in that year; if in the 8th month or later, it is celebrated the following year)
　　　　Seats for two deities (required at both Upper and Lower Shrines; facing
　　　　south, they ascend to the east);[68]
　　　　4 *shaku* each of five colors of thin silk, 2 *to* of sake (to be offered to the deities;
　　　　requested from officials in charge).

---

[65] Sacred or taboo fire, *imibi* 忌火, is fire kindled
within the menage of the princess—for lighting
and for cooking in the stoves whose indwelling
*kami* are worshiped in this festival.

[66] Azuma, 'the East', a name for the maritime
provinces of eastern Honshū.

[67] The *Ainame matsuri* 相嘗祭 was the mutual
tasting, or 'together tasting', of newly harvested
rice, an annual festival celebrated in the 11th
month. The sovereign made a ceremonial meal
together with the ancestral deities in the Palace,
and it was celebrated for 71 deities in shrines
around the capital, as outlined in *E-S*, Bk II.
As far back as Temmu Tennō's 4th year (A.D.

675), it is recorded that the Court sent offerings
to be presented to the deities at these shrines for
the *Aimube* (*Ainame*) Festival. Cf. Aida, *Chūkai
yōrō-ryō*, p. 348.

[68] As will be seen, seats are set out for two deities at each of the shrines for the 'together
tasting'. The deities on their seats face south
(royalty kept such a custom) and sat according
to their rank, with higher rank on the east. This
would indicate differing ranks for the two deities
('divine parents') enshrined in the Lower Kamo
Shrine. As to the Upper Shrine, since Kamo no
Wakeikazuchi-no-mikoto is said to be the only
*kami* at this shrine—for whom is the other seat?

### Requirements for Ceremonial Dress

For one *senji* abstainer[69] and one *uneme*: 1 *hiki* of stiff silk, 3 *mochi* of floss silk and 1 *jō* 5 *shaku* of *sayomi* cloth[70] apiece; for 7 alternates for *uneme*: 3 *jō* of stiff silk, 1 *jō* 5 *shaku* of *sayomi* cloth (all to be used for the divining) and 1 *jō* 5 *shaku* of *sayomi* cloth for three persons of the Princess's office. For one messenger of the Princess's office (for divining): 1 *hiki* of stiff silk, 3 *mochi* of tribute floss silk,[71] 1 *tan* of ordinary cloth; for the chief diviner: 1 *hiki* of stiff silk and 1 *mochi* of floss silk; for one *toneri*: 1 *tan* of ordinary cloth; and for one manservant: 1 *tan* of tax cloth.

For this, at cockcrow on the first hare day of the 11th month each year the Consecrated Princess performs lustration and abstinence. She makes distant obeisance[72] and sends up symbolic offerings to the shrines. In the evening, the deity seats in the above item are set up in the abstinence hall.[73] For each deity seat there is a seat from which the Princess is to make the offerings [of food] and the festival takes place. After the Messenger presenting offerings has made his rounds, officials of the Princess's office and the chief diviner are each given a robe. On the following day in the evening, to the men and women serving the Princess's office are given sake and food; emoluments are bestowed upon each according to their differences. After the Imperial Messenger has presented offerings at the shrines he bestows emoluments on the *negi, hafuri,* and *imiko*[74] of both shrines in front of the shrines. This is the same as is done at the festival in the 4th month. Requirements for articles for this are: 20 *hiki* of stiff silk, 200 *mochi* of tribute floss silk, 30 *tan* of ordinary cloth. Already beforehand the [*Jingi-*]*kan* should be asked to request these from the Treasury.

### Requirements for Festival to the Deity of the Stove[75]

2 *shaku* each of five colors of plain silk, 2 *shaku* of colored hemp-cloth, 1 *kin* each of bark-cloth and hemp, 1 *kin* each of abalone, bonito, dried meat, *wakame*, and assorted seaweeds; 2 *shō* each of salt, rice, and sake; 4 saucers, one jar, 1 water-bucket, 4 bundles of oak, 1 gourd.

### Requirements for the Purification on the Last day of the Month

1 *jō* 4 *shaku* of tax cloth, 2 mattocks, 10 *ryō* of Aki bark-cloth, 8 *ryō* of hemp, 2 *shō* each of rice and sake, 1 *kin* each of abalone, bonito, and *wakame*, 2 *soku* of rice-in-ear.

---

[69] *Senji* 宣旨 were the ladies personally responsible to the sovereign who transmitted his messages or commands to the outside.

[70] *Sayomi no nuno* 賛布, a coarse textile woven from fibres of bark of the *shina no ki*, a species like linden, *Tilia cordata.* The cloth was used to pay taxes in kind.

[71] That is, *chōmen* 調綿.

[72] *Yōhai* 遙拜 is obeisance from a distance; in this case, the princess bows in the direction of the shrines and claps her hands in reverence to the *kami.*

[73] The *saiden* 齋殿.

[74] The *negi* 祢(禰)宜 are high-ranking priests of the shrine, while *hafuri* 祝 are lesser priests of a shrine, although the term *hafuri* is also used as generic for all sacerdotal personnel. The *imiko* 忌子, lit. 'taboo child', were young girls attached to the shrine. They correspond to the *mono-imi* or child abstainers at the Ise and Kashima Shrines, and like them practiced abstinences and served as helpers to the priests in presenting offerings to the *kami* at those shrines.

[75] *Kamado-no-kami*, the *kami* who resides in the cook-stove which is used for preparation of food for the Princess, is here feted.

The above are required for the festival and for the purification. The *Jingi-kan* each month sends these directly to the officials in charge, requesting that they take them, and the chief diviner is made to conduct the festival and the purification. However, on the last day of the 6th and 12th months[76] a Nakatomi presents the symbolic offerings. After it is over emoluments are bestowed (the Nakatomi is given one quilt; the chief diviner a silk garment).

*Requirements for the Annual Festival of Lustration*

For the Consecrated Princess: 1 *hiki* of damask of Wu,[77] 1 *hiki* of medium-green pongee, 2 *hiki* of lined material (to carpet her route), 2 *hiki* of silk gauze, 1 *hiki* of light-green stiff silk, 5 *hiki* of white thick silk,[78] 10 *hiki* of white stiff silk, 10 *hiki* of stiff silk and 10 *hiki* of plain silk, 4 *hiki* of thin white silk,[79] 4 *kin* of violet silk thread; 2 each: violet-leather skin and scarlet-leather skin, 3 great *kin* of sapanwood,[80] 20 great *kin* of madder-root,[81] 20 great *kin* of safflower, 100 *kin* of gromwell,[82] 10 willow boxes,[83] 2 top-layer *tatami* with brocade borders (each 9 *shaku* long, 5 *shaku* wide), 12 *tatami* bound on both sides (8 to spread on the ground for daytime sitting at the hall, and 4 for seats at the two shrines), 10 *tatami* with green borders (to be spread on the floor of the sleeping quarters), 2 mattresses with brocade borders (for seats in the shrines), 4 Izumo straw-mats (2 for the shrines, 2 for summer seats), 2 *hiki* 9 *shaku* 8 *sun* of stiff silk (for the curtains for 5 *kichō*).[84]

Required for decorating the clothes and the robes for lady escorts for the day of the festival: 4 *ryō* 1 *bu* 2 *shu* of gold paint, 4 *ryō* 1 *bu* 2 *shu* of silver paint, 4 great *kin* of sapanwood, 5 *kin* 3 *ryō* 3 *bu* of Chinese white,[85] 3 *kin* 13 *ryō* of verdigris, 1 *kin* 12 *ryō* 2 *bu* of white-green,[86] 2 *kin* 3 *ryō* 2 *bu* of azurite, 2 *kin* 2 *ryō* of red lead, 5 *ryō* 1 *bu* of realgar, and 4 *ryō* 4 *shu* of same yellow[87] (on the 13th day of the 3rd month the ladies-in-waiting are assigned to request these).

[76] The Great Purification, *ōharae*, was a national festival held twice yearly on the last day of the 6th and 12th months, whereas a regular monthly *oharae* or purification was held on the last day of each month in the Princess's Office (*Saiin-shi*) as long as she served.

[77] *Kure no aya* 呉綾, silk damask, or figured silk, a weave imported originally from China and bearing the name of the State of Wu (Kure).

[78] Although the reading is *katori*, a different character from the usual is used here: 繡. See n. 51 above.

[79] A very thin, gauze-like silk is meant here: *usuginu* 紗 or *usumono*.

[80] *Suō* 蘇芳 is sapanwood (or Judas-tree?), the yellow flowers of which yielded a violet dye.

[81] *Akane* 茜草, or madder-root, which yielded a red dye.

[82] Safflower is *benibana* 紅花, a source of yellow dye. 'Gromwell' is used for the *murasaki* plant,

紫草, which yielded a violet dye.

[83] *Yanagibako* or *yanaibako* 楊筥, 'willow box': a ceremonial box made of split willow-wood bound together with vines to contain sacred articles.

[84] *Kichō* 几帳, a curtained frame put up to screen royal personages or noble ladies from direct view of those around them. 'Screens of state' Waley calls them.

[85] *Gofun* 胡粉 is a mixture of calcium carbonate prepared from seashells and glue and used as white pigment; used for priming or mixing with colors. Tokyo National Museum, *Textiles and Lacquer*, p. 174.

[86] White-green, written 白緑, a mineral pigment.

[87] *Dō-ō* 同黄, 'similar yellow'; presumably it means realgar also, but a separate amount for a different purpose from the immediately preceding item.

Required for personal supplies: 178 *hiki* 3 *shaku* of stiff silk (40 *hiki* for 3 quilts to be used for emoluments, 30 *hiki* for 80 under-robes, 86 *hiki* 3 *shaku* for Court dress on the festival day for *senji* down to pages on foot,[88] 2 *hiki* for Court dress for officials of the Princess's office and 20 *hiki* for emoluments to guards of the marching horses and for musicians); 14 *hiki* of plain silk (for six private secretaries, 4 girls on horseback, and one *uneme* and three alternates), 7 *hiki* 4 *jō* of white damask (6 *hiki* 4 *jō* for divided skirts[89] for 4 young girls, 1 *jō* 5 *shaku* apiece), 4 *hiki* of red-violet stiff silk (2 *hiki* 3 *jō* for garments for 10 girl attendants, 1 *jō* 5 *shaku* apiece; 1 *hiki* 3 *jō* are for long cloaks for the same, 9 *shaku* apiece), 5 *hiki* 5 *jō* 5 *shaku* of scarlet stiff silk (4 *jō* 4 *shaku* for robes of prescribed color for the chief, 5 *hiki* for skirts of 10 pages on foot, 3 *jō* apiece; 1 *jō* for sashes for the same, 1 *shaku* apiece), 3 *hiki* of stencil-dyed[90] blue silk (for one *senji* and two wet-nurses, 1 *hiki* apiece), 4 *hiki* 1 *jō* of white thin silk (3 *hiki* for scarves for 20 ladies from *senji* down to girl-attendants, 9 *shaku* apiece; 1 *hiki* 1 *jō* for scarves for 10 pages on foot, 7 *shaku* apiece); 40 *kin* of silk thread (20 *kin* each of white and red for various uses for the festivals), 480 *mochi* 5 *ryō* 3 *shu* of tribute floss silk (180 *mochi* for 30 quilts for emoluments, 6 *mochi* each; 15 *ryō* 3 *shu* to go with 15 *hiki* 2 *jō* of stiff silk stencil-dyed on light-blue background, 1 *ryō* to each *hiki*; 200 *mochi* are for emoluments on the day of lustration; 100 *mochi* for emoluments to the guards who lead the marching horses and to the musicians); 8 *tan* 3 *jō* 7 *shaku* of linen[91] (6 *tan* 1 *jō* 2 *shaku* for divided skirts for 36 persons from chiefs of the palanquin down to burden bearers, 7 *shaku* apiece; 3 *jō* 5 *shaku* for stockings for the pages on foot, 3 *shaku* 5 *sun* apiece; 1 *tan* 3 *jō* for divided skirts for 10 carriers on the day of lustration, 7 *shaku* apiece), 4 *tan* 8 *shaku* of dark-blue linen (for divided skirts for 14 carriage assistants and 10 followers[92] on the day of lustration, 7 *shaku* apiece), 18 *tan* of dark-blue tribute cloth[93] (4 *tan* for two wet-nurses, 2 *tan* apiece; 14 *tan* for the 14 mounted ladies, 1 *tan* apiece), 94 *tan* 2 *jō* 5 *shaku* 2 *sun* of ordinary cloth (5 *tan* for one *senji*; 4 *tan* for two wet-nurses, 2 each; 50 *tan* for 25 persons from mounted ladies down, 2 *tan* apiece; 17 *tan* 6 *shaku* for divided skirts for 44 palanquin bearers, 2 servants, 44 burden bearers—total of 90 persons, 8 *shaku* apiece; 2 *tan* 4 *shaku* for leggings for 44 palanquin bearers, 2 *shaku* apiece; 1 *tan* 1 *jō* 5 *shaku* 2 *sun* for waist-ties[94] for 44 palanquin bearers, 1 *shaku* 2 *sun* apiece; 15 *tan* for miscellaneous uses); 700 *tan*

---

[88] These pages are young girls, as can be concluded from the description of their costumes that follows later.

[89] That is, the long, loose trousers called *hakama* 袴.

[90] Stencil-dyeing, *kyōkechi* 夾纈, was a highly skilled textile art of the Nara period; the details of the process are no longer known. The fabric to be dyed was evidently pressed between boards through which the design had been cut. Examples are found in the Shōsōin repository.

[91] *Hosonuno* 細布 was very finely woven hemp-cloth that had the appearance of linen.

[92] For carriage attendants see n. 38, above. The 'followers' are *teburi* 手振, lit. 'hand-shakers' or 'hand-wavers'.

[93] Tribute cloth is used to translate *chōfu* (*tsukinuno*) 調布.

[94] The *ayui* 脚結 was a plaited string hung from the top of the trousers or divided skirt down to the knees; sometimes bells were attached to it. *Kogo jiten*.

of tax cloth (200 *tan* for emoluments on the day of the festival for officials in charge from watchmen on down; 500 *tan* for various uses at the festival of lustration); 1 great *kin* 14 *ryō* 2 *bu* 4 *shu* of sapanwood (for preparation of 15 *hiki* 2 *jō* of silk stencil-dyed with light-blue ground), 16 great *kin* 7 *ryō* 3 *bu* of yellow-bark (12 *kin* 7 *ryō* 3 *bu* to stencil-dye 15 *hiki* 2 *jō* of silk with light-blue ground and 4 *kin* for stencil-dyeing 4 *hiki* of silk with ground of Kara safflower),[95] 16 great *kin* of safflower (for stencil-dyeing 4 *hiki* of silk with ground of Kara safflower, 4 *kin* per *hiki*), 7 great *kin* 10 *ryō* 2 *bu* 4 *shu* of madder-root (for stencil-dyeing 15 *hiki* 2 *jō* of silk with light-blue ground, 8 *ryō* per *hiki*), 7 great *kin* 10 *ryō* 2 *bu* 3 *shu* of *haji*[96] (to do the same for 15 *hiki* 2 *jō* of silk, 8 *ryō* per *hiki*), 15 *ryō* 1 *bu* 2 *shu* of alum (for the same for 15 *hiki* 2 *jō* of silk, 1 *ryō* per *hiki*), 2 *to* of *fu*[97] (5 *shō* each for 4 *hiki* of Kara-safflower colored stencil-dyed silk), 3 *to* 5 *shō* of wheat (2 *to* 3 *shō* for stencil-dyeing 15 *hiki* 2 *jō* of silk with light-blue ground, 1 *shō* 5 *go* each); 1 *to* 2 *shō* for stencil-dyeing 4 *hiki* of silk colored with Kara safflower, 3 *shō* each), 100 *kin* of gromwell (plant of Tsukushi to be used for dyeing various things); 89 *kan* 72 *mon* in coin[98] (1 *kan* 200 *mon* for Court dress for the *senji*; 6 *kan-mon* for six private secretaries, 1 each; 2 *kan* 400 *mon* for two wet-nurses, 1 *kan* 200 *mon* each; 4 *kan-mon* for the four mounted girl attendants, 1 *kan-mon* each; 2 *kan-mon* for the four young girls, 500 *mon* each; 6 *kan-mon* for 6 ladies riding in carriages, 1 *kan-mon* each; 4 *kan-mon* for one *uneme* and three alternates, 1 *kan-mon* each; 16 *kan* 100 *mon* for 46 persons from chiefs of the palanquin down to burden bearers for price of caps, 350 *mon* apiece; 15 *kan* 200 *mon* for price of caps for 44 palanquin bearers, 300 *mon* apiece; 5 *kan* 800 *mon* for stencil-dyeing 19 *hiki* 2 *jō* of silk dark blue at 300 *mon* per *hiki*; 64 *mon* for stencil-dyeing 4 *hiki* of silk with Kara safflower at 8 *mon* each for 8 armloads of straw; 690 *mon* for cost of 23 armloads of firewood for doing the stencil-dyeing, at 30 *mon* a load; 4 *kan-mon* for cost of 20 *koku* of ashes at 200 *mon* a *koku*; 2 *kan* 360 *mon* for rations for 39 dyeworkers of the 19 *hiki* 2 *jō* of silk to be stencil-dyed, at 60 *mon* apiece; 1 *kan* 258 *mon* for rations for 39 helpers for the above at 32 *mon* apiece; 20 *kan-mon* for miscellaneous purposes); 5 *koku* 7 *to* 8 *shō* 6 *gō* of white rice (50 *koku* to be laid aside for the lustration festival; 7 *to* 8 *shō* 6 *gō* for half rations for the 39 workers in stencil-dyeing), 50 *koku* 7 *to* 8 *shō* 6 *gō* of dark rice[99] (50 *koku* to be laid aside for lustration festival, 7 *to* 8 *shō* 6 *gō* for 39 helpers in the stencil-dyeing), 5 *to* of oil (for various uses in the lustration festival, etc.); 4 *koku* 1 *shō* 5 *gō* 7 *shaku*

---

[95] Or, Chinese safflower. Here the character 辛 is used, the sound being the same as that of 韓.

[96] *Hiji* or *haji* 黄櫨 (also *haze-no-ki*) is mentioned in the *Man'yōshū* (no. 4465). It is a plant of the *Rhus* family, the berries of which yield a red dye.

[97] *Fu* 麩, a kind of bread made with wheat flour.

[98] The use of money as a medium of exchange did develop in the Heian period, but was mainly limited to the capital and its environs. Rice and cloth were the chief commodities and media of exchange. A *kan* 貫 was a string of 1,000 copper coins known as *mon* 文. In the 'four-figure' numbers, *kan* equals one thousand, or *kan-mon*—'a thousand *mon*'.

[99] Dark rice or black rice meant unpolished rice (*gemmai*).

of salt (4 *koku* to be laid aside for the lustration festival uses, 1 *shō* 5 *gō* 7 *shaku* for the master of stencil-dyeing and 78 workers, large ration, 2 *shaku* each), 6 *shō* of vinegar (for 4 *hiki* of silk to be stencil-dyed in Kara safflower, 1 *shō* 5 *gō* per *hiki*), 1 *koku* 5 *to* 3 *shō* 6 *gō* of sake (1 *koku* 3 *to* for use on day of festival: 2 *to* 3 *shō* 6 *gō* for master of stencil-dyeing and total of 78 workers, 3 *gō* apiece), 100 *kin* each of abalone, bonito, and dried salmon (for the lustration festival), 3 *koku* 1 *to* 5 *shō* 7 *gō* of assorted fish (3 *koku* for the festival of lustration; 1 *to* 5 *shō* 7 *gō* for the master of stencil-dyeing and total of 78 workers, at 2 *gō* apiece), 9 *kin* 13 *ryō* 3 *shu* of *wakame* (for master of stencil-dyeing and total of 78 workers, 2 *ryō* apiece), 159 complete meals (4 tables, 21 each of 1st and 2nd class bent-wood food-boxes, 25 large containers, 88 wrappers).

The officials in charge sort and prepare the above and present them on the day of the festival.

### Requirements for Presentation

50 *hiki* of stiff silk, 30 *kan-mon* in coin, 10 *koku* of white rice, 20 *koku* of dark rice.

The above is for when the Princess is first selected; the items to be accordingly requested and received.

The various things to be requested after the selection of the Princess:

*Utensils*: 1 silver rice bowl, 3 pairs of silver chopsticks, 1 silver sake cup, 2 silver spoons, 1 silver chopstick holder, 1 silver water-bowl, 1 silver pitcher, 2 silver dishes, 1 white-bronze[100] sake jar, 1 white-bronze dipper (add white-bronze stand), 1 white-bronze bathtub, 1 white-bronze brazier, 3 white-wood Kara chests (add bench and carrying poles), 3 3-*shaku* vermilion-lacquer tray-tables (add stands), two casks.

*Travel articles*: One palanquin, 1 sedan-chair (add a footstool for dismounting), 2 large sunshades[101] (placed in a *hyōmon* lacquered box;[102] with rain covers), 1 small sunshade (placed in lacquered box; with rain cover), 2 large sedge umbrellas (add lacquered handles and cord-ties), 6 portable screens[103] (4 large, 2 small), 2 lacquered silver boxes, one gilded carriage, 2 curtains, 2 frames for light curtains, 2 silk awnings (each 1 *jō* 4 *shaku* square made of 5 *jō* 6 *shaku* each of dark-violet, lavender, and yellow plain silk and 1 *hiki* 1 *jō* 2 *shaku* of scarlet plain silk; and for the linings, 4 *hiki* of scarlet plain silk; for 56 strands of braid trim, 1 *jō* 2 *shaku* 6 *sun* of scarlet plain silk; 1 *hiki* of scarlet plain silk for three large cords; for the central banners, 1 *tan* 2 *jō* of

---

[100] Lit. 'white copper'. *Hakudō* 白銅 (now an alloy of copper, zinc, and nickel) was used extensively in pre-Nara times for making mirrors. Holtom says *hakudō* was an amalgam of copper and tin with a small portion of lead in those times. *Japanese Enthronement Ceremonies* (1928), p. 12 (7). [2nd number refers to Sophia U. ed.]

[101] The *sashiba* 翳 was a round or floral-shaped screen with a very long handle, used to screen the princess from view when in procession.

[102] This refers to *hyōmon* 平文 ('flat design'), in which a design was done in silver or gold on the box and then lacquered over several times. Afterward the lacquer was polished to bring out the design. Cf. Tokyo National Museum, *Textiles and Lacquer*, p. 36.

[103] Or, movable screens, *kōshō* 行障, to be used during the movement of the procession.

plain cloth; for one bag, 5 *shaku* 4 *sun* of faced material; and for the lining 5 *shaku* 4 *sun* of stiff silk; 8 curtains (4 of them 10-widths wide and 4 8-widths)[104] made from 12 *hiki* of red-violet plain silk; for their linings: 12 *hiki* of plain silk; for 36 braided cords: 4 *jō* 4 *shaku* of violet plain silk; for their linings: 4 *jō* 4 *shaku* of plain silk; for sewing these: 1 skein scarlet silk thread, 4 *ryō* silk thread; nine mottled curtains (2 of them 5 *shaku* long, 7 of them 8 *shaku*) made from 15 *hiki* 1 *jō* 8 *shaku* of scarlet plain silk, 15 *hiki* 2 *jō* 4 *shaku* of yellow plain silk, 11 *hiki* 3 *jō* 7 *shaku* 5 *sun* 5 *bu* of pale-blue plain silk; to sew these: 1 skein 8 *ryō* of pale-blue silk thread, 1 skein 4 *ryō* of yellow silk thread, and 6 *ryō* of [undyed] silk thread; for 8 bags: 3 *tan* 1 *jō* 4 *shaku* of dark-blue plain cloth, 3 *tan* of cloth for linings (all these are requested from the *Jingi-kan* by the officials in charge; then they are given to the ladies-in-waiting to sew and prepare under the Ministry of Treasury); 7 awnings of dark-blue pongee (with scarlet linings), 5 curtains of above color (with pale-blue linings), 4 crossbeam poles (wood to be requested from the Bureau of Carpentry), 10 red-lacquered Kara chests to contain her wardrobe (to be requested from the Ministry of the Treasury), 10 *kichō* (six of them 3 *shaku* long, four 1 *shaku* 5 *sun*), 1 comb table, 6 folding screens (two 5 *shaku* long, four 4 *shaku*), 1 tub for washing the hair, 1 tub for bathing.

*Requirements for Personal Supplies*

5 metal tripods[105] (one of 5-*to*, one of 4-*to*, and three of 3-*to* capacity), 3 large sake jars (each of 2-*to* capacity); 10 service plates, 7 tray-tables (one 8 *shaku* long, six 4 *shaku* long), 4 pairs of white-bronze chopsticks; 8 [white-bronze][106] spoons; 2 white-bronze dippers; 30 covered jars for brewing the sake; 34 medicine bags.

As in the preceding item, when the foregoing articles are worn out, replacements are to be requested from the [*Jingi-*] *kan*. Articles in item below which are requested once in three years are at the same time also requested and supplied. But at the time the Princess changes office, they are all collected and stored at the house of the Princess.

*Seasonal Clothing Requirements*

40 *hiki* of stiff silk (20 for summer, 20 for winter), 40 *tan* of tribute cloth (20 *tan* for summer, 20 for winter), 200 *ton* of tribute floss silk (100 *ton* for summer, 100 for winter).

The above are announced to the *Jingi-kan* according to the season and are requested from the Ministry of the Treasury.

*For the First Day of the Year*

20 *koku* of white rice, 4 *koku* of glutenous rice, 2 *koku* each of soybeans and red beans, 1 *koku* each of sesamum and millet (all to be requested by the

---

[104] The width of material varied, but was usually about 2½ feet or 2 *shaku*.

[105] Perhaps a cauldron with three feet, *kanae* 釜; here thought to be equivalent to the Chinese cauldron or tripod of bronze, a *ting* 鼎.

[106] 'White-bronze' is supplied from the list in Bk XVII of *E-S*, Procedures for the Bureau of Skilled Artisans, *takumi-ryō*.

Bureau of Palace Kitchens), 6 *to* of oil (requested by the Bureau of Palace Caretakers), 2 *koku* of salt (requested by the Office of Palace Tables).

The foregoing are announced beforehand to the *Jingi-kan* and requested and received.

*To be Installed for Winter Use* (in the summer, articles for the festival in the 4th month are used throughout)

2 *tatami* bound in brocade (each 8 *shaku* long and 5 *shaku* wide), 8 *tatami* bound on both sides, 10 *tatami* bound in green, 2 Izumo straw-mats (for middle of the mattresses).

The foregoing are for the seats of the Consecrated Princess; every year they announce to the *Jingi-kan* and request and receive these.

10 *tatami* bound in green; 10 *tatami* bound in yellow.

The foregoing are to be supplied for personnel, and are used at the same time the seats are set up for the Princess.

*The Various Articles to be Requested Once in Three Years*

4 *shaku* 4 *sun* of *ungen* brocade[107] (for top of one cover for the comb table), 6 *hiki* of double-face material (5 *jō* 1 *shaku* for covers hung from 3 red-lacquered tray-tables for her meals, 1 *jō* 7 *shaku* apiece; 4 *jō* 2 *shaku* for covers for 3 red-lacquered Kara chests, 1 *jō* 4 *shaku* each; 4 *hiki* 2 *jō* 7 *shaku* are for 10 each of deep and shallow covers for the 10 Kara chests for her wardrobe), 3 *hiki* 4 *jō* 5 *shaku* 5 *sun* of green pongee (2 *jō* 5 *shaku* 5 *sun* for top of covering for one floor, 3 *hiki* 2 *jō* for making 20 cords for the 10 Kara chests for the wardrobe), 6 *hiki* 8 *shaku* of scarlet pongee (5 *hiki* 5 *jō* for overgarments for 10 carriers, 3 *jō* 5 *shaku* apiece; 1 *jō* 8 *shaku* for the linings of two large sedge umbrellas), 3 *hiki* 5 *jō* 2 *shaku* of red-violet plain silk (2 *hiki* for short curtains and for cover of trim for 2 summer short curtains; 1 *hiki* 5 *jō* 2 *shaku* for the same for 2 winter short curtains), 4 *hiki* 3 *shaku* 5 *sun* of deep-blue plain silk (4 *jō* 4 *shaku* for top and trim of summer wall curtain;[108] 1 *hiki* 5 *jō* 2 *shaku* for the same for winter wall curtain; 5 *jō* 2 *shaku* 5 *sun* for top and trim of 5 summer short curtains; 3 *jō* 5 *shaku* for same for winter short curtains), 7 *hiki* of yellow plain silk (5 *hiki* for garments for 10 chiefs of the palanquin, 3 *jō* apiece; 2 *hiki* for garments for maidservants, 3 *jō* apiece), 5 *hiki* of plain silk (for linings of garments of 10 chiefs of the palanquin), 238 *hiki* 1 *jō* 7 *shaku* 9 *sun* of stiff silk (5 *jō* 1 *shaku* for linings of covers for 3 tray-tables for food presentations, 1 *jō* 7 *shaku* each; 4 *jō* 2 *shaku* for same for 3 red-lacquered Kara chests, 1 *jō* 4 *shaku* each; 5 *jō* 1 *shaku* for linings of rain covers for 3 tray-tables for food presentations, 1 *jō* 7 *shaku* each; 4 *jō* 2 *shaku* for linings of rain covers for above Kara chests, 1 *jō* 4 *shaku* each; 2 *jō* for linings of bags for two boxes for carriers; 4 *hiki* 2 *jō* 7 *shaku* for 10 each of deep and shallow covers for 10 Kara chests for the wardrobe; 1 *jō* 8 *shaku* for middle panels for covers of two large sedge umbrellas, 2 *jō* for

---

107 *Ungen* 暈繝 is a polychrome silk woven with colors in gradation.

108 The *kabeshiro* 壁代 is a curtain or drape used as a wall or a partition in the residence.

linings of rain covers for two leather boxes for carriers; 2 *jō* 4 *shaku* 5 *sun* for lining of rain cover for one platform; 4 *jō* 5 *shaku* 5 *sun* for linings of 3 rain covers for one palanquin; 4 *shaku* 4 *sun* for lining of cover of 1 comb table; 3 *hiki* 3 *jō* for overgarments for six chefs; 18 *hiki* for undergarments[109] for 36 persons—10 chiefs of the palanquin, 10 carriers, 6 chefs, and 10 bearers: 3 *jō* each; 12 *hiki* for undercoats[110] for the same, 2 *jō* apiece; 12 *hiki* for undergarments for 14 carriage attendants and 10 followers on the day of lustration, 3 *jō* apiece; 8 *hiki* for undercoats for the same, 2 *jō* apiece; 36 *hiki* 4 *jō* 8 *shaku* for summer hangings for two short curtains; 2 *hiki* for facing and 2 *hiki* for edging of the same; 38 *hiki* 3 *jō* 4 *shaku* for winter hangings, 2 *hiki* for the facing and 1 *hiki* 5 *jō* 2 *shaku* for summer hangings for the wall covering; 4 *jō* 4 *shaku* for lining of the trimming; 51 *hiki* 1 *jō* 2 *shaku* for winter hangings for wall covering, 1 *hiki* 5 *jō* 2 *shaku* for lining the trimmings; 9 *hiki* 2 *jō* for 5 summer hangings for curtains; 5 *jō* 2 *shaku* 5 *sun* for lining of bands; 8 *hiki* for winter hangings, 3 *jō* 5 *shaku* for lining of bands); 323 *ton* of tribute floss silk (128 *ton* for 2 winter hangings for the curtains, 160 *ton* for 18 winter wall coverings, 35 *ton* for 5 winter curtains); 2 skeins of silk thread (to sew drapes, curtains, and short curtains), 3 *hiki* 5 *jō* 2 *shaku* of oiled pongee (5 *jō* 1 *shaku* for rain covers for 3 tray-tables for food presentations, 1 *jō* 7 *shaku* apiece; 4 *jō* 2 *shaku* for rain covers for 3 Kara chests for same purpose, 1 *jō* 4 *shaku* each; 1 *jō* 8 *shaku* for covers for 2 large sedge umbrellas; 3 *jō* for rain covers for two large sunshades; 2 *jō* for rain covers for 2 boxes for carriers; 2 *jō* 5 *shaku* 5 *sun* for rain cover for one floor; 4 *jō* 5 *shaku* 5 *sun* for 3 rain covers for one palanquin); 34 *tan* 2 *jō* of dark-blue linen (22 *tan* for overgarments for 44 palanquin bearers, 2 *jō* each; 12 *tan* for garments for 14 carriage attendants and 10 followers on the day of lustration, 2 *jō* apiece); 23 *tan* 2 *jō* 4 *shaku* of linen (5 *tan* for overgarments for 10 burden bearers, 2 *jō* apiece; 8 *tan* 2 *jō* for cloth sashes on the day of lustration for 14 carriage attendants, 10 followers, and 10 carriers, 1 *jō* apiece; 5 *tan* for overgarments for 10 carriers, 2 *jō* 4 *shaku* apiece; 4 *shaku* to make 4 bags to soak safflower in; 5 *tan* for cloth sashes for 10 chiefs of the palanquin and 10 burden bearers, 1 *jō* apiece); 4 *jō* of dark-blue tribute cloth for overgarments for two servants, 2 *jō* apiece; 28 *tan* 2 *jō* 3 *shaku* of ordinary cloth (5 *tan* 1 *jō* for cloth sashes for 44 palanquin bearers, 1 *jō* for every 2 persons; 2 *tan* 1 *jō* 6 *shaku* for middle layer of 20 cords for Kara chests for the wardrobe; 20 *tan* for garments for 44 porters, 2 *jō* apiece); 15 *tan* 2 *jō* 4 *shaku* of 6-*jō sayomi* cloth[111] (for undergarments for 44 palanquin bearers, 2 *jō* 1 *shaku* apiece); price of 40 loads of firewood (17 loads for dyeing short

---

[109] The *kazami* 汗衫 was a long undergarment with sleeves and a narrow sash worn by both women and men in the Heian period. Ema, *Shinshū yūsoku kojitsu* p. 110–11.
[110] The *hampi* 半臂 was a sleeveless tunic-length garment worn by men under their Court

dress (*gohō* 御袍). Ema, op. cit. pp. 75–6.
[111] Here, the length of a bolt (6 *jō*) of *sayomi* cloth (see n. 70) is given since it differs from the usual bolt of cloth measuring from 2 *jō* 8 *shaku* up to 4 *jō* in length.

curtains and wall coverings yellow, white, and grey, 3 loads for dyeing one hanging for the curtain with Kara safflower; 20 loads for dyeing of the garments for the various functionaries and servants), price of 14 *koku* 2 *to* of ashes (10 *koku* 2 *to* for dyeing short curtains and wall coverings, 3 *koku* for dyeing the garments of various functionaries and 44 porters), 82½ armloads of miscanthus[112] (31½ for dyeing 20 *hiki* 4 *jō* of stiff silk for 18 wall coverings; 27 armloads for dyeing 5 *hiki* 4 *jō* of stiff silk for 7 short curtains; 10 armloads for dyeing the hanging of the short curtain; 12 armloads for dyeing the garments of various functionaries; to be requested from the Bureau of Palace Storehouses); price of 37 armloads of straw (for heat treating and dyeing the silk with safflower), 69 large *kin* of safflower (61 *kin* for dyeing the short curtains, wall curtains, and garments of functionaries, 8 *kin* for dyeing overgarments for 10 carriers for the day of lustration; to be requested from Ministry of the Treasury), 30 large *kin* of yellow-bark (for dyeing stiff silk for the short curtains and wall coverings; to be requested from Ministry of Treasury); 17 *kan* 730 *mon* of coin (9 *kan* 816 *mon* for cost of dyeing short curtains, 18 wall coverings, surface of 7 short curtains—to dye 32 *hiki* 4 *jō* 2 *shaku* of stiff silk with indigo, 300 *mon* per *hiki*; 7 *kan* 720 *mon* for dyeing the linings for the same—for 25 *hiki* 4 *jō* 4 *shaku* of light-blue silk, at 300 *mon* per *hiki*; 120 *mon* for work of 4 hired-men, at 30 *mon* each; 80 *mon* for work of 4 hired-women, at 20 *mon* each); 6 *to* 1 *shō* of vinegar (5 *to* 6 *shō* for dyeing silk with safflower for the short curtains; 5 *shō* for dyeing Court robes for various functionaries); 6 *koku* 4 *to* 2 *shō* 8 *gō* of white rice (2 *to* for starching the facings of the hangings for the short curtains; 1 *to* for starching the garments of the various functionaries, 6 *koku* for food for a total of 500 persons in the palaces who do the sewing, 1 *shō* 2 *gō* apiece; 8 *shō* for food for 4 hired-men, 2 *shō* each; 4 *shō* 8 *gō* for food for 4 hired-women, 1 *shō* 2 *gō* each); 2 *koku* 4 *shō* of sake (2 *koku* for a total of 500 persons, 4 *gō* each; 2 *shō* 4 *gō* for 4 hired-men, 6 *gō* apiece; 1 *shō* 6 *gō* for 4 hired-women, 4 *gō* apiece); 1 *koku* 2 *shō* of fish (1 *koku* for total of 500 palace personnel who do the sewing, 2 *gō* apiece: 1 *shō* 2 *gō* for the 4 hired-men, 3 *gō* apiece; 8 *gō* for the 4 hired-women, 2 *gō* apiece); 5 *to* 2 *shō* of soybean dregs (5 *to* for the 500 persons who sew, 1 *gō* apiece; 1 *shō* 2 *gō* for the 4 hired-men, 3 *gō* apiece; 8 *gō* for the 4 hired-women, 2 *gō* apiece); 80 *tatami* for the use of all those from Imperial Messenger down to girl attendants (10 with green borders, 10 with yellow borders, 30 of Azuma straw matting, 30 of Suō straw matting;[113] all with binding on the back side); 12 mattresses (2 with violet binding, 5 with green binding, 5 with yellow); 1 5-*shaku* bed (for use at both Upper and Lower Shrines), 4 casks (each of 2-*to* capacity; add dippers); 20 shelf-tables; 3

---

[112] The gray dye is obtained from the *tsuru-bami* (see n. 27 above) and the pale yellow dye is from the *kariyasu* 刈安 (*Miscanthus tinctorius*), a wild grass; 14 *koku* 2 *to* should read 13 *koku* 2 *to* and is so emended in some mss. It will be

noted that the armloads of miscanthus total only 80½.

[113] Straw matting from Suō Province, west of Aki Province, at southwest tip of Honshū. See map.

lamps of white wood, 10 boards for august food; 10 lampstands, 6 single beds, 10 raised beds, 2 large sedge umbrellas, 6 willow boxes, 4 mats, 104 straw raincoats, 98 thick straw-hats (16 straw-coats for the horses of the mounted ladies, 98 *kera* raincoats[114] and 98 thick straw-hats for chiefs of the palanquin and below; all these to be requested from the Bureau of Palace Storehouses).

At all times, the Consecrated Princess ascends to the festival at both Upper and Lower [Kamo] Shrines. On the day [of the festival] she makes her entrance in the evening and pine-knot torches are lit in Yamashiro Province. An official of the 3rd or 4th class does the official greeting. His name[115] is forwarded to the *Jingi-kan* a day in advance.

At all times, [to be provided:] 192 *hiki* 3 *jō* of stiff silk for clothing for 40 men and 41 women functionaries (71 *hiki* for summer and 121 *hiki* 3 *jō* for winter), 283 *ton* of tribute floss silk (for winter), 23 *tan* 5 *jō* 5 *shaku* of 6-*jō sayomi* cloth (for 41 women in summer), 82 *tan* of ordinary cloth (for 41 women in winter), all these to be requested from the Ministry of Treasury.

At all times, to be provided for clothing for 8 artisans: 32 *ton* of tribute floss silk (for winter), 56 *tan* of ordinary cloth (24 *tan* for summer and 32 for winter), 6 *tan* of tax cloth for clothing for 2 restituees[116] (2 *tan* for summer; 4 *tan* for winter), 8 *ton* of tax floss silk (for winter), all these to be requested from the Ministry of Treasury. For their food: 6 *to* of dark rice (to be requested from Ministry of People's Affairs), 6 *shō* of salt (requested from Office of Palace Tables).

At all times, the headquarters of the Gate Guards builds an encampment; the Bureau of Carpentry builds the fire-kindling shelter.

At all times, on days when the official buildings of the Princess's Residence are repaired by the Bureau of Carpentry, officials of her Office go and inspect them. If in less than 10 years any of them suffer damage, officials of 5th Rank and above are deprived of rank stipends, while those of 6th Rank and below are deprived of seasonal emoluments.

*    *    *    *    *    *

End of Book Six of the *Engi-shiki*

Enchō 5th Year [A.D. 927], 12th Month, 26th Day

Outer Rank[117] Junior 5th Rank Lower Grade, Left Great Secretary *omi*[118] Ato no

---

[114] *Kera* 螻 is the mole cricket (*Gryllotalpa africana*) common in Japan. As it frequently lives in harvested rice-straw, that may account for the raincoat name; or it may be because the plaiting and shape of the raincoat resembles the shape of the insect: its forewings are short; its hindwings are broad but capable of folding up narrowly like a Japanese fan, and pointed at the end.

[115] i.e. his 'card', *myōbu* 名簿, a piece of wood with his name inscribed on it.

[116] *Tsukunoi-bito* 客作兒 means persons who have been recompensed for service or paid restitution for some accommodation made to the Office of the Princess.

[117] 'Outer officials', *gekan* 外官, were those holding provincial appointment, as opposed to inner officials, *naikan*, who held appointment in the capital.

[118] *Shin*, or *omi* 臣, was a *kabane* 姓, or clan-rank title. After Temmu's restructuring of the *kabane* titles it was 6th in a list of eight.

Sukune[119] Tadayuki; Junior 5th Rank Upper Grade Assistant Provisional Examiner and Senior Private Secretary, Provisional Governor of Kii, *omi* Tomo no Sukune Hisanaga; Junior 4th Rank Upper Grade, Chief of the *Jingi-kan*, *omi* Oonakatomi no Ason[120] Yasunori; The Great Counselor, Senior 3rd Rank, Chief of People's Affairs, *omi* Fujiwara no Ason Kiyotsura; Great Minister of the Left, Senior 2nd Rank, Major Captain of the Left Palace Guards and Protector of the Heir Apparent, *omi* Fujiwara no Ason Tadahira.

---

[119] *Sukune* 宿祢(禰) was also a former *kabane* title and was third in Temmu's list.

[120] *Ason*, or *asomi* 朝臣, was the second *kabane* in the list of eight. Although the system of Court ranks by numbers and grade superseded the old *kabane* system, nevertheless nobles whose families had held the *kabane* titles persisted in using both the old and new titles with their names.

## Chapter Two

## INTRODUCTION TO BOOK SEVEN

### THE GREAT NEW FOOD FESTIVAL OF
### THE ENTHRONEMENT

THERE ARE three elements in the Japanese enthronement ceremonies of the Nara and Heian periods which are distinguished by name. The first is the accession, or succession to the throne, called *sokui*. It literally means 'attaining rank', although the Heir Apparent in truth rises above all ranks to the high level of emperor upon the demise or the abdication of the previous sovereign.[121] The second element is the *senso* or 'treading the throne' ceremony, as Dr Holtom has called it.[122] The actual characters (*kanji*) of *senso* have almost the same meaning as *sokui*, for they signify ascending to honor or happiness or rank. It is just as well, for as we study the procedures in Book VII of the *Engi-shiki* we do not find that the sovereign treads or even sits upon a throne, nor does he become crowned with any crown. The third element is the great feast of the enthronement. This commences with the *Daijō* (Great New Food), a feast of communion by the sovereign with the *kami* of the imperial line. It is followed by the partaking of sacred food by the princes, princesses, Court nobles, and all officialdom, as well as by the representatives of the selected provinces and taboo districts which have produced the sacred rice and other foods for the communion feast. The pageantry and conferring of ranks and the singing and dancing to celebrate the great event of a new reign follow the sacred feasting. The 'throne treading', if we wish to call it that, is part and parcel of the *Daijō* ceremonies, and hence the name, *Senso Daijō-sai*, for this greatest of festivals.

The festival of the sovereign's tasting the first-fruits of the rice harvest in the presence of the ancestral *kami* was an annual event of the Yamato Court. When that same festival was held for the first time after the accession of a new sovereign it was called the Great New Food Festival of the Enthronement, *Oonie no matsuri* or *Oomube no matsuri* (*Daijō-sai* in Sino-Japanese pronunciation). On the other

---

[121] According to the law, the sovereign is above the ranks. The Taihō civil code set up four upper-echelon ranks called *hon* 品. The first *hon* included imperial princes (sons or brothers of the sovereign). Others related to him in less degree came in the 2nd and 3rd *hon*. No rank is assigned to the sovereign. See Kubomi, *Taihō-ryō shinkai*, p. 2.

[122] D. C. Holtom, *Japanese Enthronement Ceremonies* (1928), p. 57 (47).

hand, the annual festival was called the *Niiname no matsuri* (*Niiname-sai*). In
both names the element *nie, mube, nahe,* or *name* is represented by the same
character, which meant food offered to the *kami*. The festival of first-fruits had
its beginnings in the earliest days of the agricultural society of Yamato. Did not
the Sun Goddess, Amaterasu-ō-mikami, celebrate the harvest festival in her
'Hall of First Fruits', as told in the *Kojiki* and *Nihongi*? Again, did not Jimmu
Tennō, the first earthly sovereign, celebrate in the fourth year of his reign the
tasting of the first-fruits of the harvest together with the *kami*? According to the
*Nihongi* the tradition was that for 38 reigns, from the legendary Suisei to Temmu,
each sovereign held at the commencement of his reign a banquet of the first-
fruits of the rice harvest dedicated to the *kami*.[123] In the record of the Takahashi
Uji, a noble family, descriptions of the 'first' celebration of the festivals of 'Divine
Tasting' and 'Great New Food' (*Kamunie* and *Oonie* respectively) by Keiko Tennō
are given in the first year of his reign.[124] There is no question that the offering
of the first-fruits of the harvest to the ancestral *kami* and the *kami* of food was
intricately bound up in the life of the sovereign and of the people in this agricultural society of pre-Nara.

When we come to the time after the codes of law were drawn up—the *ritsuryō* period starting in the latter seventh and continuing into the eighth century—
we find that the *Taihō-ryō* (Taihō codes) of A.D. 701–2 were quite vague about any
distinction between the accession and the celebration of the Great New Food
Festival. The *Yōrō-ryō* (Yōrō civil code) of 718 stated only that the *Daijō-sai* must
be held at the commencement of a new reign. This is stated in the section on
*jingi-ryō* (laws concerning *kami* affairs) and also in the *shokuin-ryō* (laws for administrative personnel).

But by the time the *Gishiki* were compiled in the Jōgan era (859–77) the two
separate terms, *Niiname-sai* and *Daijō-sai*, had come into use. Therefore the distinction between these two forms of the festival was established some time between the completion of the Yōrō Codes in 718 and the Jōgan era in the Heian
period. This points to a growth and development in the celebration of harvest
festivals, and incidentally coincides with the growth and development of celebrations at the Ise Shrines, where an additional festival, the *Kanname-sai*, or *Kamunie
no matsuri*, festival of first-fruits to the deities, was celebrated (only at the Ise
Shrines) annually in the 9th month.

The particular procedures that characterize the *Daijō-sai* are testimony to the
sacredness of rice and to the reverence for the *kami* shown in the ceremonies in
which the sovereign offers a feast of the new rice, sake, and other products of the
field and ocean to the *kami* in a kind of sacred communion. The preparation for
this feast must begin in the early spring, when the rice paddies which are to produce the sacred grain to be used in these particular ceremonies must be selected.

---

[123] Amaterasu-ō-mikami had a 'new palace'
in which to celebrate the first-fruits festival.
Aston, *Nihongi*, pp. 40–1. See note on *Shinjō-sai*,
p. 86; for the celebration attributed to Jimmu

Tennō, p. 122; for that of Nintoku Tennō, p. 292,
etc.
[124] D. E. Mills, *Takahasi uzibumi*, p. 132. Keiko
was the 12th sovereign.

Purified paddies were selected in different parts of the country for two respective crops of rice—the *yuki* and *suki*, respectively. In the early stages of the celebration of the *Daijō-sai* the *yuki* paddies were variously located in Tamba, Inaba, Mino, Mikawa, Ise, and Echizen, showing a scattering to east and west of the capital. Similarly, the *suki* fields were selected in the provinces of Harima, Owari, Echizen, Misaka, Hizen, Bitchū, Tamba, and Inaba, the distribution being both east and west of the capital. But after the reign of Daigo Tennō, it became regularized to a pattern of choosing *yuki* paddies in districts (or provinces) east and south of the capital, while *suki* were selected to the north and west of the capital.[125]

One of the values of the seventh book of the *Engi-shiki* is that it gives some information about the functions of the sovereign. In all the other books based on the *jingi-ryō* we find almost no mention of the participation of the sovereign in religious ceremonies. For instance, the function of the Court in the worship of the ancestral Great Deity at the Ise Shrines is delegated to the Consecrated Princess, who spent only a part of her career in residence at the Shrines. The national festivals whose procedures appear in Books I–III mention only 'officialdom' and occasionally include mention of the imperial princes who participate in festivals. In Book VII we find the special vocabulary used only for an emperor and we find a description of his movements during the elaborate ceremonies which span several days. The *yuki* and *suki* rites took place on two successive nights; for it is during the dead of night that the *kami* descend to receive offerings of food and drink in sacred communion with the incarnate *kami*, the sovereign. The sacredness and solemnity of the entire proceedings are evident from the language and the rigidity of procedures.

Comparison of the procedures written in the *Engi-shiki* to those used for enthronement ceremonies of modern times will reveal great differences. Performance of ceremonies declined in the late Heian and Kamakura periods and dwindled into oblivion during the Oonin Wars of the fifteenth century. Later, under Tsunayoshi, the fifth Tokugawa shogun, there was a partial revival of imperial ceremonies. The full revival did not come about until the Meiji Restoration. By that time, however, both nomenclature and the form of the ceremonies, buildings, and procedures were markedly altered. The enthronement ceremonies of the Meiji, Taishō, and Shōwa emperors are not exact replicas of what took place in the Nara and Heian periods. The imperial visits to the Grand Shrine of Ise and to imperial mausolea are among the additions of recent times.

To facilitate understanding of the succession of events for the Great New Food Festival of the Enthronement, an outline is given below of the items of Book VII which are analyzed by Miyagi Eishō as having historical precedent at the time of compilation of the *Engi-shiki*.

[125] *Kokugakuin zasshi*, vol. 34, 1935, p. 2.

## The Items of Book VII

1 Matter of selecting the month [for the festival]
2 Messengers for the Great Purification
3 Presentation of offerings
4 August Lustration (*gokei*)
5 *Kami* along the way
6 Abstinences
7 Rice-in-ear for various purposes
8 Plucking the grain
9 Deities to be worshiped in the Sacred Districts
10 Details of plucking the grain
11 The *tametsu* rice
12 Protection of moors
13 The cooking enclosure
14 The sacred areas
15 Kanhatori [weavers of sacred raiment]
16–21 Various utensils to be made and furnished by the provinces of Kawachi, Izumi, Owari, Mikawa, and Bizen
22 Ceremonial vessels to be made
23 Tribute goods from Kii Province
24 Articles to be made by Awaji Province
25 Tribute goods from Awa Province
26 Messengers to procure ceremonial articles
27 Sake and rice
28 Ashes (to be prepared)
29 The Daijō-gū (temporary palace for the Great Food Festival)
30 The Kairyū-den (Sovereign's Ablution Hall)
31 Shields and spears for the *kami*
32 Sacred raiment (*miso*)
33 August *tatami* mats
34 Cooking procedures
35 Narrators (*kataribe*)
36 Ceremonial clothing (*saifuku*)
37 Distribution of symbolic offerings (procedures on the day of the hare)
38 Offerings of coarse-cloth raiment (*aratae no miso*)
39 Procedures on the day of the dragon
40 Procedures on the day of the snake
41 Procedures on the day of the horse
42 Depuration (*gesai*)
43 Great Purification (*ōharae*)
44 *Ootono-hogai* (Luck-wishing for the Palace)[126]

---

[126] E. Miyagi, *Engi-shiki no kenkyū*, I, pp. 129–57.

# ENGI-SHIKI, BOOK SEVEN

## Senso Daijō-sai[127]

### THE GREAT FOOD FESTIVAL OF THE ENTHRONEMENT

### Translation

WHENEVER the accession to the throne takes place by the 7th month of a given year the *Senso Daijō-sai* is held in that year; if in the 8th month or later, then the festival is held in the following year. (This refers to accession after abdication and does not mean enthronement after national mourning for the death of a Sovereign.)[128] In the given year, the officials in charge determine by divination beforehand the provinces and districts for the *yuki* and *suki*.[129] When the announcement has been made the orders are handed down according to precedent, and then they determine who shall supervise and who shall conduct the ceremonies.

At all times, there are Imperial Messengers for the Great Purification. In the first decade of the 8th month these are selected by divination and then dispatched: one to Left and Right Capital Offices, one to the five inner provinces, one for each of the seven circuits.[130] In the second decade once more Imperial Messengers are selected by divination and again dispatched: one to Left and Right Capital, one to the five inner provinces, one each to the provinces of Oomi and Ise. On the last day of the month the civil officials residing in the capital assemble and perform purification as they do for the ceremony for the two seasons.[131]

---

[127] The native reading for *Senso Daijō-sai* is *Senso-ōmube-no-matsuri*, or, according to *Nihon kigen* 日本記諺, 'Amanohitsugi wo fumu ōnae no matsuri'. Translation is 'Great food for the treading of the succession of heavenly light'. The element *jō* 甞 may be read *nahe, name, nie,* or *mube*, any one of which is an archaic word for food. Since *ahe* alone meant 'food', the *n-* may mean 'new'; in any case, the connotation is of food offered to the *kami*: sacred food.

[128] National mourning after the death of a sovereign lasted one year.

[129] The etymology of *yuki* and *suki* is not altogether certain, and the terms are written with different characters in different texts. The *E-S* uses 悠紀 and 主紀, respectively, in this book. In Bk VIII 由貴 is used for *yuki*. According to D. C. Holtom, *yuki* most probably meant 'consecrated-purified' [from *yufu*, to taboo, and *ki*, pure], while *suki* appears to be related to *tsugi*, meaning 'following' or 'next'. Thus the first food-offerings are *yuki* and the second are *suki no yuki* (*tsugi no yuki*). (*Suki* is written 次 in the *Nihongi*.) See *Japanese Enthronement Ceremonies* (1928), pp. 117-18 (90, 93-4).

[130] The five inner provinces (*kinai*) were Yamashiro, in which the capital was situated, Yamato, Kawachi, Izumi, and Settsu. The seven circuits (*shichidō*) were the groupings of provinces into regions: Tōkaidō, Tōsandō, Hokurikudō, San'indō, Nankaidō, San'yōdō, and Saikaidō.

[131] Meaning the twice-yearly Great Purification, *ōharae* 大祓, performed for the Court and the nation on the last day of the 6th month and the last day of the 12th month. In Bk VIII the ritual for this ceremony appears: the *ōharae no kotoba*.

At all times, after the Imperial Messengers for the Great Purification have left, the messengers are dispatched with offerings to the Deities of Heaven and Earth.[132] To the Shrine of the Great Deity[133] are sent: one Prince of 5th Rank or higher, one Nakatomi, one Imbe, one *urabe* diviner; and to the five inner provinces and the seven circuits, one person each. (Members of Nakatomi and Imbe Uji serve for these latter.) The procedure for these symbolic offerings at each of the major places[134] is: 5 *shaku* of stiff silk, 1 *shaku* each of five colors of thin pongee, 1 skein of silk thread, 1 *ton* of floss silk, 2 *ryō* of bark-cloth, 5 *ryō* of hemp; and for each of the minor places: 3 *shaku* of stiff silk, 1 skein of silk thread, 1 *ton* of floss silk, 2 *ryō* of bark-cloth, 5 *ryō* of hemp, and, altogether, 90 leaf-mats for wrapping. For all these Treasury goods are to be used.[135] (Major places and minor places refer to the various shrines which celebrate the *Toshigoi* Festival.)[136] Also 70 *ryō*[137] of rope, 52 porters, 52 carrying-poles.

At all times, when the Sovereign[138] goes down to the streamside to perform lustration in the last decade of the 10th month, the requirements are: 8 *shaku* each of five colors of thin pongee, 8 *shaku* each of five colors of stiff silk, 4 *tan* of tax cloth for august garments, 2 *tan* of tax cloth for kneeling-cushions for [reciting] the ritual,[139] 8 *kin* of Aki bark-cloth, 2 great *kin* each of bark-cloth and hemp, 19 sheets of yellow-bark, 4 mattocks, 6 *kin* each of abalone and bonito, 2 *to* of dried salmon, 8 *shō* of salt, 8 *kin* of assorted seaweeds, 4 *to* each of sake and rice, 4 *soku* of rice-in-ear, 4 food-mats, 20 bundles of oak, 8 saucers, 8 jars, 2 gourds, two palanquins, 6 porters.

At all times, when the Sovereign progresses to perform lustration symbolic offerings are to be presented to the *kami* along the way; for each: 1 *shaku* each of 5 colors of thin pongee (5 *shaku* for major and 3 *shaku* for minor presentations); 1 skein of silk thread, 1 *ton* of floss silk, 2 *ryō* of bark-cloth, 5 *ryō* of hemp; porters to wrap [articles] in leaf-mats (these last two are in proportion to the number of offerings).

At all times, when the Sovereign progresses, the Sacred Maidens and diviner's assistants[140] who serve as escorts are provided with riding horses.

[132] This is the double binomial *tenshin chigi*, or *amatsu-kami kunitsu-kami* 天神地祇, the *kami* that dwell in heaven and the *kami* that dwell on earth, or heavenly *kami* and earthly *kami*.

[133] Meaning the shrine of the Sun Goddess, Amaterasu-ō-mikami, in the Province of Ise.

[134] 'Places' means shrines, but the categories of 'major' (*dai* 大) and 'minor' (*shō* 小) actually refer to the *kami* that are enshrined therein. These distinctions are made in the list of shrines comprising Bks IX and X of the *E-S*, below. (See Introduction to Bks IX and X.)

[135] That is, tax goods which are stored in the Treasury (*ōkura-shō*) are used to supply these symbolic offerings. This paragraph makes clear the method of distributing official symbolic offerings from the *Jingi-kan* to government-supported shrines throughout the country.

[136] The *Toshigoi* Festival is the first festival of the agricultural year, celebrated on the 4th day of the second month, with offerings made to 3,132 *kami*, of which 492 were major deities and 2,640 were minor. Again, this information is given in the list of shrines in Bks IX and X.

[137] This *ryō* 丁 is a unit of length, not weight, believed to have been 7 *shaku* (approx. 8½ ft). Headnote in *Kokushi taikei* ed. of *E-S*, p. 143.

[138] Here the title 'sumeramikoto' 天皇, also read *tennō*, is used for the sovereign.

[139] The kneeling-mat is used when the Nakatomi recites (i.e. reads aloud) the *norito* (ritual) for the *Daijō-sai*, text of which is given below in Bk VIII, ritual no. 14, The Great New Food Festival.

[140] *Heza* 戸座 were young boys who assisted the *urabe* diviners with making fires and doing other tasks connected with the heating of tortoise-shells for divination.

At all times, there is to be one month of partial abstinence[141] (starting the first day of the 11th month and lasting through the last day); total abstinence is for three days (starting on the ox day and ending on the hare day). This month of abstinence is announced in advance to the officials in charge, and when the order[142] is handed down to the inner provinces no one may participate in Buddhist fasts or maigre feasts. The language to be used is: 'death' is called 'getting well', illness is called 'slumber', to weep is 'to shed salt', to strike is 'to caress', blood is called 'sweat'; meat is called 'vegetables', and a tomb is called 'clod of earth'.[143]

At all times, the rice-in-ear required for the *Daijō* celebration is furnished to the extent of 10,000 *soku* from each province as regular taxes,[144] as well as tribute and taxes and crops produced by the males[145] in the district where divination is done; if there are sustenance villages[146] in that district then villages of other districts combine some of their rice with the former. But if both provinces are asked for more rice-in-ear, they deal with it on a temporary basis, supplying in accordance with what is asked for. (To substitute therefor the regular taxes are raised; the increase is then used to make up the need.)

At all times, the paddies for grain to be plucked number 6 *tan* in each province. (Paddies worked by the farmers are to be used; to substitute, let it be made up out of regular taxes.) In the first decade of the 8th month the [*Jingi-*] *kan* is asked to send one chief diviner and three *urabe* diviners, who are to be dispatched two to each of the two provinces. One of them is named the diviner of the rice-ears[147] and one is named priest diviner.[148] Upon reaching the respective provinces they each go to the sacred district,[149] where they perform purification rites. (For this are required: 1 horse, 1 sword, 1 bow, 1 deerhide, 1 *tan* of tax cloth, 1 *kin* of bark-cloth, 4 *kin* each of bonito and abalone, 4 *kin* each of *wakame* and *arame*,[150]

---

[141] Partial abstinence, *ara-imi* 散齋, was practiced for a whole month prior to this 'great' festival. Total abstinence, *ma-imi* 致齋, was practiced for the three days prior to the festival day. The *Daijō-sai* is the only festival of the 'great' category, according to *E-S* Bk I. In contrast, for festivals of 'middle' category (*Toshigoi, Tsukinami, Kanname, Niiname,* and *Kamo*), the requirement was three days of partial abstinence and one day of total abstinence preceding the festival day.

[142] The order is a *fu* 符, an official government directive. Most such orders were handed down from the *Dajō-kan* and were called *dajō-kampu*, though occasionally the *Jingi-kan* issued a *jingi-kampu*.

[143] It will be noted that this list is the same as the one given in Bk VI as words tabooed in the presence of the Princess of Kamo. See n. 23 above.

[144] *Shōzei* or *ōchikara* 正税 is the regular tax on the land, paid in rice to government collectors. Rice so collected was stored in government granaries in the capital and used for general

expenses. R. K. Reischauer, *Early Japanese History*, A, p. 222. Sansom calls it 'tax proper'; *TASJ*, ser. 1, XI, p. 127.

[145] Namely, *chūnan* 中男 (same meaning as *shōchō* 少丁)—who, according to the Taihō code, were the young workers—males of ages 17 through 20. In the 9th year of Tempyō-shōhō (757) it was changed to 18 through 21. *Nihonshi-jiten*.

[146] The *fugō* 封郷 were villages (*sato*) designated to furnish sustenance rice (or goods) to support the Imperial House.

[147] *Ina-no-mi-no-urabe* 稲實卜部, a diviner appointed to determine the ripening of the rice-ears.

[148] That is, a *negi-no-urabe*. For *negi*, see n. 74 above.

[149] *Saigun* 齋郡, 'taboo' district, set aside for the cultivation of sacred rice for the *yuki* and *suki* feasts.

[150] *Arame* 滑海藻 or 麁布, an edible seaweed, *Ecklonia bicyclis* or *Eisenia bicyclis*; modern-day *manakashi*.

4 *to* each of rice and sake, 4 *shō* of salt, which the respective districts prepare; moreover, for each village: 1 knife, 1 quiver, 1 mattock, 1 *kin* of hemp, 1 *soku* of rice-in-ear.) That completed, they select by divination the rice paddies and the various functionaries for the sacred area. (Men and women singers are not determined by divination.) One *sakatsuko*[151] (an unmarried daughter of the prefect or assistant prefect of that district is selected by divination for this). One honorable *sakanami*,[152] one sifter of flour, 2 helpers, one *tametsu*[153] *sakanami* (the foregoing all women); one lord of the rice-ears,[154] one ash-burner, four firewood-cutters, 20 singers, 20 women singers. When these are ready, the sacred area is propitiated.[155] For this the symbolic offerings are: 5 *shaku* each of five colors of thin pongee, 3 *kin* each of bark-cloth and hemp, 5 *shaku* of colored hempen cloth, 2 mattocks, 2 each of axes, hatchets, and sickles, 2 *hiki* of pongee for lustrous robes[156] for two diviners, 2 *tan* of tribute cloth, 8 *ton* of floss silk; and for the *sakatsuko* and *sakanami*: 3 *tan* 1 *jō* 4 *shaku* of tribute cloth, 1 ½ *ton* of floss silk, 1 *ryō* 1 *bu* 2 *shu* of sewing thread. For all these Treasury goods are to be used. (But the sake and food for the propitiation festivals are furnished by the respective provinces.) A Hall of Eight Deities[157] is to be built (4 *jō* long, 1 *jō* wide), and one sacred shelter for the rice[158] (2 *jō* long, 8 *shaku* wide), one administrative building (4 *jō* long, 1 *jō* 2 *shaku* wide), one shelter for the lord of the rice-ears, one shelter for the *sakatsuko* and others (each 2 *jō* long and 1 *jō* 2 *shaku* wide), all to be made of unpeeled wood and thatched with grasses; the side walls to be made of grasses. One well is to be dug (a roof built over it). There are to be 16 square *jō* within the compound; brushwood is to be used for the fences, and wood to make the doors. Within this sacred compound eight *kami* are to be worshiped (Mitoshiro-no-kami, Takami-

---

[151] The *sakatsuko* 造酒兒, lit. 'brewer', was the young girl entrusted with the sacred duties of initiating the plucking ceremony, in which the ripened rice plants are plucked whole (not cut off) out of the paddies; of initiating the preparation of a sacred site for storing the rice; and of initiating the cutting of wood used for the buildings erected for the ceremonies, and the cutting of grass to thatch them.

[152] The *on-sakanami* 御酒波, 'honorable sake women', were those who serve the sovereign by brewing sacred sake under the direction of the *sakatsuko*.

[153] *Tametsu* (多明) means 'having delicious flavor'. *Tametsu-mono* are delicacies. The term appears in the *Kojiki* for the viands which came forth from the head and body of the Food Goddess, after she was slain. See Philippi, *Kojiki*, p. 87.

[154] *Ina-no-mi-no-kimi* 稻實公 may be the 'lady' or the 'lord' of rice-ears.

[155] *Shizumu* 鎭む is to pacify or to calm the spirits of the area in order to prevent any evil influences, natural disaster, or pollution from endangering the cultivation of the pure rice.

[156] Lustrous robes, *akawa* or *myōe* 明衣, were

a type of sacred dress (*saifuku*) worn to maintain ritual purity during festivals. They were white robes of lustrous raw silk, worn over the customary clothing. *Kōgaku sōsho* ed. of *E-S*, III, p. 62; *Shintō daijiten*, III, p. 325.

[157] Hasshin-den 八神殿, a building within the sacred compound of buildings in which the *kami* connected with food and the growing of rice are enshrined. The list is given in the text and includes Mitoshiro (Mitoshi-no-kami), a god of rice cultivation; Takami-musubi, an ancestral spirit worshiped by the Imperial House; Niwa-takatsuhi, offspring of Ootoshi-no-kami, an agricultural and land-protecting deity; Oomiketsu, the Food Goddess; Oomiya-no-me, another ancestral deity of the Imperial House, worshiped within the Imperial Sake Office; Kotoshironushi, offspring of Ookuninushi-no-kami, and associated with Izumo myths; Asuha, also offspring of Ootoshi-no-kami, and a protector of land and gardens; and Haigi, protector of houses and buildings. See also nn. 170 and 309.

[158] *Imiya* 齋屋 is a 'taboo dwelling' or hut. I use 'shelter' to translate *ya* in this passage, as they are small and temporary buildings.

musubi-no-kami, Niwatakatsuhi-no-kami, Oomiketsu-no-kami, Oomiya-no-me-no-kami, Kotoshironushi-no-kami, Asuha-no-kami, and Haigi-no-kami). The symbolic offerings for each presentation: 4 *shaku* of stiff silk, 1 *shaku* of each of five colors of thin pongee, 1 *shaku* of colored hemp-cloth, 1 *ryō* of bark-cloth, 1 skein of silk thread, 1 *ton* of floss silk, 1 *tan* of ordinary cloth, 1 mattock, 1 *soku* of rice-in-ear, 4 *shō* each of rice and sake, 2 *kin* each of abalone, bonito, and *wakame*, 2 *shō* each of dried meat and salt. For all of these the products of the province are to be used.

At all times, eight *kami* are to be worshiped in the sacred compounds of the sacred districts (the two provinces provide lustrous robes and quilts to each).

At all times, for plucking the rice plants the diviners lead the governor of the province, the prefects of the districts and on down to lower functionaries to the rice paddies to pluck the grain. First the *sakatsuko*, then the lord of the rice-ears, then the *sakanami*, then the lower functionaries, then commoners, in succession pluck the grain. Then it goes to the sacred compound where it is dried and stored. Then they begin to divide it up, taking the first 4 *soku* which were plucked (4 bundles making a *soku*).[159] They measure the amount for the august cooked-rice offerings, the rest they measure for the two kinds of sake, both dark and light. Then it is all heaped into baskets, 1 *soku* in each basket. Two baskets make a load; supports are put under each load. Covers are made from woven reeds,[160] and on them *sakaki* branches are inserted and bark-cloth festooned. When that is done workers on foot take up the loads; for every 10 loads there is one junior attendant to urge them on. Diviners, governors, and prefects lead the lower functionaries and others. Forward and backward they supervise the transportation. In the procession the rice-in-ear for the august cooked rice is carried first, the remainder follows this. The lord of the rice-ears wears a bark-cloth headdress[161] and shows the way. They reach the capital in the last decade of the 9th month. Divination is done outside the limits of the sacred area. A temporary shelter is built beforehand and the august rice is stored therein for a while.

At all times, in the *yuki* and *suki* provinces the districts selected by divination must apportion and furnish 30 *koku* of *tametsu* rice (for *tametsu* sake), 40 short *tatami* mats, 70 seat-mats, 70 long mats, 50 split-bamboo mats, and 300 workers on foot who are sent to transport this rice and are to be urged on in the same way as those for the plucked rice plants.

At all times, the mountains where materials for the *Daijō* buildings[162] and oak leaves for sacred food offerings are to be gotten, as well as the moors where reeds for thatching are to be cut, and ground to be used for the sacred areas, are all to be

---

[159] Usually one *soku* 束 equals 10 *wa* 把, or bundles. Here *soku* of only 4 *wa* are specified, probably because they were uncut sheaves, roots and all.

[160] *Kaya* 茅, an arundo, *Miscanthus sinensis*.

[161] *Yuukazura* 木綿鬘 are sacred fillets of bark-cloth (not a 'wig'). The use of them attests to the great sanctity of this festival. They had the form of a narrow band of bark-cloth around the head tied in a double bow at the back.

[162] This means the lumber for constructing the buildings—Yuki-den and Suki-den—within the *Daijō* enclosure set up for this festival in the capital.

selected by divination by the members of the *Jingi-kan* and the governors of the provinces together in the first decade of the 8th month. (In divining the sacred area, first it is exorcized; required articles for this are forwarded by the respective provinces.) When that is done, the fact is announced to the *Jingi-kan*. And the prefect in whose district the mountains and moors are situated is made to keep them under taboo and prevent any defiled person[163] from entering them. The mountain from which materials for the august *koto* for the Pacification of August Spirits[164] are gathered is subject to the foregoing procedure; there are to be four kite-tail *koto*[165] which the *Jingi-kan* orders the Bureau of Skilled Artisans to construct and send up.

At all times, the compound where the august foods are to be cooked and the food for the officials under particular taboo[166] is to be prepared must be selected by divination at a place conveniently near the Palace. When that is done the festival of propitiation takes place. Symbolic offerings for this are: 1 *shaku* each of 5 colors of thin pongee, 1 *shaku* colored hemp-cloth, 1 *kin* each of bark-cloth and hemp, 2 *ton* of floss silk, 4 *tan* of commercial cloth,[167] 5 mattocks, 4 *shō* of rice, 1 *to* of sake, 1 *kin* each of abalone and *wakame*, 2 *tan* of tribute cloth for emoluments to *hafuri*; for all these, products of the province are to be used. (For the other festivals the kinds and amounts of offerings are not stated, as all duplicate these.) To be built: 1 shelter for food offerings, 1 sake shelter, 1 shelter for offerings to the *kami*, 1 for utensils, 1 for Palace cooks, 1 for serving the august foods, 1 for cooking the different kinds of fish, and 1 for preparation of foods (for the foregoing shelters: the number and dimensions of them may vary according to the demands of the affair). All are to be built of boards and thatched. One well is to be dug. The compound is to have a gate opening on each of the four sides. When the building of these is done, the diviners of the rice-ears enter the compound and perform exorcism. Articles required for this are sent up by the respective provinces.

At all times, the sacred area in the capital is set up in advance and divided in two: the *yuki* is to the left and the *suki* to the right. The two provinces are to send the plucked grain. When it has reached the capital, first the ground is hallowed. When that is done the *sakatsuko* first takes the sacred spade;[168] then they begin

---

[163]  *Kegare-bito* or *enin* 穢人 is a person who is unclean, having suffered a defilement. Ceremonial defilement occurred if one came into contact with pollution from birth, death, illness, blood, burial service, etc., as outlined in Bk III of *E-S*.

[164] The *Chinkon-sai* or *Mitama-shizume-no-matsuri*, or *Oomitama-furi-no-matsuri*, was the festival for pacifying or calming the spirits of the sovereign and the ancestral *kami*, held in the 11th month. See Bk VIII, no. 15.

[165] The *shibi-no-ongoto* or *tobi-no-o-goto* was in ancient times a kind of zither with six strings, the narrow end in the form of a large bird's tail. A latter-day one with 13 strings may be seen in the Chōkokan Museum of the Grand Shrine of Ise.

[166] *Omibito* 小齋人 ('lesser avoidance persons')

are the participating officials who are under the strictest abstinence because they serve in the intimate presence of the *kami* and the sovereign during the *Niiname-sai* and *Daijō-sai* festivals. They wear purified clothing, *omigoromo*; are selected to serve by divination; refrain from use of any of the taboo words (*imikotoba*); abstain from eating meat. The *omibito* are contrasted with *ōmibito*, persons under general taboo or general avoidance.

[167] *Tan'i*, or *shōfu* 商布, was hemp-cloth used as a medium of exchange. (See tax cloth, n. 31, and tribute cloth, n. 71.)

[168] The 'taboo spade' or 'taboo mattock' is *imi-suki* 齋鍬. Similarly, below we find the *imi-ono* 齋斧 'taboo axe' or cult axe.

to sweep the ground; then holes for the posts at the four corners of the enclosure are dug. The diviners lead the provincial governors and prefects of the districts and all those down to laborers. They go into the mountain selected by divination and cut the wood; then they worship the *kami* of the mountain, and that done, the *sakatsuko* first takes a sacred axe and commences to chop a tree. After this the different laborers lay hands to the work. (Cutting the timber for the Daijō-gū duplicates this.) Again, the diviners lead the prefects and lower functionaries to the moors selected by divination to cut the reeds.[169] Then they worship the *kami* of the moors. That done, the *sakatsuko* first cuts the grass, then the various others lay a hand to it. (Cutting the grasses for the Daijō-gū duplicates this.) The sacred enclosure is divided into inner and outer compounds, for which brushwood is used to make the fences and wood to make the gates. In the inner compound the Hall of Eight Deities[170] is to be built, 1 shelter for the rice-ears, 1 shelter each for dark sake and light sake, and 1 storehouse, 1 shelter for sacred food offerings, 1 for mortars, 1 for Palace cooks, and 1 fermenting room. In the outer compound a shelter is to be built for *tametsu* sake, 1 storehouse, 1 shelter for cooking august offerings, 3 shelters for *tametsu* cooking, and 1 fermenting room (dimensions of the foregoing buildings are according to need). For all of them unpeeled wood is to be used, and reeds for thatching. The screening is done with reeds (but, for the fermenting rooms, walls must be painted). For the interiors, lengths of straw matting are to be used; for the sake shelters and fermentation rooms, straw matting is used for the ceilings[171] and bleached cloth for the interior. For the two wells: when the divining has been completed the *sakatsuko* commences to dig the august well and the diviners of rice-ears commence to dig the well which is for the *sakatsuko*. When the building of the two compounds is completed the august rice-ears are gathered into the rice-ear shelter, but the grain for the august cooked rice is separately stored on shelves built for it. The Eight Deities of August Food are to be worshiped inside the inner compound. (The symbolic offerings for this are the same as those preceding.)[172]

At all times, for the weaving of deity raiment,[173] the *Jingi-kan* dispatches one shrine chief[174] of the shrine of the Kanhatori in the first decade of the 9th month, and giving him a post-station bell,[175] sends him to Mikawa Province, where he

---

[169] The character 草 is interpreted to mean *kaya* (see n. 160) as in *fuki-kaya* 葺草, thatching grass or thatching reeds.

[170] Hasshin-den here enshrined the same eight *kami* for whom the hall in the fields was erected (n. 157 above). They differ from the eight gods of the *Jingi-kan* in respect to five, while Takamimusubi, Oomiketsu, and Kotoshironushi are common to both sets of eight. See the celebration of *Mitama-shizume* Festival, *E-S*, Bk II.

[171] A *nageshi* or *shōjin* 承塵, which is straw matting stretched overhead in place of a ceiling.

[172] The list of offerings appears above in the ninth paragraph after the list of names of the

eight *kami*.

[173] The reading is *kammiso* (*wo oru*) 神服 (織) but the same characters are used for the Kanhatori (also written 神服部) Uji who were the hereditary group of weavers of divine raiment for presentation to the *kami*.

[174] *Kannushi* or *kamunushi* 神主, 'deity chief', or the chief priest of a shrine; in this case the family shrine of the Kanhatori Uji. See n. 297.

[175] The post-station bell, *ekirei* 驛鈴, was received by public messengers when riding from one province into another to permit them the use of post-station horses.

gathers together members of the deity households.[176] Then two chief weavers of deity raiment and six weaving women and two artisans are selected by divination. When that is done, the shrine chief leads the ten persons, from chiefs downward, and carrying 10 skeins of tribute silk-thread that the Kanhatori of said province have forwarded, he returns to the sacred area in the capital. First a worship service is held at the weaving house; after that they commence to weave. For building they need: 4 axes, 4 chisels, 4 knives, 4 planes, 3 gimlets,[177] and 3 fire-kindling sets (required for the foregoing: 3 *tei* of iron), 2 deerhides, 3 *kin* 4 *ryō* each of bark-cloth and hemp, 1 quiver, 4 mats, and 4 *tan* 8 *shaku* of tribute cloth for lustrous robes for the 10 men and women, all to be supplied from official goods. As for the halls for Kanhatori, there is 1 for each province, and 1 resthouse each for the men and the women Kanhatori, 1 resthouse for *hafuri* (dimensions of these are according to need), all to be built of unpeeled wood and thatched with reeds.

At all times, as to utensils which are required for the presentation of sacred offerings (in sacred language: *yukamono*):[178] the officials in charge must take careful note of the number of utensils needed and notify the [*Jingi-*] *kan* beforehand. In the first decade of the 8th month they depute scribes of the Imperial Household Ministry[179] and send them to oversee manufacture in five provinces: one scribe to Kawachi and Izumi, one to Owari and Mikawa, and one to Bizen. When they reach the province they first perform purification, then the manufacture commences. Symbolic offerings in each province are:

1 *jō* each of five colors of plain silk, 6 *kin* 10 *ryō* each of bark-cloth and hemp, 4 mattocks, 2 bearskins, all to be supplied from Treasury goods.

*Kawachi Province* is to make 20 rush boxes, 18 clay hand-basins, 18 large jars, 9 small hand-basins, 16 short-stemmed dishes, 16 jars for hot water, 16 small dishes, 20 coverless dishes, 120 tray-tables, 16 salt saucers, 8 rice-gruel dishes, 56 large dishes with front lip, 8 sake cups, 20 cups, 80 tray-tables, 80 stands for them, and 30 clay bowls.

*Izumi Province* is caused to make 9 rush boxes, 1 Ike large jar, 10 great jars, 1 kettle, 6 oil dishes, 6 oil-dish stands, 2 oil jars, 6 chopping bowls.

*Owari Province* is caused to make 8 jars, 50 jugs, 40 box-stands, 8 shallow earthenware vessels, 10 bowls, 32 short-stemmed dishes, 8 sake jars, 16 spouted vessels, 40 coverless saucers, 8 ceramic mortars, 8 decorated earthenware jars, 40 pedestalled dishes, 12 ritual clay urns,[180] 12 sake cups, and 8 sake pourers.

---

[176] *Shinko* 神戸, also pronounced *kambe*, were the households engaged in working or raising produce for a shrine; here, the households of Kanhatori. See n. 7 above.

[177] Some texts say: 'two gimlets'. These tools appear to be for the construction of their looms, and the other articles for ceremonial dress and for offerings.

[178] Sacred language, *shingo* 神語, is another way of saying archaic language. *Yukamono* breaks down into *yu*, meaning 'sacred' or 'taboo'; *ka*, ceremonial clay utensil; and *mono* 'things'. It is written here 雑器 (various utensils), or 由加物.

[179] *Kunai-shō no fubito* (*fumbito*) 宮內省史生.

[180] Translation for *tsubaha* 都婆波.

*Mikawa Province* is caused to make 40 *torosuki*,[181] 32 ritual clay urns (16 large and 16 medium sized), 8 ritual water-pitchers,[182] 60 each of *yamatsuki* and small saucers, 60 each of *itsuki* and spouted vessels.[183]

*Bizen Province* is caused to make 30 shallow earthenware vessels, 30 water-jugs and 60 ritual clay urns (30 large and 30 small), 30 earthenware jugs, 30 standing jugs, 30 sake pourers, 30 spouted vessels, 30 waste jars, 30 short-stemmed dishes, 30 *yamatsuki*, 30 coverless dishes, 30 sake cups, 30 small wine jars, 30 ceramic mortars, and 30 *itsuki*.

At all times, materials for the ceremonial utensils required for offerings to the *kami* are to be requested for the *Jingi-kan* in the first decade of the 9th month. Three diviners are deputed and dispatched to the three provinces.[184] They first perform great purification, then the affair takes place. Requirements: 1 horse, 1 sword, 1 bow, 20 arrows, 1 mattock, 1 deerskin, 1 *tan* of tax cloth, 8 *ryō* of bark-cloth, 1 *kin* of hemp, 2 *kin* each of abalone, bonito, *wakame*, and *arame*, 2 *shō* of salt, 2 *to* each of rice and sake (the foregoing are to be sent by the respective districts),[185] 1 horse, 1 sword, 1 bow, 20 arrows, 1 mattock, 1 deerskin, 1 *tan* of tax cloth, 1 *kin* each of bark-cloth and hemp, 4 *kin* each of bonito and abalone, 4 *kin* each of *wakame* and *arame*, 4 *to* each of sake and rice, 4 *shō* of salt (foregoing are to be sent by the two districts of Oe and Naka in Awa Province). For symbolic offerings and articles to be made for presentation to the *kami*, as well as require-ments for the robes for the girl divers[186] (1 *jō* 4 *shaku* of ordinary cloth apiece), Treasury goods are to be used. But the provisions are to be supplied from regular taxes of those provinces, at 2 *shō* of rice per person per day. (Kii to provide for 7 days, Awa for 10 days.) When they have finished making the articles, the diviners forward these to the sacred area, dividing them between the two [*yuki* and *suki*] provinces; but the *arame* and bark-cloth presented by Awa Province are to be sent to the *Jingi-kan*.

As for the items to be presented by *Kii Province*, the 4 strings of thin-sliced abalone, 6 baskets each of fresh abalone and fresh periwinkle, 6 baskets each of *tsujimo* and *komo*,[187] 10 *ka* of salt-broiled periwinkle, are all to be gathered, weighed, and prepared by 10 girl divers of Kata [District]. Symbolic offerings for this require: 1 *shaku* each of 5 colors of thin pongee, 1 *shaku* of colored hemp-cloth, 5 *ryō* each of bark-cloth and hemp, 1 leaf-mat, 10 chisels, and 2 knives to be used by the girl divers.

*Awaji Province* is to make 20 jars (each holding 1 *to* 5 *shō*), 100 shallow vessels (each holding 1 *to*), and 200 jars (1-*to* capacity). The symbolic offerings for

---

[181] *Torosuki* 等呂須伎, ceremonial clay dish.

[182] Translation for *tashiraka*, 多志良加.

[183] *Yamatsuki* and *itsuki* are varieties of pedes-talled dishes; a spouted vessel is *hazō* (*hanzō*) 匜.

[184] The three provinces are Awa 阿波 on Shikoku, Kii (part of present Wakayama Pref.),

and Awaji, the island in the Inland Sea.

[185] The districts (*kōri* 郡) in which the cere-monial articles are made, as Oe and Naka, which are mentioned.

[186] The *katsukime* 潜女, who dive for shellfish.

[187] These are two kinds of freshwater plant.

this are: 3 *shaku* each of 5 colors of thin pongee, 3 *shaku* of colored hemp-cloth, 1 *kin* each of bark-cloth and hemp, 1 leaf-mat. Tools for making articles: 2 each of large mattocks, axes, hatchets, and sickles. When manufacture is finished, one member of the Ooshi of *atae* rank[188] of that province dons the bark-cloth headdress, carries the *sakaki* branch, and shows the way. *Awa Province* is to present 1 *tan* of *arame*, 6 *kin* of bark-cloth, 15 vessels of trout, 15 jars of pickled blossom and root of garlic, 15 baskets each of dried *shikukusa*,[189] sweet potatoes,[190] and citrus fruits[191] (Imbe prepare the foregoing); 45 nets of abalone, 15 jars of abalone sushi,[192] and 20 jars of small shellfish, sea-urchins, and oysters combined[193] (the foregoing gathered by 10 girl divers of Naka). Symbolic offerings for this are: 6 *shaku* each of 5 colors of thin pongee, 6 *shaku* of colored hemp-cloth, 2 *kin* each of bark-cloth and hemp, 1 leaf-mat. Tools for preparing these: 4 each of large mattocks, axes, hatchets, and sickles, 12 chisels, 4 knives, 2 planes, and 3 fire-making sets, all of which the Imbe and diving girls measure out, make up, and prepare.

At all times, messengers from the three provinces of Kii, Awaji, and Awa take the ceremonial utensils. On the day they go up to the capital, the streets in the provinces on the way are swept and a welcome is given.

At all times, the rice for dark and light sake is to be pounded. The *sakatsuko* commences this and then the other women join in the pounding. When it is done the *kami* of the wells are worshiped, then the *kami* of the stoves. On the day they begin the brewing of the sake the *kami* of sake are again worshiped. Each province must have 4 great jars and 4 shallow clay vessels (2 each for dark sake and 2 for light sake; all to be furnished by the Office of Palace Tables), 4 large containers, 4 mortars, 4 pestles, 8 winnowing baskets, 3 rice-steamers, 8 large carrying-baskets, 8 flat boxes, 3 sake vats, 4 white-wood boxes, 2 split cypress-wood boxes, 2 large tables, 2 Kara chests, 1 large white-wood chest, 6 small boxes, 7 gourds, 4 dippers, 2 sieves for ashes, 2 sieves for flour; the great jars and shallow clay vessels are to be covered with bleached hemp-cloth. When brewing the *tametsu* sake 30 *koku* of rice prepared in the province are to be used.

At all times, one master brewer[194] of august sake in the Imperial Sake Office leads ash-burner and 5 underlings[195] and they go to the mountain for divining. First they worship the *kami* of the mountain, then they do the burning and get 1 *koku* of lye. They are to carry with them 1 each: hatchet, adze, and sickle, 2 white-wood boxes, and 2 rush-mats.

---

[188] One person of the Ooshi Uji of *atae* rank. These were formerly the local chieftains, *kuni-no-miyatsuko*, of Awaji and Sanuki provinces. A. Oota, *Nihon jōdai shakai soshiki*, pp. 569–70.

[189] *Shikukusa*, or *shiuno* 乾羊蹄.

[190] *Ie-no-imo* 蹲鴟.

[191] Small, thin-skinned sour oranges: *tachibana* 橘子.

[192] Sushi is fish or meat pickled and eaten with rice.

[193] Shellfish are here *shitatami* 細螺; the sea-urchins, *uni* 棘甲蠃; and oysters, *kaki* 石花.

[194] *Miki no miyatsuko* 酒部: older name for brewers of august sake for the sovereign's use. (Later pronunciation: *sakabe*.)

[195] The *hasetsukai* 駈使 are those who work under shrine attendants or staff as brewers and assistants.

At all times, seven days before the festival, those who build the Daijō-gū, two officials, a Nakatomi and an Imbe of the *Jingi-kan*, in order of rank, lead the governor of the *yuki* province and the various functionaries, forming a single line. Again, the Nakatomi and Imbe separate from them and lead the governor of the *suki* province and those under him in manner similar to the others, all in a single file. These lines start from the east- and west-side gates of the Chōdō-in[196] and arrive at the palace ground (in the south garden of the Ryūbi-dō),[197] then the lines divide to left and right (*yuki* to the east and *suki* to the west). That ground is ceremonially pacified.[198] The respective provinces are made to prepare these symbolic offerings: 4 *tan* of tax cloth, 1 *kin* of Aki bark-cloth, 2 *kin* of Oshi bark-cloth, 2 *kin* of hemp, 8 mattocks, 1 *to* of rice, 2 *to* of clear sake, 8 *shō* of dark sake, 4 *kin* of abalone, 10 *kin* of bonito, 10 *kin* of *wakame*, 1 *to* 6 *shō* of dried meat, 4 *shō* of salt, 10 jars, 10 saucers. The *sakatsuko* from both provinces take *sakaki* branches, deck them with bark-cloth, and set them up in the four corners of the enclosure and at the gates. When that is done they take the consecrated spades (4 for each province, wrapped in cloth bags and tied with bark-cloth). They commence to dig the holes for the posts at the four corners of the hall, 8 spades to each hole; afterwards the various workers take over the digging at one time. That palace measures 21 *jō* 4 *shaku* from east to west, and 15 *jō* south to north. In the middle on the east side is the *yuki-in*, and on the west side is the *suki-in*. In the palace fence due south there is a gate. Within it there is a brushwood fence. On the east there is a gate; outside it a brushwood fence is to be built. (The *yuki* province builds this.) Again, there is a gate due north, inside it a brushwood fence; and there is a gate to the west, outside it a brushwood fence (the *suki* province builds this). The middle fence between the two structures is built by the two provinces. On the south end of the central fence 1 *jō* from the brushwood fence is a small gate (built by the two provinces). For the fences brushwood is used. Spears are planted in the eight fence-ends. Into them the branches of oak (*shii*) are inserted. (In ancient language they are called *shii no wae*.)[199] The various gates are 9 *shaku* in height, 8 in width (small gate less). *Shimoto*[200] is woven to make the doors. The Yuki Hall is to be built with one main hall (4 *jō* long, 1 *jō* 6 *shaku* wide), ridge going south to north. The 3 *ken* to the north form one room and the 2 to the south a chamber. On the south is a door. Screen matting forms the door. Across the roof-ridge are placed 8 crossbeams[201] and the gable-boards[202] are extended. For construction unpeeled wood is to be used, and for thatching, green miscanthus.

---

[196] The Chōdō-in, also called Hasshō-in, was the first building directly in front as one entered the Palace precinct (*dai-dairi*) at the Suzaku Gate.

[197] Lit. 'dragon's tail walk,' a route in an ornamental garden of the palace.

[198] *Shizume-matsuru*—the spirits of the ground are appeased and quietened so that no evil force or pollution may enter.

[199] *Shii no wae* 志比乃和惠

[200] *Shimoto* 椅, a native tree, also called *sarugaki* 猿柿 (*Diospyrus lotus*), wild persimmon; also equated with *beni-ringo* 紅林檎.

[201] *Katsuogi*, the ornamental crossbeams set on top of the ridgepole.

[202] *Chigi* or *higi* are the crossed barge-boards or gable-boards so prominent in the architecture of the Ise Shrines. This feature of shrine architecture occurs and reoccurs in the *norito* of Bk VIII.

Beams of cypress are used for the ceiling, horizontal trabeation is of straw matting, and the partitions are of miscanthus. Straw matting is used over the exterior and interior. On the ground tufted grasses[203] are spread. Added to the foregoing are coverings of split bamboo, and in the chamber straw matting is spread over the covering of split bamboo. On top of the straw matting are laid white-edged august *tatami*. On the *tatami* are placed triangular pillows.[204] (*Tatami* and pillows are installed by the Bureau of Housekeeping; the making of them is in the procedures for that Bureau.)[205] Curtains of ordinary cloth are hung before the doorways (to be hung by the Bureau of Palace Storehouses). On the east, south, and west sides of the building hang reed blinds on the outside, and on the inside are sliding doors of straw matting. But for 2 *ken* on the west side the blinds are furled up, leaving an open interval. In the northeast corner of the enclosure the house for the kitchen is built. (Length and width thereof are the same as for the main sanctuary.) The eaves run east to west. The eastern eaves are screened with oak brushwood. Under the east wall shelves are constructed. Along 3 *ken* of the west eaves foods are stored. On the north of the kitchen house the mortar house is built (1 *jō* 4 *shaku* long and 8 *shaku* wide). It is screened with oak brushwood and has a door on the west side. On the south and west sides of the two structures brush-wood fences are to be built, making this a separate enclosure. To the southeast of the main sanctuary an august privy is to be constructed (1 *jō* long and 8 *shaku* wide). Its walls are like those of the main sanctuary. On its west side is a door.

The hall of the *suki-in* is made to conform to the foregoing. The construction of it is to be completed within five days. The Nakatomi and the Imbe lead the Sacred Maidens and others in consecrating the buildings and the gates. The symbolic offerings for this are: 3 *shaku* of each of 5 colors of thin pongee, 2 *ryō* of silk thread, 1 *kin* of Aki bark-cloth, 2 round boxes, 2 tables, 2 *shō* of rice, 2 *shō* of sake, 2 jars, and 2 saucers, all of these to be requested from the *Jingi-kan*. (Same for requirements for the propitiation ceremony later on.)

At all times, the Bureau of Carpentry builds the main sanctuary of the Kairyū-den[206] to the north of the Daijō-gū (4 *jō* long, 1 *jō* 6 *shaku* wide, the ridge running east to west; 3 *ken* of its west side are straw matting; doors are on the east and south.) It is built of unpeeled timbers and thatched with rushes. The horizontal timbers are covered with straw matting. (The various august items are all offered according to precedent by the officials in charge.)

At all times, 4 august shields are put up at the south and north gates of the Daijō-gū (each 1 *jō* 2 *shaku* long, upper width 3 *shaku* 9 *sun*, middle width 4 *shaku* 7 *sun*, bottom width 4 *shaku* 4 *sun* 5 *bu*; thickness 2 *sun*) and 8 spears likewise (each 1 *jō* 8 *shaku* long).[207] The Left and Right Outer Palace Guards request

---

[203] The particular type of grass is *atsuka* grass.

[204] This is the *sakamakura* 坂枕, a sloping pillow or bolster used by the sovereign when reclining on the august couch of thick mats.

[205] Procedures (*shiki*) for the Bureau of House-keeping, *kamon-ryō* (under the Ministry of the Imperial Household), are given in Bk XXXVIII of the *E-S*.

[206] The *shōden* of the Kairyū-gū 廻立宮正殿.

[207] These cult shields and spears are of colossal size, as they are intended for the use of the *kami*.

these from the *Jingi-kan* in the first decade of the 9th month. The Bureau of Military Storehouses is caused to fashion and prepare them according to precedent. (Shields are made by the shield-makers' *uji* of Tamba Province; the spears by the Imbe Uji of Kii Province. After the celebration is over they are gathered up by the Outer Palace Guards.) Again, 6 great shields are set up at the Suzaku, Ooten, and Kaishō Gates,[208] as well as 12 spears, and the same Bureau is caused to prepare those.

At all times, 2 august garments are to be worn at the time of entering the Daijō-den; and also 3 quilts, 3 quilts to sleep on, 2 triangular pillows, 3 silken coronets,[209] 2 unlined garments of Mōda cloth,[210] 2 curtains, and 3 boxes, all to be cut, sewn, and made ready beforehand by the Bureau of Needlework (all put into chests). Further, the 8 quilts and 4 unlined garments to be presented to the *kami* in the same hall are to be sewn and prepared by the same Bureau.

At all times, there are required for the Daijō-den 12 long *tatami*, 6 short *tatami*, and 16 blinds, which are to be fashioned and made ready beforehand by the Bureau of Housekeeping.

At all times, august articles to be offered to the *kami* are to be prepared by the Office of Palace Tables: 80 pedestalled dishes (5 *sun* 5 *bu* in height, 7 *sun* in diameter, without covers and having 4 folding legs, each piled with 14 *ryō* each of Oki abalone and squid, 15 *ryō* of dried *bêche-de-mer*, 1 *shō* of dried fish, 10 *ryō* of seaweeds, and 5 *shaku* of salt). All these are placed on leaf-dishes which are covered with peaked leaf-mat covers, decoratively tied with strings of bark-cloth. And 80 flat dishes (height, diameter, and decoration same as the pedestalled dishes, but no folding legs; on each to be piled 5 *gō* of each of the various items to be offered), 40 *yamatsuki* (on each one, 1 *shō* each of mussel sushi and abalone sushi, decoration same as for flat dishes); 300 white boxes for coarse foods (1 *shaku* 5 *sun* long, 1 *shaku* 2 *sun* wide, 3 *sun* deep); 5 boxes to hold Azuma abalone (10 *kin* in each); 16 boxes to hold dried *bêche-de-mer* (12 *kin* each), 12 boxes to hold squid (6 *kin* in each); 4 boxes to hold Sado abalone (10 *kin* each); 15 boxes to hold boiled bonito, 1 unopened basket in each; 24 boxes to hold bonito (12 *kin* each), 55 boxes for dried meats, an unopened basket in each; 11 boxes for *yorito*[211] fish (1 *to* 5 *shō* in each); 2 boxes for salmon (10 in each box), 4 boxes for kelp (15 *kin* in each), 6 boxes for tangle (6 *kin* in each), 4 boxes for laver[212] (1 unopened basket each), 6 boxes for *wakame* (6 *kin* in each), 10 boxes for citrus fruits (10 *kage* in each), 5 boxes of pounded chestnuts (1 *shō* each), 5 boxes of flat chestnuts (20 baskets in each), 2 boxes dried persimmons (50 strings to a box), 5 boxes *nashi*[213] (1 *to* in each), 6 boxes boiled chestnuts (1 *to* in each), 2 boxes peeled chestnuts (2

---

[208] Three of the twelve main gates of the Imperial Palace.

[209] Hats of stiff silk, *katori no kōburi* 絹幞頭, which have a small crown and a large loop of fabric erect in the back, and are wrapped around with a fillet of white silk. T. Ema, *Shinshū yūsoku kojitsu*, p. 61.

[210] Mōda 望陀 cloth, from the district of that name in Kazusa (Kamitsufusa) Province.

[211] A small fish, perhaps whitebait.

[212] These three kinds of marine algae are kelp, *hirome* (or *kombu*) 昆布; tangle, *miru* 海松; and laver, *nori* 紫菜.

[213] *Nashi* are the round Japanese pears.

*to* in each), 3 boxes of ripe persimmons (1 *to* in each), 2 boxes of limes (3 *ka* each), 5 boxes of twisted *mochi*,[214] 5 boxes of *mametsuki*,[215] 10 boxes of soybean *mochi*, 10 boxes of redbean *mochi*, 5 boxes of *mukikata*,[216] and 5 boxes of rice-gruel (of the foregoing 6 items, in each box 6 portions). When the festival is over, all items up to and including the *yamatsuki* are placed in pure places in mountains or moors. The remainder are distributed among the officials in charge. The Imperial Sake Office is made to prepare 16 *torosuki* (each holding 5 *shō*), 32 ritual clay urns (16 to hold 1 *to* of sake each and 16 to hold 5 *shō*; 8 to be placed on each table), 8 shallow clay vessels (each holding 1 *koku* 5 *to*, and set on a table), 60 spouted vessels, 60 small sake cups (each to be placed in a box on top of the table), and 1 box of oak leaves[217] (placed on table). When the festival is finished, all items up to and including ritual clay urns again are placed in pure places in mountains or moors. The rest are distributed as above.

At all times, there must be 170 knives for use in cooking (88 long ones, 2 medium, and 80 small, all contained in boxes) which are to be made ready by the officials in charge, as well as 18 *kin* of bark-cloth and 3 *tan* 2 *jō* 4 *shaku* of tribute cloth for handcloths from official goods to be divided among [the personnel of] the two provinces.

At all times, the Mononobe,[218] Gate Guards,[219] and Narrators[220] who serve as Left and Right Outer Palace Guards, report to the *Jingi-kan* in the first decade of the 9th month. They are to count up the number and gather them together. The Mononobe [are assigned] 20 each to the Left and Right Offices of the Capital; the Gate Guards 2 each to Right and Left Offices of the Capital and 8 to Yamato Province, 3 to Yamashiro, 2 to Ise, 1 to Kii; and the Narrators are 8 to Mino, 2 to Tango, 7 to Tajima, 3 to Inaba, 4 to Izumo, and 2 to Awaji.

At all times, sacred robes are bestowed on the middle tiger day of the 11th month. Thirteen persons, from the chief of the *Jingi-kan* down to and including players of august *koto* (1 chief, 2 assistant chiefs, two secretaries, 2 recorders, 1 chief diviner, 2 masters of divination, 1 Sacred Maiden, 2 players of august *koto*), each receive a wadded silk tunic with design printed in blue[221] and one white divided skirt; 137 persons from scribes down to Kanhatori (4 scribes, 24 *kambe*,

---

[214] *Magari-mochi* 勾餅, a cake made of glutenous rice flour rolled in thin strips and twisted back and forth.

[215] *Sora-mame* ('horse beans', *Vicia faba*) cooked, peeled, and sweetened.

[216] Lit. 'twisted head' 捻頭, a confection.

[217] *Nagame-kashiwa* 長女柏, a variety of *kashiwa* oak (*Quercus dentata*).

[218] The Mononobe were hereditary 'armorers' attached to the Imperial Court. They were in charge of military matters and administering justice. As a family, the Mononobe Uji was of *muraji* rank (*kabane*) and were classed as *tomo-no-miyatsuko*, 'Court Chieftains'.

[219] The Gate Guards are Kadobe 門部, who guarded the gates of the Imperial Palace.

This appeared to be either an hereditary or a temporary appointment, as seen by their role in Bk VI.

[220] The *kataribe* 語部 were narrators or reciters, an occupational group which had long functioned to transmit by word of mouth the myths, legends, and traditions of the Yamato Court and of local ruling families.

[221] These tunics, worn over the Court dress, were a form of sacred or ceremonial garb (*saifuku*). Instead of being pure white, these garments have a design rubbed on with blue dye, *aozuri* 青摺, the process being something like a silk-screen rubbing, though for convenience it is translated 'blue-printed'.

16 diviners, 12 official attendants,[222] 5 Imbe from Awa Province, and 76 Kan-hatori) receive one blue-printed and unlined hempen garment each. For the Sacred Maidens and Sarume Maidens[223] clothing is as for the *Niiname* [Festival]. From princes who are under particular taboo downward, all have blue-printed tunics, while those of 5th Rank and above wear the red hanging sash (combining both light and dark color), and the rest all wear tied sashes. Princesses and palace women down to girl attendants also wear blue-printed tunics and red hanging sashes (5th Rank and above combine both light and dark colors). The rest all wear tied sashes. (Princes and down to girl attendants all wear *hikage* vines on their heads.[224] When the divining is completed these are all bestowed. On the night of the hare day 50 each of white-silk quilts and plain-cloth quilts are put in the place where those under particular taboo are on duty. (When the affair is over these are returned.) The Gate Guards, Narrators, and players of the Nara flute all receive blue-printed, plain-cloth, unlined tunics. The Mononobe receive dark-blue, plain-cloth, unlined tunics. The Ministry of Central Affairs requests in advance and receives the materials from the *Jingi-kan*. Sacred robes for *Jingi-kan* personnel are sewn and made ready by the Bureau of Needlework; the other articles to be sewn are sent to this bureau and then distributed. The two diviners of the rice-ears and the two *negi* diviners are each given Court robes of color prescribed for their rank.[225]

At all times, before the middle tiger day of the 11th month (if the hare day falls on the 1st of the month use the first tiger day), when the entire array of things, inside and out, is properly set in order (similarly to the usual arrangement at the beginning of the Pacification of August Spirits), at dawn on the day of the hare the *Jingi-kan* officials distribute the symbolic offerings for the various *kami* (that is, those to whom offerings are placed on top of the tables at the *Toshigoi* Festival); for each: 5 *shaku* of pongee, 1 *shaku* each of 5 colors of thin pongee, 1 *shaku* of colored hemp-cloth, 2 *ryō* of bark-cloth, 5 *ryō* of hemp, 1 *yokura-oki*

---

[222] *Shibu* or *tsukaibe* 使部 were petty officials attached to the *Dajō-kan* and various ministries to perform clerical and other tasks. R. K. Reischauer, *Early Japanese History*, B, p. 421.

[223] It says in the *Kogoshūi* that the Sarume-no-kimi are descendants of Ame-no-uzume-no-mikoto (also known as Sarume-no-mikoto) and Saruda-hiko, both of whom are worshiped as phallic deities. Katō and Hoshino, op. cit. pp. 29–30. It also says the sacred symbolic dance or pantomime was the hereditary duty of the Sarume Family (ibid. p. 36). Their dancing may have added rhythmic and religious ecstasy to this solemn occasion. The dance of Ame-no-uzume-no-mikoto in the myth of the Sun Goddess hiding in the cave was indeed a dance of deity possession.

[224] The *hikage no kazura* 日蔭鬘 was a garland of *hikage* vine, a low-growing, bright-green plant with heart-shaped leaves. Makino gives *Lycopodium clavatum*. It is mentioned several places in *Man'yōshū* poems, for example, 19: 4278 . . . . 'hikage no kazura keru, uhe ni ya sara ni ume wo shino-hamu'—showing that on top of the garland of *hikage* vine were added plum blossoms. Komura, *Man'yō shokubutsu zukan*, p. 386.

[225] *Tōjiki* 當色, 'appropriate color', refers to the system of prescribed and prohibited colors, *tōjiki kinjiki no sei*, which was set up at the time of the Taika Reforms to prescribe the wearing of certain colors to denote certain Court ranks. Regulations were later modified when more ranks were added.

and 1 _yakura-oki_,[226] 1 shield, 1 spear, 6 _shaku_ of leaf matting for wrapping, 1 _jō_
4 _shaku_ of tax cloth (cloth omitted for the first _kami_). On the appointed day the
Nakatomi officials lead the diviners to the Ministry of the Imperial Household
to determine by divination who from the various departments shall be under
particular taboo. That done, they return to their respective quarters. They perform ablutions and don their sacred robes and gather together. Besides them,
one Nakatomi and one Imbe official are sent to lead officials of the Needlework
Bureau and the Ministry of Treasury in placing the quilts and unlined garments
in the Yuki-den of the Daijō-gū and to lead Palace Storehouse officials in placing
the divine raiment and silken coronets in the Kairyū-den. Members of the
Bureau of Palace Caretakers offer the august hot water three times. One time is
for personages under general taboo at the usual place in the Palace; then hot
water is offered twice to those under particular taboo (both times in the Kairyū-
den). The various guards stand up their staves and the various officials line up the
articles for solemn presentation in the same way as for New Year's Day ceremonies. Two persons each from the Isonokami and Enoi Uji, wearing Court
dress, lead 40 of the Inner Mononobe (dressed in unlined tunics of dark-blue
cloth). They set up shields and spears for the _kami_ at the north and south gates of
the Daijō-gū (2 shields and 4 spears at each gate; the Bureau of Carpentry prepares frames for them in advance at left and right of both gates; when the celebrations are finished, the Left and Right Outer Palace Guards gather them up).
When that is done they divide and go to left and right to the frames under the
shields. (At each gate are 20 Inner Mononobe, 10 on each side, in lines of five
at intervals of 6 _shaku_.) Two each of the Tomo and Saeki Uji separate and go to
the frames at left and right of the south gate and wait until the time of opening
the gates. The Left and Right Captains of the Inner Palace Guards and below
each lead a squad and, dividing right and left, guard their respective sides. The
Chiefs of the Left and Right Military Guards and below each lead a squad, and
dividing, guard that side. The Chiefs of the Outer Palace Guard and below each
lead a group, they divide and guard that side and the gates. Gate Guards control[227]
those going in and out of the various gates. The officials of the Hayato[228] lead
the Hayato; they divide and stand in front of the Left and Right Chōshū-dō.[229]
They wait until the opening of the gates and then give a shout. The Assistant Chief
and the Secretary[230] of the Ministry of Central Affairs lead the Bureau of Oodoneri
and the _toneri_ nobles. The Assistant Chief and Secretary of the Imperial House-

---

[226] _Yokura-oki_ and _yakura-oki_ were types of
offering tables made up of four and eight pieces
of wood, respectively. _Yokura-oki_ stood 1 _shaku_
2 _sun_ high (about 1½ ft) and _yakura-oki_ stood
2 _shaku_ 4 _sun_ high. They were used for expiatory
offerings at the time of exorcism and purification
rites. For 'offerings placed on top' see n. 483.

[227] Lit. 'disciplinary investigation', _kyūsatsu_
糾察, carried out by the Gate Guards (Kadobe).

[228] The Hayato 隼人, originally a tribe from
south Kyushu, were brought under the rule of

the Yamato people late in the 5th century A.D.
and were then organized into a corporation of
guards for the Palace. They also were engaged
to perform their own traditional songs and dances
for the Court, and made their own folk crafts.
The Hayato were under the Office of Hayato in
the Ministry of War (_hyōbu-shō_).

[229] The Chōshū-dō 朝集堂.

[230] The second (_suke_) and third (_jō_) officials of
that Ministry. See n. 47 above.

hold lead the caretakers and housekeepers of the Bureaus of Palace Caretakers and Housekeeping, all dressed in ceremonial attire and carrying the solemn offerings;[231] they separate to left and right and arrange them in order. The Ministry of Ceremonial puts up the posting-board of ranks[232] for Heir Apparent and on downward in the outer garden by the south gate of the Daijō-gū. (For the distance from the gate see the *Gishiki*.) At the hour of the snake the Bureau of Palace Caretakers presents the august hot water for the persons under general taboo. At the same time, offering goods from the two provinces are moved from the sacred area to the Daijō-gū; *yuki* in the left column and *suki* in the right. Four *kambe* form the vanguard of this procession. (They wear blue-printed robes and carry *sakaki* branches.) One official of the *Jingi-kan* is at the mid-point of the column (wearing Court dress of color prescribed for rank and bark-cloth headdress). Next come two chiefs of the Kanhatori separated to left and right (wearing blue-printed robes and carrying *sakaki*), and one *sukune* of the Kanhatori is at the mid-point (wearing Court dress of color prescribed for rank, bark-cloth sleeve-ties,[233] and *hikage* vines). Next, tables for the raiment of soft cloth[234] (the which are wrapped in linen and placed on top of the offering table; 2 Kanhatori carry them on their shoulders, and wear blue-printed robes). Next come 72 Kanhatori men divided in left and right columns (wearing blue-printed robes and *hikage* vines); next 50 Kanhatori women divided in left and right columns (wearing blue-printed robes and *hikage* vines; both men and women carry sake oak leaves[235] and 4 fronds of *yuzuruha*[236] fastened onto each of 4 white staves); next come the 4 persons forming the vanguard from *yuki* province, dividing to left and right (and wearing blue-printed robes and carrying *sakaki* branches); next the diviner of the rice-ears in the middle (wearing robes of color prescribed for rank, bark-cloth headdress, and *hikage* vines, and carrying green bamboo fronds). Next comes the *sakatsuko* (wearing lustrous robes of linen and *hikage* vines, and riding in a white palanquin borne by 4 bearers); next comes the august rice palanquin (the rice is packed in hempen bags; 2 porters for the palanquin). Then the lord of the rice-ears (wearing blue-printed robe, bark-cloth headdress, and *hikage* vines); next come 8 women who carry on their heads the tables for the august food offerings (wearing linen garments, bark-cloth sleeve-ties, and *hikage* vines on their flowing tresses). Then comes 1 table for sacred sake (4 bearers), then 2 shallow earthenware vessels of dark sake (8 porters for each), next 2 shallow earthenware

---

[231] The *igibutsu* 威儀物.

[232] The posting-board is *hen'i* 版位 (also pron. *han'i* or *henni*), on which the order of Court ranks and the promotions in rank were posted at times of great convocations, such as festivals, at which the host of officials participated.

[233] *Tasuki* are back straps or sleeve-ties. Here it is *yūdasuki*, the ceremonial sleeve-ties of bark-cloth fibre which are donned by those persons preparing or presenting offerings to the *kami*, or preparing and serving sacred food to the sovereign. They are mentioned in the myths, as

in the above-mentioned (n. 223) episode: Ame-no-uzume-no-mikoto, before performing the deity-possession dance, bound up her sleeves with a cord of heavenly *hikage* vine and tied around her head a head-band of the heavenly *ma-saki* vine, and so forth. Philippi, *Kojiki*, p. 84.

[234] The *nigitae no miso*, sacred raiment of either soft bark-cloth or of silk.

[235] *Sakakashiwa* are decorative leaves of *kashiwa* oak served with ceremonial sake.

[236] 弓綏葉, *Daphniphyllum macropodum*, according to Brinkley.

vessels of clear sake (8 porters for each); these four vessels are each borne in an unpeeled wood palanquin decorated with *hikage* vines. Next come 8 palanquins filled with large ceremonial jars (4 porters for each palanquin; jars in white-wood boxes placed upon large tables), next 4 short tables and 2 split-wood boxes to hold knives (bleached cloth for wrapping, 1 table to a load, 2 porters to a load), next 1 fire-kindling set (packed in 2 boxes with legs of Kure bamboo, covered with green tie-dyed silk; one bearer). Next comes the mortar (put into a cloth bag tied at the top with cloth band, and with a cover of white wood; wrapped with fine straw matting; one porter); next 4 pestles (packed in cloth bags; stands of Kure bamboo; one porter); next 2 dust baskets (wrapped in bleached cloth; stands of Kure bamboo; one porter); next, 10 loads of firewood (both ends covered with fine straw matting; 10 porters); next, 4 platforms for fire (whitewashed,[237] and covered with fine straw matting; 2 porters for each platform); next 4 pineknot torches (each end wrapped with fine straw matting; 4 porters); next, 4 clay braziers (whitewashed, with camellia-wood frames; covered with fine straw matting, 4 porters for each); next, 2 bundles of oak leaves (wrapped in fine straw matting; 2 porters); next, 1 load of food-mats and bamboo mats (wrapped in bleached cloth, packed in white-wood boxes, placed on large table; 2 porters); next one Kara stove (packed in a white-wood box, placed on a large table, covered with oiled silk; 6 porters); next, 6 shallow clay vessels for water (each covered with lid of white wood; carried on a palanquin of unpeeled wood and decorated with leaves of plants and trees; 4 porters for each); all the foregoing are for offering to the *kami* and are decked with *sakaki*). Next come the *negi* and diviners marching in the middle (in Court dress of color prescribed for rank, bark-cloth sleeve-ties, *hikage* vines; all these to be provided by the *Jingi-kan*). Next the provincial governors and district prefects, dividing in left and right columns (all wearing Court dress of color prescribed for rank, and *hikage* vines; those who assist the kinsmen of the governors each inspect the articles for presentation, and separate into left and right columns, wearing green cloaks, blue-printed robes; these garments and silk for the porters all to be supplied by the province). Next comes 1 table for sake cups (4 porters); next 10 jugs of dark sake (20 porters); then 10 jugs of light sake (20 porters); next 10 shallow clay vessels of decorated august sake[238] (8 porters for each); next 40 portable storehouses[239] (8 porters each; items from dark sake on use palanquins of unpeeled wood that are decorated with delicate plants). Next 100 jars with varieties of fish sushi (200 bearers for these, and stands of cypress wood; the jars to be covered with bleached cloth); next 10 loads of fish, vegetables, and fruit (4 bearers per load); next 100 boxes of cooked rice (200 bearers); next 100 jugs of sake (200 bearers); next 100 jars of fish and green vegetables (200 bearers; the burden bearers for the foregoing all to be dressed in blue-printed robes; the foregoing all are *tametsu* foodstuffs). The procedure for the *suki* province which follows is the same as this.

---

[237] Text says 'white earth' (白土)—perhaps lime or chalk to cover the platforms.

[238] *Kazari no miki* 飾酒, sake decorated with leaves. See n. 235.

[239] *Kurashiro-mono*, 'substitute for storehouse', may mean a miniature one.

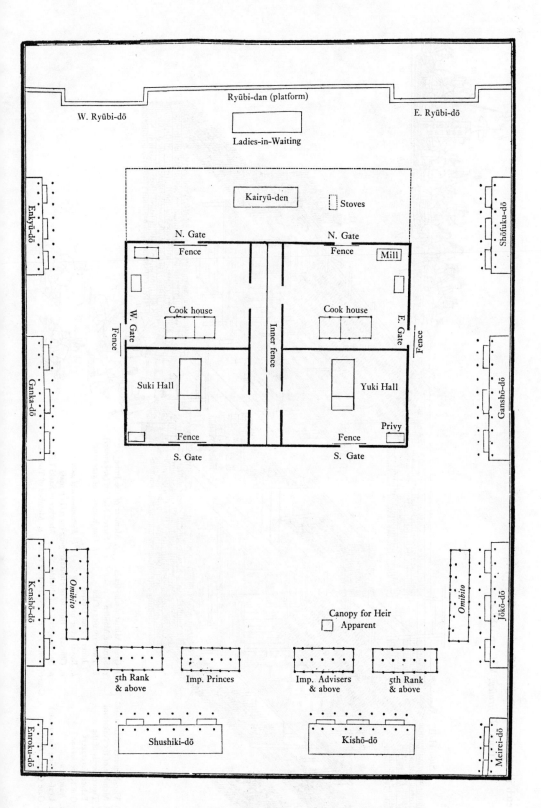

*Jōgan-gishiki* Diagram of the Daijō-gū from *Kojiruien*, VII., pp. 16–17.

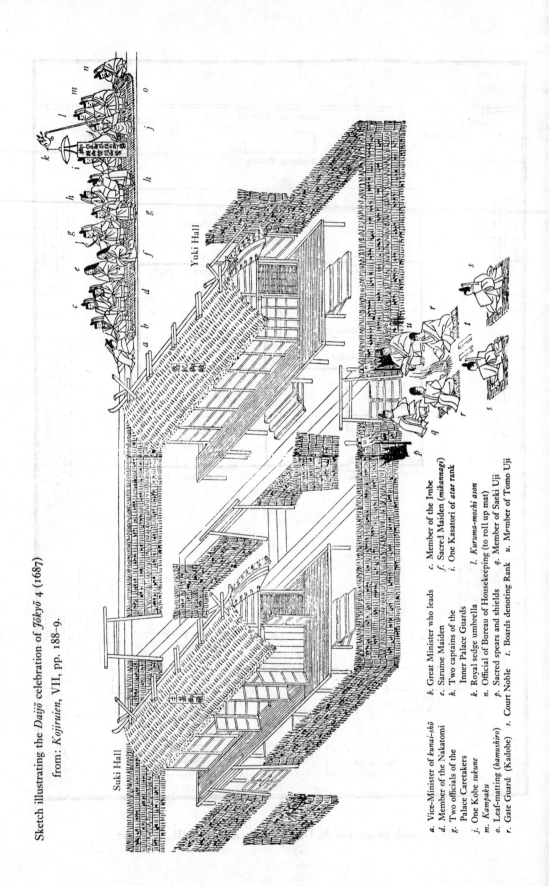

Sketch illustrating the *Daijō* celebration of *Jōkyō* 4 (1687)

from: *Kojiruien*, VII, pp. 188-9.

Suki Hall

Yuki Hall

*a.* Vice-Minister of *kunai-shō*    *b.* Great Minister who leads    *c.* Member of the Imbe
*d.* Member of the Nakatomi    *e.* Sarume Maiden    *f.* Sacred Maiden (*mikannagi*)
*g.* Two officials of the    *h.* Two captains of the    *i.* One Kasatori of *atae* rank
     Palace Caretakers      Inner Palace Guards
*j.* One Kobe *sukune*    *k.* Royal sedge umbrella    *l. Kuruma-mochi ason*
*m. Kampaku*    *n.* Official of Bureau of Housekeeping (to roll up mat)
*o.* Leaf-matting (*hamushiro*)    *p.* Sacred spears and shields    *q.* Member of Saeki Uji
*r.* Gate Guard (Kadobe)    *s.* Court Noble    *t.* Boards denoting Rank    *u.* Member of Tomo Uji

The Imbe of Awa Province[240] are caused to weave coarse garments[241] (in sacred language these are called *aratae*). These are made up ahead of time at the *Jingi-kan*. They are packed in finely woven baskets and placed on top of the offering-tables. At the four corners they set up *sakaki* branches and deck them with bark-cloth. One Imbe bearing a *sakaki* branch decked with bark-cloth leads the way; four of them raise up the offering-table; all wear bark-cloth headdresses. Before the hour of the sheep the articles to be offered reach the Suzaku Gate.[242] The Kanhatori are in front as they were in the beginning. The Imbe of Awa Province take the table with offerings of coarse cloth, go out from the *Jingi-kan*, and go to the back of the table with raiment of soft cloth. They stand in order and wait until the Inner Controllers[243] have finished. The Outer Palace Guards open the three south gates just as at the ceremony of New Year's Day.[244] One offcial of the *Jingi-kan* leads the men and women of the Kanhatori to the kitchen-house of the Daijō-gū. They place the sake oak leaves and then go out. Again, the *Jingi-kan* officials separate to the left and right and lead the presentations from both provinces as they approach. (Except for articles to be offered to the *kami*, all are kept in the garden of the Chōshū-dō, where they are separated and placed in offering in the east and west buildings.) When they reach the outside of the south gate of the Daijō-gū the *yuki* come around from the left and the *suki* come around from the right, reaching the north gate together. The *Jingi* official leads the Kanhatori of *sukune* rank. They enter in and offer up the table with the offerings of soft cloth at the deity seat[245] in the *yuki* hall. Then an official of the Imbe enters and offers up the table with offerings of coarse cloth at the same deity seat. That done, both withdraw. Thus the offerings from both provinces are respectively assembled in the hall of offerings. That completed, the Outer Palace Guards close the gates. The *Jingi-kan* officials attend inside the north gate on the left. The *sakatsuko* begins to pound the rice for the august cooked rice; next the *sakanami* women together finish the pounding without changing hands. The Court chieftains kindle the fire. Members of the Office of the Sovereign's Table[246] lead the Court chieftains of various *uji*, who respectively assist the members of the Office in cooking the august foods. Officials of the Imperial Household Ministry divide into left and right columns and lead the members of the Office

---

[240] Again, Awa Prov. in Shikoku; this shows that a branch of the Imbe 忌部 Uji came from there, and they were not necessarily attached to the *Jingi-kan*.

[241] *Aratae no miso* is coarse raiment, of hemp or other fibre, as contrasted to the soft raiment mentioned in n. 234. The soft and coarse symbolism, as well as dark and light symbolism, is seen throughout.

[242] The Suzaku (or Sujaku) Gate, one of the twelve main gates of the Palace. The hour of the sheep corresponded to 2 p.m.

[243] Inner Controllers, *naiben* 内辨. See n. 35, above.

[244] The procedures for the Outer Palace Guards (Left and Right), the *sayū emon-fu*, are contained in *E-S*, Bk XLVII. As to who served in this capacity on this occasion, see nn. 218, 219, and 229, above.

[245] The *shinza* 神座 is the sacred couch which is made up of layers of thick *tatami* mats and occupies the center of the chamber of the Yuki-den. It is reserved for the ancestral *kami*, and the sovereign does not use it. See D. C. Holtom, op. cit. p. 122 (94-8).

[246] The *naizenshi* under the Imperial House-hold Ministry (*kunai-shō*).

of the Palace Tables and Imperial Sake Office,[247] who each line up in that place and make ready the articles to be offered to the *kami*. One Takahashi *ason* and one Azumi *sukune* each raise up a tray-table; the chefs and brewers again stand in order of rank. They all enter the Daijō-gū. Together they ascend into the hall and stand beside the offering-tables. Their positions arranged, those in front begin to place the offerings on the tables, after which the others in turn assist in presenting the offerings. This completed, exchanging bows, they withdraw. (The next day the procedure for ending the feast is the same.)

At the hour of the cock the Bureau of Palace Caretakers, using fire from the Bureau, lights the lamps and courtyard fires in each of the *yuki* and *suki* courtyards; for each: 2 lamps and 2 courtyard fires. One Tomo of *sukune* rank, one Saeki of *sukune* rank, each respectively lead eight Gate Guards (who wear blue-printed silk tunics) outside the south gate to keep the courtyard fires through the night. The *yuki* and *suki* provinces each send 2 *to* of oil to the august hall (5 *shō* each for each night). Required: 8 each of lamp-oil cups and trays, 8 *shaku* of ordinary cloth for wicks (2 *shaku* for each night), 8 *koku* of charcoal ash (2 *koku* for each day), 320 torches (8 *shaku* long; 80 for each night), 1,200 *kin* of kindling wood (300 *kin* for each day).

At the hour of the dog the way is cleared[248] and the first warning given of the Imperial approach to the Kairyū-den. The Bureau of Palace Caretakers proffers the august hot water. Then the ceremonial garments are assumed [by His Majesty] and he enters the Daijō-gū. As for the route thither, the Ministry of Treasury beforehand lays a double width of unlined ordinary cloth on the route. The Bureau of Housekeeping prepares leaf-matting, and also lays it on top of the cloth runner where the august footfall will tread—rolling it out before and rolling it up after. (Two persons, Vice-Minister of the Imperial Household or above, spread it, and two persons, Secretaries of the Bureau of Housekeeping or above, roll it up.) No one shall dare to step on it. On the return the same procedure is followed. As for the route in the Palace and through the garden, 8 layers of ordinary cloth 8 widths wide are laid. One Great Minister or Great or Middle Counselor and one Nakatomi and one Imbe (Nakatomi on the left and Imbe on right), then Sacred Maidens and Sarume on left and right proceed in line. (The Great Minister stands in the center, the Nakatomi and Imbe lead the lines to left and right on the street outside the gates.) The Sovereign[249] deigns to come forth; two of the Caretakers carry the lights and worshipfully approach, one Court noble who is carriage attendant carries the royal sedge umbrella;[250] one Kobe of *sukune* rank[251] and one Kasatori of *atae* rank[252] together carry the cords of the umbrella and push

---

[247] The *daizen-shiki* and the *mikizukasa*, respectively; both under the Imperial Household Ministry.

[248] *Tenhitsu* 天蹕 is 'clearing the way'. There were four intervals between nightfall and midnight, the first being the 'hour of the cock' (above). The next interval was 'hour of the dog', at the beginning of which the progress of the sovereign commenced. See Diagram of Intervals of Day and Night.

[249] Here the expression 'shingi' 宸儀, for the august person of the sovereign, is used.

[250] The umbrella is the *sugegasa*, a sunshade made of sedge grass, suspended from the end of a long pole.

[251] The Kobe Uji 子部氏.

[252] Kasatori is the name of an *uji* which likewise was an hereditary group of umbrella-bearers, as the name shows: 笠取.

themselves forward on their knees as they perform their duty (the same is done on the return). As the progress is made to the august *yuki* communion hall, the group of officials under particular taboo each take their seats therein (the group of officials under general taboo may not enter the Kairyū-den enclosure or into the Daijō-gū). When that is done two persons each of the Tomo and Saeki Uji open the south gates of the Daijō-gū. The Outer Palace Guards open the south gate of the Chōdō-in. Officials of the Imperial Household Ministry lead 12 persons of the Kuzu of Yoshino Province and 12 Nara flute players[253] (all wearing tunics of blue-printed cloth). They enter from the east side gate of the Chōdō-in, and on reaching their places they play an ancient air. The governor of the *yuki* province leads the singers and enters through the same gate; on reaching their places they sing an ancient air. One Tomo of *sukune* rank and one Saeki of *sukune* rank each lead 15 Narrators (wearing blue-printed tunics). They enter from the east and west side gates, and on reaching their places they recite ancient legends. The Heir Apparent enters from the southeast side gate. The Imperial Princes enter through the west gate; Great Ministers and down to 5th Rank courtiers enter through the south gate. All take seats under the awning. Those of 6th Rank and below remain behind the Kishō and Shushiki buildings.[254] They stand in line in order of rank. When the host of officials first make their entrance the Hayato raise their voices. When everyone is standing in place they cease. They proceed to a point in front of the shields. They clap their hands; they sing and they dance.[255] Those of 5th Rank and above rise together and go to the posting-board in the middle courtyard. They kneel and clap their hands four times. Each time there are eight claps (in sacred language this is known as *yahirade*). The Heir Apparent first claps hands and then steps back, then those of 5th Rank and above clap their hands. Those 6th Rank and below clap hands in concert and repeat it in the same way (but those under particular taboos do not enter this procession). That completed, they all withdraw, but those of 5th Rank and above retire to their places under the awning and, their seats determined, two persons of 5th Rank of the Abe Uji and six persons of 6th Rank, dividing to left and right, advance simultaneously to the posting-board. The civil and military officials keeping the night watch announce the register of nobles down to the level of guards on duty.[256] (The chief ritualist and above use their *kabane* title and name; the guards on duty are announced only by number; at all times, those who report the matters to the Throne all kneel; except that in case it is rainy or wet they may stand.) When this is completed, the *yuki* feast is presented (it is presented at the beginning of the hour of the boar and retired at the fourth). The order of succession (in presenta-

---

[253] The Kuzu 國栖 were called upon for their tribute of local products and their performance of singing and flute music at the annual festival of first-fruits and at the feast of the *Daijō-e*. In the *Kojiki* are recorded two songs of the Kuzu of Yoshino which show their association with trees and with the brewing of sake for festal purposes. These are recorded in the reign of Oojin Tennō. See Philippi, *Kojiki*, pp. 282–3.

The Nara flute (*narabue* 楢笛) is distinct from other flutes of bamboo.

[254] Kishō 暉章 and Shushiki 修式 halls (堂).

[255] The succession of entertainment includes various folk songs and dances and the traditional songs and dances of the Hayato. See n. 228 above.

[256] *Bumban* 分番 refers to those palace nobles who are doing sentry duty.

tion) is that in the very front are the chefs of the Office of the Sovereign's Table, 1 Court chieftain[257] (who carries the fire-kindling set) and 2 *uneme* of *ason* rank from the Office of *Uneme* (forming left and right vanguards), next a chief diviner (wearing the bark-cloth headdress and sleeve-ties and carrying a bamboo rod), next 1 water-carrier of *muraji* rank from the Office of Water (who carries the ritual elongated basin),[258] then 1 water-carrier (who carries the ritual water-pitcher), then 10 *uneme* (1 carries the box of brushes, 1 the box of towels, 1 the food-mats for the *kami*, another the food-mats for the Sovereign, 1 the box of august leaf-dishes,[259] 1 the box of cooked rice, 1 the fresh seafood, 1 the dried foods, 1 the chopstick box, and another the box of fruit). Next comes a Takahashi of *ason* rank of the Sovereign's Table Office (who carries the abalone sauce pickle), 1 Azumi of *sukune* rank (who carries the seaweed sauce pickle), 5 chefs (1 carries the vessel of hot abalone soup, 1 the vessel of hot seaweed soup; 2 carry the offering-table with pots of soup; but the one who guards the shelves does not enter the procession), 4 sake brewers (2 carry on their shoulders the offering-table for sake and 2 carry the tables for dark and for light sake). All are in pre-scribed order and stand for the presentation. As soon as it is over everything is taken away in like manner. At the hour of the rat, *Jingi-kan* officials lead the chefs of the Sovereign's Table Office and move to the *suki* Food Hall[260] to cook the sacred food-offerings for the *kami*.[261] The Sovereign returns to the Kairyū-den. (This ceremony is the same as the first one.) The august hot water is proffered. That done, the august garments are changed and [the Sovereign] progresses to the *suki* Food Hall. The ceremonial for this is the same as for the *yuki*. Again, the Kuzu perform an ancient air, and the clapping of hands by Heir Apparent and those below and the other procedures are all the same as in the *yuki* ceremonies. At the first moment of the tiger hour the *suki* august feast is presented. The pro-cession and recession are as before. (For the affair see the *Gishiki*.)

On the dragon day in the first quarter of the hare hour[262] the return to the Kairyū-den is made. (This ceremony is the same as the first one.) The august garments are changed and [the Sovereign] returns to the Palace. The warning to clear the road and the military guard are the same as for ordinary ceremonies. When the festival affairs are finished the host of officials severally withdraw. The members of Tomo and Saeki Uji close the gates. At the second quarter hour the Nakatomi and Imbe of the *Jingi-kan* lead the Sacred Maidens in the festival of propitiation of the build-ings of the Daijō-gū. Symbolic offerings for this are the same as at the first cere-mony. This completed, the people of the two provinces are ordered to break the

---

[257] *Tomo no miyatsuko* 伴造, a chieftain over a group of people, as opposed to a chieftain over the land (*kuni no miyatsuko*). They were hereditary officials in charge of *be* (occupational groups) who were owned by the Imperial House. After the Taika Reforms they still continued to have influential roles in Court.

[258] The *ebi-no-hatafune* (lit. 'shrimp-fin boat') was an oval-shaped basin used only by the sovereign or a member of his family for cere-monial hand-washing.

[259] Leaf dishes, *hirade* 枚手, were made of oak leaves and used to serve ceremonial foods.

[260] *Suki no kashiwadono* 主基膳殿.

[261] Foods prepared for offering to the *kami* are called *kami no o-mono* 神御饌.

[262] The intervals of day and night were divided into quarters, known as *ten* 點, which varied in duration according to the season of the year. See Diagram of Intervals of Day and Night.

ground and then retire; after which the area of the propitiation ceremony is leveled; then they ceremonially pacify that ground. Requirements for this are: 4 *tan* of tax cloth, 2 *kin* of bark-cloth, 2 *kin* 10 *ryō* of hemp, 8 mattocks, 8 *shō* of rice, 8 *shō* of turbid sake, 4 *kin* 10 *ryō* of abalone, 10 *kin* 6 *ryō* of bonito, 10 *kin* 6 *ryō* of *wakame*, 1 *to* 6 *shō* of dried meats, 4 *shō* of salt, 8 each of jars and saucers. The august garments, quilts, tunics, narrow *tatami*, seats, and the things for offerings at the Kairyū-den and august hot water are bestowed on the Imbe and various articles which have had contact with fire are bestowed on the chief diviners. The remainder of multiple articles and the various buildings are all bestowed on the Nakatomi. At the 4th quarter-hour the officials of the *Jingi-kan* according to precedent worship in the Jijū-den. Again, the various articles of the portable storehouses of *yuki* and *suki* provinces are lined up in the garden of the Buraku-in.[263] The officials in charge will have already cleansed the Buraku-in before this. Both *yuki* and *suki* provinces provide and hang august curtains in the palaces[264] (the *yuki* on the east and the *suki* on the west). The arrangement for the host of officials inner and outer is the same as for ordinary ceremonial. The Ministry of Ceremonial[265] sets up the posting-board of ranks beforehand. In the 2nd quarter-hour of the dragon, the Imperial carriage approaches the Buraku-in and the Sovereign progresses to the *yuki* curtain. The disposition of the various guards is as for ordinary ceremonies. The Heir Apparent enters from the gate on the northeast side. (From Imperial Princes on down, their highnesses wait until ranks have been conferred and then enter.) Those of 5th Rank and above enter through the south gate and each goes to the posting-board. Those of 6th Rank and below make their entrance in double file. They stand in their places and the *Jingi-kan* Nakatomi bear the *sakaki* branches and carry batons. They enter through the south gate and go to the posting-board. They kneel and recite the congratulatory words to the deities of heaven.[266] The Imbe now enter and present the items of divine regalia:[267] the sacred mirror[268] and the sacred sword.[269] When that is done they withdraw. (If rainy or wet, they may present them while standing.) Next, one Controller of 5th Rank or higher again goes to the posting-

---

[263] The Jijū-den 仁壽殿, located behind the Shishin-den or 'Throne Hall' of the Imperial Palace, was for the use of the sovereign when watching performances. The Buraku-in 豐樂院 was also a pavilion for watching performances and entertainment.

[264] In this text *denjō* 殿上, 'palaces', means the buildings of the Daijō-gū.

[265] The Ministry of Ceremonial (*shikibu-shō*) supervised matters of protocol and procedures for Court ceremonies.

[266] *Amatsu kami no yogoto wo mawosu*: 奏天神之壽詞; this is the *norito* or ritual recited by the Nakatomi. See no. 14 of the rituals, Bk VIII. First historical mention of its recitation is in the *Nihongi*, 4th year of Empress Jitō, at her accession ceremony.

[267] Only two of the imperial regalia are mentioned. The first of the three, the sacred curved jewels (*magatama*), do not appear here or in the text of the ritual for the *Daijō-sai* or in the Nakatomi *yogoto*. They are mentioned in the *Kojiki* in the story of Ninigi-no-mikoto, when Amaterasu-ō-mikami bestowed the three sacred regalia upon him before his descent to earth. Philippi, *Kojiki*, p. 139.

[268] Here it is simply *mi-kagami*, 'august mirror'. But in the expression '*yata-kagami*' of mythology, *ya* means 'eight' or 'many', *ta* is 'hand' or 'span', and *kagami* is 'mirror'.

[269] The sword is *mi-tsurugi*, 'august sword', but in the myths is called *kusa-nagi* 'herb-queller'. See Philippi, *Kojiki*, pp. 90, 139.

board, he kneels and announces to the Throne the gifts presented by both provinces and the list of *tametsu* offerings. The Heir Apparent first claps his hands,
then withdraws. Then those of 5th Rank and higher all clap their hands. Those
of 6th Rank and below clap their hands in concert. The whole is like the previous
ceremony. Then they withdraw and go out. (Officers of Ceremonial take the post-
ing board and go out.) Officers of the Imperial Household lead the staffs of Offices
of Palace Tables and of Imperial Sake to go and inspect tray-tables and flat dishes
which were made ready in the garden. That done, they are led away. At this hour
the Great Ministers[270] who are attending the palace summon those of 5th Rank
and above (first they call the *toneri*, then the Lesser Counselors,[271] as in the case
of ordinary ceremonies). Then together with them they enter and take places in
the two halls—Ken'yō and Jōkan.[272] Those of 6th Rank and below make their
entrance. They arrive and enter the Kantoku and Meigi halls.[273] That completed,
the separate tribute goods from the *yuki* province are brought in. In the first quarter-
hour of the snake, persons of the *yuki* province offer the august meal and serve
the banquet to those of 5th Rank and above. (*Yuki* province personnel serve it
to nobles under particular taboo and the Office of Palace Tables serves those
under general taboo.) This is done in the same way as ceremonial for palace
banquets. The *tametsu* foodstuffs from the two provinces are distributed by the
Controllers to the host of officials. The *yuki* province persons offer at the proper
time the delicacies of fresh seafood. Then the governor of the province leads out
the singers, who render a provincial air. When they finish, the morning food
offering is presented. In the 2nd quarter-hour of the goat, His Majesty removes
to the august *suki* curtain. The Heir Apparent and those under him go to their
*suki* seats. The separate tribute offerings are brought in. At the appropriate time
the delicacies of fresh seafood are offered. The august feast is offered. The performing of provincial airs and so forth is all the same as for the previous ceremony.
When it is finished, emoluments are bestowed on the *yuki* province personnel.

On the day of the snake, in the 2nd quarter-hour of the dragon, the Imperial
Progress is made to the *yuki* curtain. In the 3rd quarter-hour the august feast is
offered. Next, the *Yamato-mai*[274] is performed. All those of 5th Rank and above
are invited, and a banquet is bestowed. Then those of 6th Rank and below make
their entrance. Popular music and dance is performed. All is the same as on the
dragon day. In the 2nd quarter-hour of the goat, the Imperial Progress is made
to the *suki* curtain. August food is offered and after that *Ta-mai*[275] is danced.
The various details are the same as in the previous ceremony. When it is finished,
emoluments are bestowed on the *suki* province personnel.

---

[270] 'Great Ministers', *ō-omi* 大臣, includes
the Great Minister of State (*dajō-daijin*), Ministers of Left and Right (*sadaijin* and *udaijin*), etc.

[271] *Shōnagon* 少納言.

[272] 顯陽 and 承觀 (堂)

[273] 觀德 and 明義 (堂)

[274] The *Yamato-mai* 和舞 was a traditional
dance performed after important festivals. It
was performed for the *Daijō-sai* and for festivals

at the Grand Shrine of Ise (*E-S*, Bk IV). The
performers consisted of two dancers, two singers,
and one each of musicians playing the wooden
clappers (*shakubyōshi*), bamboo flute (*fue*), fife
(*hichiriki*), and the horizontal harp or zither
(*wagon*).

[275] The *Ta-mai* 田舞, or *dembu*, was a traditional dance of rice-transplanting, performed now
to celebrate the harvest of new rice.

On the day of the horse in the first quarter-hour of the hare, the curtains of each province are taken away. The officials in charge set up the usual august curtains. At the 2nd quarter-hour of the dragon the Imperial Progress is made to these curtains. Nobles of 5th Rank and above as well as those of 6th Rank and below are invited. They all make their entrance as on the preceding day. In the 4th quarter-hour Court Rank is conferred on the governors of the two provinces and titled families.[276] (The number of persons for rank conferral is according to disposition of Imperial Command.) At the 2nd quarter-hour of the snake, the officials in charge present the august food offering. (As utensils for this and the various sacred articles, utilize as convenient those provided by both provinces for august food offerings on the preceding day.) The *Kume-mai*[277] and *Kishi-mai*[278] are performed. At the first quarter-hour of the monkey, the grand chorus sings, and the *Gosechi* dances[279] are performed. In the 3rd quarter-hour the depuration dance[280] is presented. Kanhatori women perform first (number limited to four persons). Next the Nakatomi and Imbe of the *Jingi-kan* as well as chamberlains under particular taboo, and down to guards, enter divided into left and right columns. They bestow oak leaves on each of the members of the Imperial Sake Office. Thereupon they receive sake and drink it. When that is done, they don headdresses and perform the dances. In the 2nd quarter-hour of the cock, the Heir Apparent and all nobles down through the 5th Rank are given emoluments, each being different. Moreover, on the host of officials of 6th Rank and below, and on the personnel from both provinces down to the outrunners,[281] are bestowed emoluments (the chief and assistant chief of the *Jingi-kan* and on down to vice-chieftains[282] of sacred districts each receive one horse also). The 4th-class officials of the *yuki* and *suki* provinces and on down to the prefects and 4th-class officials of the districts all carry batons and are recipients of Court Rank by Imperial Command, by extraordinary disposition. (The host of officials from 6th Rank down receive emoluments; on 4th-class officials and below of both provinces rank is conferred; it may be done on the day of the goat. See the *Gishiki* for the affair.) On this day the chamberlains and below under particular taboo advance to the Imperial Household Ministry and carry out depuration. The singing and dancing

---

[276] Governors: *kuni-no-tsukasa*; title families: *ujibito*. One infers that the governors and the leading families of the two (*yuki* and *suki*) provinces are promoted in Court rank as a reward for their contributions of rice, personnel materials, and tribute products.

[277] 久米舞, a dance relating to the rice harvest originally performed by members of the Kume Uji. After the disappearance of that clan, it was danced for the Court by members of the Ootomo (changed in 821 to Tomo) Uji and Saeki Uji. This dance was performed for such special Court occasions as the *Daijō* and *Kigen-setsu* festivals up to World War II.

[278] A dance done by members of the Kishi (吉志 or 吉士) Uji, and subsequently by members of the Abe Uji.

[279] The *Gosechi-mai* 五節舞 were part of the repertoire of Court dances (*bugaku* 舞樂) and were performed by five young dancing girls on the ox, tiger, hare, and dragon days of the 11th month to celebrate the festival of first-fruits (*Niiname-sai*), and the *Daijō-sai* when it took place.

[280] The *gesai-no-mai* 解齋舞 to celebrate release from the restrictions of abstinence (*imi*); abstinence was to have been observed by all participants until this point.

[281] The *hasetsukai no yohoro* 馳使丁.

[282] The text says *saigun no shōryō* 齋郡少領.

is as usual. To chefs, cooks, and brewers, and to personnel of both provinces, sake and food are given. When that is done, they doff their ceremonial robes and return to the usual.

At all times, when the celebration is finished the various structures in the sacred area of the north moor[283] are destroyed.

At all times, when the *Daijō* Festival is over, two persons, *negi* and diviner, are dispatched to the two sacred provinces to worship the eight *kami* of august food. Then they carry out depuration. The following day they burn the sacred area. Offerings to the *kami* are to be supplied by the two provinces respectively. [At all times,] on the last day of the month the host of officials in the capital gather for the purification ceremony. This is done the same as purification at the two times of year.

At all times, requirements for the *Ootono-hogai*[284] include: 16 sheets of Aki bark-cloth, 2 [rice] boxes, 4 *shō* of rice, 2 *shō* of sake, 1 jug, 2 small dishes, 1 table. Again, the festival to the august stoves of the *Daijō* Festival and the propitiation of the kitchens, and so on, are carried out in the same way as for the regular New Food celebration.[285]

✳　✳　✳　✳　✳　✳

End of Book Seven of the *Engi-shiki*
　　Enchō 5th Year, 12th Month, 26th Day
　　　[Same signatures as at end of Book Six]

---

[283] The *kitano no saijō* 北野齋場 is the sacred area, just north of the palace, in which the *Daijō* ceremonies have taken place.

[284] The *Ootono-hogai* is the blessing or luck-wishing festival for a palace. See n. 352 below, and no. 8 of the rituals in Bk VIII, below.

[285] Here text says *Shinjō-e* 新嘗會, referring to the feast of the First-Fruits Festival, *Niiname-matsuri* 新嘗祭 (or *Shinjō-sai*).

## Chapter Three

### INTRODUCTION TO BOOK EIGHT

#### THE *Norito*, OR RITUALS

THE eighth book of the *Engi-shiki* begins with a short introductory paragraph to explain who is to recite the various *norito*; this is followed by the texts of 27 *norito*, or rituals, for recitation at certain of the religious festivals. The development and the composition of the *norito* have been the object of research and speculation by Japanese scholars from the national learning scholars (*kokugaku-ha*) of Tokugawa times up to the present. It has been commonly held that the *norito* were the oldest portion of the *Engi-shiki*, but this broad statement must be carefully examined. The language of the *norito* differs from the Chinese style (*kambun*) of the other books of the *Engi-shiki*, showing that *norito* had entirely different sources—some of which are earlier than the time of the Taika Reforms (mid-7th century) and some of which are later. Even though the procedures for some of the national festivals, notably the *Toshigoi* and *Tsukinami* and the Great Purification, were extremely old, the regularizing of these festivals into a national cult and the writing down of the texts of rituals appear to belong to the post-Taika age. They belong to an age when the political scheme of things demanded the formalization of a national cult centered around the Court and the *Jingi-kan*, or department of *kami* affairs.

Certain outstanding characteristics of this collection of *norito* will be noted by the reader of these texts. First, the various *norito* are not uniform in language, but differ in style and phraseology, combining elements from different periods or different sources. Second, the various *norito*, and the passages within a given *norito*, are not of uniform antiquity. Third, the collection is not all-inclusive, but is a representative selection. In this regard, the opening paragraph of Book VIII acknowledges that *norito* for some of the national festivals are omitted from the collection. This perhaps was written for a preliminary collection and not revised later, for it makes the distinction between the *norito* to be recited by the Imbe (the Mikado and Ootono) and those to be recited by the Nakatomi, but fails to mention the incantation to be recited by the *fubito* (recorders) of Yamato and Kawachi, respectively, when presenting offerings of swords (no. 11). Nor does it mention the Chieftain of Izumo, who was to recite a very lengthy Laudatory Ritual to the Deities upon his visit to the capital to receive honors and congratulatory gifts (no. 27). Also not mentioned is an incantation, the *Na-no-matsuri no kotoba*, recited by masters of the Bureau of Yin-yang Divination *(on'yō-ryō)*, the text of which is given in Book XVI of the *Engi-shiki*.

The first known compiling of *norito* was in the procedures of the Kōnin era, *Kōnin-shiki*, in the ninth century, and subsequently some were included in the *Jōgan-shiki*.[286] Later on, the compilers of the *Engi-shiki* assembled a larger and more developed collection of *norito*. But before any *norito* were written into the *shiki* portion of the law they had long existed in the shrine liturgy of individual shrines. References to prayers, rituals, and spells or incantations appear in the *Kojiki*, the *Nihongi*, official chronicles which appeared early in the 8th century, as well as in the *Kogoshūi* and *Takahashi ujibumi*, house chronicles composed during the century following. For example, in the Sun Goddess myth, it is related that one of the means used to lure Amaterasu-ō-mikami out of the cave where she was hiding was the intoning of 'a solemn liturgy', i.e. *futo-norito-goto*, by the deity Ame-no-koyane-no-mikoto, revered as ancestor of the Nakatomi Uji.[287] Again, in the Izumo myth of Ookuninushi, there is mention of the deity Kushi-yatama, who 'pronounced words of blessing' *(negi-mawoshite . . .)* as he presented the offering of food to the *kami*, following it with the recitation of a poem of some 15 lines of dedication of various food offerings from the sea. Since this story appears to be an account of the founding of the Great Shrine of Izumo, the verses may represent a *norito* used for presentation of offerings at that shrine.[288] In the *Takahashi ujibumi*, a retainer to the Emperor Keikō named Ihaka Mutsukari cast a spell *(noroi)* upon some birds, turning them into fish, which he called bonito *(katsuo)* and later used as part of the divine food offerings prepared for the emperor. This incidentally caused Mutsukari to be credited with the first performance of the divine feasts of *Kamunie* and *Oonie*, which became the annual Deity New Food Festival and the Great New Food Festival, respectively.[289]

In the proto-historic agricultural society of Yamato the principal celebrations of farm villagers and fishermen had to do with petitioning the *kami* for successful planting, the protection of crops from natural disasters, and a bountiful harvest from the land and the sea. Elements of prayers concerning products of the fields, moors, mountains, and ocean, and the presentation of offerings of these products, are the core of most of the *norito* texts. These are thought to be the oldest passages of the *norito*. Invocations to the *kami*, prayers of presentation and dedication, and praises of the *kami* were certainly uttered long before the composition of the chronicles, much more so of the *shiki*. In the post-Taika period when the

---

[286] N. Aoki, 'Norito-shiki no seikaku', *Geirin*, III, 4 (1952), p. 30. In the *Norito jiten* of T. Uda are reproduced the texts of seven *norito* from the *Kōnin-shiki*, namely those of *Hirano matsuri*, *Kudo* and *Furuseki*, *Hirose no Oomi*, *Tatsuta Kaze-no-kami*, *Minazuki Tsukinami*, *Minazuki no tsugomori no ōharae*, and the Spell of the *Fumi no Imiki* of Kawachi.

The Kōnin era was the reign of Saga Tennō, 810–24, and the Jōgan era was the reign of Seiwa Tennō, 859–74.

[287] Katō and Hoshino, *Kogoshūi*, p. 22. D. Philippi, *Kojiki*, p. 85. The accounts in the *Nihongi* declare that both Ame-no-koyane and Futotama-no-mikoto recited the liturgy. Aston, op. cit. pp. 44, 49.

[288] D. Philippi, *Kojiki*, pp. 135–6.

[289] D. E. Mills, 'Takahasi uzibumi', pp. 131–2. There is a short version of the story in Aston, *Nihongi*, p. 213. The *Kamunie* (*Kanname*) Festival was held exclusively at Ise Shrines.

centralized government began issuing legislation and controls to strengthen its authority, the village agricultural festivals and other local cults of particular *kami* gradually came to be incorporated into the national worship for the people as a whole. The formulae for invoking the local *kami* beneficial to crops and harvest had to be repeated regularly and annually at the right season, and they had to be repeated without error. Hence, they came to be written down so that all shrines in the national system under the *Jingi-kan* could recite the formula that would bring blessing and bounty to the sovereign and the nobles, and even to the commoners. As the language used in some of these prayers or invocations was already archaic in the latter seventh century, the task of setting down the rituals was not easy. At that time the method used for writing was 'one symbol for one sound', the symbols being a limited selection of Chinese characters. In general, the writing was done in the manner used for setting down a decree of the sovereign which was uttered in Japanese (as opposed to those in Chinese), and hence the style was called 'imperial decree writing' (*semmyō-gaki*). In practice the stems and undeclined words were in large characters (mostly phonetically used) and the terminations and particles in small-size characters. The style of the *norito* for religious festivals closely resembled the language of the Court. The content of the *norito*, moreover, was developed to include the praises of the sovereign, the Imperial Court, and the ancestral *kami* of the Imperial Family and of the families of the highest nobility, who were associated with the Court and its religious festivals. The primary purpose was to invoke the *kami* and supplicate them for prosperity and protection from all types of ills, disasters, and defilements. But more than this, the archaic and majestic-sounding verbiage was to be intoned with solemn and sonorous syllables designed to please the *kami* and also to be awe-inspiring and magic-provoking within the minds of the celebrants and audience.

Some scholars believe that, because of the references to charms, spells, magic, and divine possession (*kamu-gakari*) in the anecdotes of the chronicles, the prevalence of shamanism in the religion is proven. It is difficult to determine how great a role shamanistic possession and communication with spirits played in the Yamato religion. From the literary evidence available it is nevertheless certain that the Yamato people believed in the magical power of words. The belief in this word-power (*kotodama*) is an outstanding trait of the *kami* worship and is borne out in the language of the *norito*. The proper recitation of the correct words in correct formulae had to be carried out in order to bring desired results. The uttering of auspicious words and laudatory phrases addressed to the *kami* was designed to bring beneficial results. The uttering of imprecations, evil spells, or curses would bring rout and destruction upon evil creatures or harmful *kami*. One finds in the chronicle references to 'divine words' (*shingo*) supposedly uttered by persons under divine possession.

But the accounts of divine possession and inspiration are rather rare in the chronicles.[290] The term *shingo* is used in the *Engi-shiki* text in interlinear glosses

---

[290] N. Aoki, op. cit. p. 31.

which give pronunciations in alternate characters for archaic religious terms, attesting to the kind of editing which the process of setting down old oral traditions necessitated.

Spells and magical formulae are incorporated in the texts of *norito*. The striking examples of magic-producing incantations in which the sound of the syllables uttered was to have magical effect are the spell intoned by the *fubito* of Yamato and Kawachi and the aforementioned *yin-yang* incantation to drive out devils (not included in this study, as it appears in Book XVI). The special vocabulary of the *norito* often employs words to induce calm, to bring good luck, to produce long life, and to drive out bad influences. The verb *hogu* and its substantive, *hogai*, were especially potent in casting a spell of good fortune upon the object in question. The adjectives *kushi* and *kusushi* meant more than 'marvelous'; rather, 'miraculous', or 'miracle-working'. Also, *iwau* or *iwai* in those rituals meant 'to cast a good spell' or 'to consecrate'. This may explain the frequent use of the word *iwa* ('rock' or 'firm') in auspicious formulae because of the similarity of sound to the lucky word *iwau*. Punning on words of magic import and use of alliteration was effective. In no. 9, the gods of the gates are besought to 'expel with words' any evil influences—evidence of the belief in word-power (*kotodama*).

One can see a combination of style elements in the various *norito* and even within a single *norito* text. Many phrases occur which have a curiously Chinese sound and a regular one-two one-two rhythm. This is obvious, for example, in the incantation, no. 11. In the Prayer for Harvest ritual for the *Toshigoi* Festival there comes the oft-repeated formula at the end of each section, '*tatae-goto-oematsuru to mawosu . . .*', illustrating the sound value of the strong vowels *a* and *o* in a refrain designed to engage the ears of benevolent *kami*. Other recurring phraseology comes forth in poetic stereotypes and flowing metaphors, such as: offerings of 'sweet herbs and bitter herbs' of the moors and mountains, and of 'creatures wide of fin and narrow of fin from the blue sea-plain'. Other figures and parallelisms give the recitation a psalm-like quality. In return for the protection or the bountiful gifts of the *kami*, the reciter promises a hyperbole of offerings: '. . . the first ears of the grain—a thousand, yea ten thousand, ears shall be offered.' Some of the phrases addressed to the *kami* are metrical, lyrical, and lofty; thereupon the subject matter, the object of address, and the style may suddenly change. For instance, in the ritual for the *Hirose no Oomi* Festival, after extolling the *kami* (here the goddess of food and related *kami*) the reciter turns at the close to call by name upon certain participants who will make the presentations of offerings. The object of address likewise changes at the end of those *norito* in which the members of the Imbe Uji are called upon to consecrate the offerings.

Many phrases and figures occurring in the *norito* are found in nearly identical form in poems of the *Man'yōshū*. The age of compilation of those poems appears to coincide roughly with the writing down of the *norito*. If there are some poems composed (or recited) as far back as the fifth century, there are also portions of some of the *norito* which go back as far. No doubt there were oral traditions which were common to both the *norito* and the poetry or songs that were handed down before the compilations which appeared in the eighth century. In the Ritual for the Great Purification (*Ooharae no kotoba*), no. 10, there are lists of what offenses (*tsumi*) against the *kami* and what defilements (*kegare*) must be driven out in this great exorcism. The *tsumi* were listed in almost the identical words in the *Kojiki*. These are the evidences of old tribal taboos of the Yamato people, and the setting down of these lists in writing may have occurred for both the chronicles and the texts of the *norito* in about the same period—the compilation having been commenced in the early seventh century and finally completed in the early eighth.

Not of such ancient origin, however, are passages which extol the reigning sovereign and the imperial line as descendants of the Heavenly Grandson (Ninigi-no-mikoto), the legendary descendant of the Sun Goddess whose progeny, Jimmu Tennō, was the first earthly sovereign. The political motivation back of all the eulogies of the imperial line and its divine forebears in use for national religious festivals ties directly into the development of the *Jingi-kan* as department of *kami* affairs for the Court and the nation, and with it the strengthening of the major shrines connected with the Imperial House and the noble families close to the Court. These developments worked together to enhance the Court and the ruling family and build up the influence of the central government—of Nara and later of Heian—over the people of the whole nation.

For this study of the *norito* the modern scholarship of Tsugita Jun (Uruu) in his *Norito shinkō*, and of Kaneko Takeo, in his *Engi-shiki norito-kō*, has been relied upon heavily. Their analyses and explanations of the vocabulary and content of *norito* are based on their own researches plus a comparative study of Kamo no Mabuchi's *Norito-kō* and *Norito-kai*, Motoori Norinaga's *Ooharae no kotoba kōshaku* and his voluminous *Kojiki-den*, and especially the work of Suzuki Shige-tane (1812–63): *Engi-shiki norito kōgi*, with its supplement, *Nakatomi yogoto kōgi*. As Motoori Norinaga leaned greatly on his own intuition and conjecture, the works of Shigetane are more reliable in respect to linguistic analysis. Mabuchi's interpretations are useful because they treat the *Engi-shiki* as a whole and make more extensive contributions, while Norinaga's detailed study is limited to the Great Purification Ritual. Other very useful modern studies include the *Norito jiten* of Uda Toshihiko, and *Norito no kenkyū* by Shiraishi Mitsukuni.

As to the etymology of the term *norito*, the characters used for it have a tendency to mislead us. But confusion may be dispelled by reading the compound 祝詞 *norito-koto*, or 'words of norito'. This leaves the single character 祝 to be read as *norito*. We find the term *norito* written 詔刀 in the *Kojiki*, 法刀 in the *Ryō no shūge*; again 法刀言 for *norito-koto* is found in the *Ryō no shūge* and 能理等 appears in the *Man'yōshū*; all of which illustrate the fact that *norito* is separate from *koto* and that *norito* is itself a compound word. The first part, *nori*, is the conjunctive stem of the verb *noru*—to tell, recite, command (superior to an inferior), reveal (as the divine will), decree—and the second part is *to*, a noun. *To* has been taken by some scholars of the past to stand for *koto*, but that would be redundant in this case. The theory of modern scholars, as Uda and Shiraishi, is that *to* means a spell or magical device. Thus the compound *norito* would mean the chanting or reciting of the spell. The combined form *norito-koto* then is 'words for reciting a spell'. The translation 'ritual' is commonly accepted and is used to include all types of *norito* in the collection. Some of these, however, are called by names other than *norito*. For example, the ritual for the Great Purification is the *Ooharae-no-kotoba*, 'Words for the Great Purification'; the ritual for the *Ootono-hogai* is the 'luck wishing' (Satow) or 'Blessing the Palace'; the *kamuyogoto* of the Chieftain of Izumo are 'divine laudatory words', while the incantation recited by the Fubito of Yamato and Kawachi is called *zu* or *majinai*, a magical spell.[291]

The longer *norito* in the collection include the initial one, for the *Toshigoi* Festival, the Great Purification Ritual, and the Laudatory Ritual to the Deities recited by the Chieftain of Izumo. These long recitations are composed of a number of parts, and were punctuated by pauses on the part of the reciter with an anti-phonal shout from the audience of participating priests and divine chiefs. A look at the subjects of these component parts will reveal the vast scope of invocation and supplication in a single *norito*. The following is the list of twelve parts of the *Toshigoi no matsuri no norito* (no. 1):

1. Introductory
2. Invocation of all the many *kami* of heaven and earth
3. Words addressed to Mitoshi-no-kami (Deity of Crops)
4. Words addressed to *kami* worshiped by the Great Sacred Maidens of the Imperial Palace
5. Words addressed to *kami* worshiped by the Igasuri Maidens
6. Words addressed to *kami* worshiped by the Mikado Maidens
7. Words addressed to *kami* worshiped by the Ikushima Maidens
8. Offerings to Amaterasu-ō-mikami
9. Words addressed to *kami* of the Imperial Districts
10. Words addressed to *kami* at the Openings of the Mountains (*yamanokuchi*)
11. Words addressed to water-dividing *kami* (*mikumari*)
12. Dedication by *kannushi* and *hafuri*

By addressing all *kami* of whatever locality in heaven and earth, the ritual takes in every worshiper in the nation. The address to Mitoshi-no-kami, who was a local god of the rice crops, elevates him to a national *kami*. The next four sections are addressed to the various *kami* worshiped in the Imperial Palace, and the address to Amaterasu-ō-mikami, the Sun Goddess, plainly places the divine ancestress of the imperial line in a position to be worshiped by all the people. The 9th section prays for crops in the districts which purvey to the Imperial House, and the succeeding two sections address the *kami* of the mountains and of water-supply and irrigation.

Finally, the Nakatomi who are reciting the ritual address the Imbe, who are official 'abstainers', to bless and purify the offerings before they are distributed and carried by the priests to their various shrines.

---

[291] Cognates of *noru* are: *inoru*, to pray; *nori*, law, rule; *norou*, to curse, to imprecate; *noroi*, a curse, a malediction; *noberu* or *noburu*, to tell, express, relate, narrate, state; *notama(f)u*, to speak, to tell (superior to inferior), and so forth. Cognates of the archaic word *to*, a spell, are: *tona(f)u*, to make sounds, and the verb *tonaeru*, to name or call.

This twelve-part ritual is used for the second most important annual festival, the *Tsukinami no matsuri*, as well. There is only one slight difference, in that the address to Mitoshi-no-kami, the god of crops and harvest, is not included in the *Tsukinami* ritual. See no. 7 of the rituals. This makes it apparent that the *Tsukinami* or 'monthly' festival was held to invoke the care of the *kami* upon the progress of the crops up until the time of harvest. It may have been held every month in prehistoric times, but our information in available sources shows that it was celebrated twice during the agricultural year—on the eleventh day of the sixth and twelfth months of the lunar calendar.

Present-day *negi* reciting the *norito* (ritual)

# ENGI-SHIKI, BOOK EIGHT

## *Norito*

### THE RITUALS

A T ALL times, regarding *norito* for religious festivals: the Imbe Uji recite the *norito* for the festivals of *Ootono* and *Mikado*. For the various other festivals the Nakatomi Uji recite the *norito*.[292]

At all times, at annual festivals for which *norito* are not included here, the *kambe*, according to established precedent, recite.[293] As for *norito* for the extraordinary festivals,[294] the officials in charge make a selection in advance of the festival to suit the occasion and present this to the *kan*[295] for a decision, which is subsequently carried out.

[292] According to the tradition of the Nakatomi family, they were the descendants of Ame-no-koyane-no-mikoto, the deity who offered the prayer to induce the Sun Goddess, Amaterasu-ō-mikami, to come out from the cave where she had hid herself, and that they therefore were entitled to conduct the prayers or ritual dressed to the *kami*. On the other hand, the Imbe (Imube) family, who traced their descent from Futotama-no-mikoto, through Ame-no-tomi-no-mikoto, who built the palace for the first earthly emperor, Jimmu Tennō, claimed their right to recite *norito* at the festivals connected with the palaces of the sovereign. Hence, the Imbe recited the ritual for the *Ootono-hogai* (Luck-wishing for the Palace) and for the *Mikado-hogai* (Luck-wishing for the August Gates), rituals nos. 8 and 9. For the story of Ame-no-tomi-no-mikoto's building, together with all branches of the Imbe Uji, the 'august abode' (*mi-araka*) of the sovereign and making mirrors, jewels, spears, shields, and offerings of cloth for presentation, see Katō and Hoshino, *Kogoshūi*, pp. 31–2.

[293] Festivals which according to the *E-S* did not require the recitation of *norito* were: Hana-shizume, Saigusa (or Saegusa), Sono and Kara Deities, *Ainame, Kammiso, Kamo*, and Inari festivals. There were occasions when the *kambe* (*kamutomo*) officials of the *Jingi-kan* had to prepare prayers according to the need. For example, when the *Amagoi* (Prayers for Rain) Festival had to be held, special prayers were made for rain; when the *Amadome* (Rain-stopping) Festival was held, or the gods of thunder had to be appeased, supplications were made for the occasion. J. Tsugita, *Norito shinkō*, pp. 48–9.

[294] The extraordinary, or occasional, festivals (*rinjisai*) are covered in *E-S* Bk III. They include those for thunder gods and deities of water, wells, stoves; festivals for propitiating the ground for a new palace or a new dwelling; presentations when the Sacred Maidens change office; festivals of deities of boundaries, the deities of Yasoshima in the Palace, the gods of Sumiyoshi, and those of Ooyosami, Watatsumi, and Sumuchi; festivals to deities of epidemic, of rain, of travel routes, for despatching envoys to foreign countries; and, finally, the celebration when the local Chieftain of Izumo came to the capital.

[295] Here is meant the *Dajō-kan*, the Great Council of State.

## [I]

### Toshigoi Festival[296]

[1] Oh ye assembled shrine chiefs[297] and all ye priests,[298] hearken unto what we say. (Shrine chiefs and all priests are to respond 'Ooh!' to this and to all succeeding pronouncements.)[299]

[2] Before the mighty ancestral gods and goddesses[300] who augustly reside in the Plain of High Heaven, before the many *kami* enshrined in heaven and earth,[301] we raise our words of praise; and to the mighty *kami* we make bold to say: In this second month of this year,[302] at the beginning of the sowing of seed, with choice offerings from the divine descendant[303] at this moment of the majestic and brilliant dawning of the morning light, we humbly raise our words of praise.

[3] Before the presence of the *kami* who govern the crops we do humbly speak, praying that the mighty *kami* may vouchsafe to us the late-ripening harvest of grain[304]—with foam on the water up to the elbows and muddy water up to the

[296] The *Toshigoi no matsuri* (or *Kinen-sai*) 祈年祭 was held on the 4th day of the 2nd month, the first festival of the agricultural year. The officials of the *Jingi-kan* led the officialdom of the capital and the provinces in petitioning the *kami* for successful planting and the ripening and harvesting of the rice. In the old Yamato language *toshi* meant the crops, especially the rice crop (Mitoshi-no-kami and Ootoshi-no-kami were deities of the rice crop); and the secondary meaning of *toshi* is the (agricultural) year. *Toshi* is used in both senses in this *norito*. In the *Kogoshūi*, Imbe no Hironari tells the story of worshiping Mitoshi-no-kami in order to secure a good harvest of rice—a tale which is probably the prototype or precedent for the *Toshigoi* Festival. Katō and Hoshino, op. cit. pp. 51–2.

[297] *Kannushi* or *kamunushi* in the early phase meant the chiefs (*nushi*) among all those nobles, from the sovereign on down, to whom was entrusted the conduct of *kami* affairs (*kamu-goto*). Later, it came to mean the chief priests of individual shrines.

[298] 'All priests' is *hafuri-be* in the generic sense; see n. 74 above. *Ugonaharu* is an archaic word meaning 'gather together' or 'come together'; it is related to modern *ugoku*, to move, and *ugomeku*, to wriggle.

[299] The participating priests were to chorus in unison: 'Ooh!', equivalent to English 'Aye!', at each interval of the *norito*, as indicated by the cadence phrase: '. . . we humbly raise our words of praise'. (. . . *koto-oe-matsuru*).

[300] This translates the phrase: '*Sumemutsu* [or *sumeragamutsu*] *kamurogi no mikoto, kamuromi no mikoto*. . . .' *Kami* alone has no gender, but this archaic term *kamurogi* has the masculine ending *gi*, and *kamuromi* has the feminine ending *mi*. *Sume*, the stem of *sumeru* (or *suberu*), to rule or have supremacy over, is translated 'mighty'. *Mutsu* had the meaning of 'familiar', 'intimate', or 'beloved' (*mutsumajii*, in modern language).

[301] Here are used the expressions *amatsu-yashiro* and *kunitsu-yashiro*, metaphors for the oft-used *amatsu-kami*, *kunitsu-kami*, a literary device to include all *kami*, known and unknown, wherever they may abide in the heavens or on earth.

[302] Text says: '*ko (no) toshi no kisaragi ni mitoshi no hajime*', in which the first *toshi* means '(this) year' and the second, *mitoshi*, the august crop.

[303] The oft-recurring expression '*Sume-mima-no-mikoto*' (lit. the Prince, the mighty, divine Grandson) is an eponym for the whole line of sovereigns or for the ruling sovereign; even though the title is that of the 'Heavenly Grandson' of Amaterasu-ō-mikami, the Ninigi-no-mikoto of the myths, who sired the line of earthly sovereigns. Therefore, a translation like 'divine descendant' can be used whether Ninigi-no-mikoto is meant or any of the line of sovereigns, though usually the reigning sovereign is thus addressed or referred to in the *norito*.

[304] *Okitsu* (or *okutsu*) *mitoshi*, meaning 'august late-ripening crop', alludes to rice, which takes longer to mature than other grains.

thighs as the rice is cultivated—may it grow into countless bundles of long-eared grain, of vigorous grain. If the mighty *kami* grant that it ripen, the first-fruits of the grain, a thousand, yea, ten thousand ears shall be offered up to them. Let the offering jars be filled to the brims, yea, let the full-bellied jars be arrayed in rows; the liquid and the grain shall we offer up with our words of praise.[305] Of things that grow in the broad meadows and moors—sweet herbs and bitter herbs; of things that live in the blue sea-plain—those wide of fin and narrow of fin, even unto the seaweeds of the deep and seaweeds of the shore;[306] and for divine raiment —bright cloth, shining cloth, soft cloth, and coarse cloth—all these we humbly offer up with our words of praise.

Before the presence of the mighty *kami* of the crops we prepare to offer a white horse, a white boar, a white cock, and all manner and variety of things.[307] These we offer as choice offerings from the divine descendant, with the words of praise which we humbly speak.

[4] Before the mighty *kami* to whom the great Sacred Maidens[308] offer words of praise, we humbly speak. We utter the hallowed names of Kami-musubi, Takami-musubi, Iku-musubi, Taru-musubi, Tamatsume-musubi, Oomiya-no-me, Oomiketsu-no-kami and Kotoshironushi,[309] to all of whom we now offer our praises. May this age of the divine descendant of heaven be an everlasting age, as firm as solid rock, as unchanging as enduring rock. That it may flourish and be a happy reign, we present the choice offerings from the divine descendant to these mighty ancestral gods and goddesses as we offer up our words of praise.

[5] Before the presence of the mighty *kami* to whom the Igasuri Sacred Maidens raise their words of praise, we make bold to utter the hallowed names of Ikui,

---

[305] The two main uses of the rice crop are for eating and for making sake. Here, the offering-jars, *mika*, refer to the great jars in which the sake is fermented and stored. The brim is *he* 閊. See J. Tsugita, op. cit. p. 75.

[306] The list of offerings to be made at the *Toshigoi* Festival is given in *E-S*, Bk I, and reads in part: 'At 198 shrines: for each presentation: 5 *shaku* of pongee, 1 *shaku* each of five colors of thin pongee, 1 *shaku* of colored hemp-cloth, 2 *ryō* of bark cloth, 5 *ryō* of hemp, 1 *jō* 4 *shaku* of tax cloth.... [sword cases, shield, spearhead, bow, quiver, deer antlers, mattock, sake, abalone, bonito, jerky, seaweeds, salt, etc.]' The symbolic offerings include the streamers of bark-cloth, hemp, and cloth in five colors—though *goshiki* 五色 may mean 'five kinds'. In the case of '*goshiki no usuashiginu*' it probably means five colors of thin pongee: blue, red, yellow, white, and black.

[307] In addition to the foregoing list of offerings made to the *kami* worshiped in the *Toshigoi* Festival, Bk I stipulates that at the shrine to Mitoshi-no-kami in Takechi District, Yamato Province, there must be added a white horse, a

white boar, and a white cock. At the Shrine of the Great Deity (Amaterasu-ō-mikami) in Ise and also at the Watarai Shrine, additional offering of a horse is required; so also to certain small shrines and to Takami-musubi-no-kami and Oomiya-no-me-no-kami, who are worshiped in the Imperial Palace.

[308] The character 巫 by itself is read *kamuko* (or *miko*), and an honorific precedes when it is used for the maidens which serve in the *Jingi-kan* and the Imperial Palace. They are called *mikamunagi* or *mikamuko*. Here the addition of 'great' (大) sets apart these Sacred Maidens who serve the eight *kami* worshiped by the Imperial House.

[309] These eight *kami* were worshiped as protectors of the Imperial Palace and were enshrined in the *Jingi-kan* (in the Palace precinct). Satow has translated their names thus: 'Divine Producer, Lofty Producer, Vivifying Producer, Fulfilling Producer, Soul-lodging Producer, Woman of the Great House, Great Goddess of Food, and Events-symbol-lord.' *TASJ*, ser. I, VII, pp. 109–10.

Sakui, Tsunagai, Asuha, and Haigi, and offer unto them our praises.[310] By the command of the mighty *kami*, the columns of the divine palace are firmly set upon the bedrock beneath the land, and the crossed gable-boards reach up toward the Plain of High Heaven, as we humbly serve and worship at the sacred dwelling of the divine descendant.[311] May it be sheltered from the gaze of heaven and from the blazing sun.[312] Vouchsafe that from it the land in all directions may be governed and made a peaceful land, a tranquil land by the grace of the mighty *kami*. So we offer up the choice offerings from the divine descendant together with our words of praise.

[6]    Before the presence of the mighty *kami* to whom the Mikado Sacred Maidens raise their words of praise, we make bold to utter the hallowed names of Kushi-iwamado-no-mikoto and Toyo-iwamado-no-mikoto[313] and offer up to them our words of praise. May they defend with strength like a magic-working mound of rock[314] the august gates of the four directions; may they open the gates in the morning and close the gates in the evening. If things to be shunned come from below, let the *kami* protect below; if things to be shunned come from above, let the *kami* protect above. May they watch by night and watch by day we humbly pray, as with choice offerings of the divine descendant we offer up our words of praise.

[310] These deities are listed in the *E-S*, Bk IX, the *Jimmyō-chō*, among the 36 *kami* worshiped in the Imperial Palace. In their names the element *i* means drinking-water; some of them are deities of wells, the others are related to water-supply. The Igasuri (or Igazuri) Maidens conduct the worship of these *kami*. The name Igasuri was a place name in Settsu Province where Nintoku Tennō had his palace; a *kami* of that name, connected with a well, was worshiped in Nintoku's palace, and that worship later moved to Yamato and Yamashiro provinces. J. Tsugita, pp. 90–1. Satow translates their names: 'Vivifying Well, Blessing Well, Long-rope Well, Foot-place, and Entrance Limit'. *TASJ*, ser. I, VII, p. 110. Imbe no Hironari refers to 'The Gods of Ikasuri—the Guardian Spirits of the Imperial Court Grounds'. Katō and Hoshino, op. cit. p. 34.

[311] The Imperial Palace of the present reigning sovereign is meant. The almost identical passage is found in the *Kogoshūi* where it is describing the Palace. See Katō and Hoshino, op. cit. p. 31. And in the *Man'yōshū*, Bk I, 136, beginning 'Akitsu minobe ni', comes the passage: 'miyaba-shira futoshiki maseba, momoshiki no ōmiyabito wa fune namete....'The latter is translated: 'Here she builds herself a mighty pillared palace, and imperial courtiers row their barges.'

[312] *Ame no mikage, hi no mikage*, 'in the shade of heaven, the shade of the sun', appears to mean that the august dwelling of the sovereign is built to protect him or cover him from the sky and from the direct rays of the sun. If the sun was the supreme object of worship, its emanations must have been the most awesome thing in nature, from which one must be shielded. Is this perhaps the purpose of the royal umbrella for an imperial progress?

[313] The *Mikado-matsuri* is held to fete the gods who dwell in the Palace gates and oversee the coming and going into the sacred area. The name Kushi-iwamado is made up of *kushi*, wondrous; *iwa*, firm or auspicious; and *mado*, true door (or perhaps eye-door). The other deity is Toyo-iwamado, with *toyo* meaning abundant or provident. These two gods are worshiped by the *mikado-no-kamunagi*, Sacred Maidens of the August Gates. In the myth of the descent of the Heavenly Grandson (Ninigi-no-mikoto) to earth, Amaterasu-ō-mikami sent along Ame-no-iwatowake-no-kami, the Deity of the Gates. Alternate names for this *kami* were given as: Kushi-iwamado and Toyo-iwamado-no-kami. See Philippi, *Kojiki*, pp. 139–40.

[314] Another adjective with magical potency was *yuzu* or *yutsu*. It is applied to something which has superior or miraculous power. Here it says: '*yutsu-iwamura no gotoku*' (like a magic-working mass of rock).

[7]   Before the presence of the mighty *kami* to whom the Ikushima Sacred Maidens raise their words of praise, we make bold to utter the hallowed names of Ikukuni and Tarukuni and offer up to them our words of praise.[315] In all the many lands far and wide over which the mighty *kami* hold sway, to the uttermost corners whither creeping creatures may crawl, and as far as the salt foam of the flood tides reaches, may the narrow places be made wide and the steep places be made level, and may there be no escaping of waters in the lands far and wide. Let the mighty *kami* vouchsafe this to us, as with the choice offerings from the divine descendant of heaven we now raise our words of praise.

[8]   And we turn now to the mighty presence of Amaterasu-ō-mikami who resides in Ise,[316] making bold to say: In all the lands through which this mighty *kami* clearly sees, as far as the heavens stretch above and as far as the ground stretches beneath, to the uttermost heights of clouds in the blue, to the limits reached by the white clouds a-massing, to the uttermost reaches of the plain of the blue sea, on which with pole and helm never dry the prows of ships do ply, yea, on the great ocean[317] where sail heavy-laden ships and on the land routes where ropes are pulled taut over the loads of tribute cargo, may the mighty goddess vouchsafe to the divine descendant that treading over rough rocks and roots of trees, as far as horses' hooves can travel, the narrow places may be made wide and the steep places made level, and may the distant countries send tribute pulled by dozens of hawsers.[318] If the great ancestral goddess grant us this, before the presence of the great ancestral goddess we shall heap up our tribute of first-fruits like unto a range of hills,[319] and if any be left over, may the divine descendant partake thereof. Moreover, may the reign of the divine descendant be an everlasting reign and may it be firm as hard rock, and enduring as solid rock, we pray. That it may flourish and be a happy reign, we humbly bow our necks way down like the cormorant in obeisance to the mighty ancestral gods and goddesses, and offer up the choice offerings from the divine descendant as we raise our words of praise.

[9]   Before the presence of the mighty *kami* who dwell in the august districts[320] we humbly speak. We make bold to utter the hallowed names of Takechi,

---

[315] The deities Ikukuni and Tarukuni are among the 23 *kami* worshiped in the *Jingi-kan*, which was within the Imperial Palace precinct. *Kuni* refers to the land of imperial domain; thus their names: 'Living Land' (or, after Satow, 'Vivifying Land') and 'Fulfilling Land'. They are also called Ikushima-no-kami.

[316] The particular invocation of Amaterasu-ō-mikami, who is also the ancestral deity and the *ujigami* of the Imperial House, illustrates the importance put upon nation-wide reverence for this deity in the celebration of the *Toshigoi* Festival.

[317] In this passage the character 艣 (which in modern language is read *tomo*, 'stern') was, according to the *Wamyōshō*, used for *hesaki*, 'prow'; 'ocean' is for the term *ō-umi*.

[318] How suggestive this passage is of Isaiah 40:4 'Every valley shall be exalted, and every mountain and hill shall be made low: and the crooked shall be made straight and the rough places plain.'

[319] In this paragraph the first 'tribute' is *ni* 荷, which Tsugita interprets to mean *kōbutsu* 貢物, tribute goods. The subsequent uses of tribute are supplied from the context and *nosaki* 荷前 means first fruits. Elsewhere in the *E-S* the expression *mitsugi nosaki*, 'first-fruits as tribute', is found.

[320] The six 'august districts', *mi-agata* 御縣, were the ones which raised rice and produce for the Imperial Table. The names given are the names of the local *kami* from which the districts get their names. T. Kaneko, p. 54.

Katsuragi, To-ochi, Shiki, Yamanobe, and Sou. As we come humbly bearing the sweet herbs and the bitter herbs that grow in these six districts, may the *kami* vouchsafe that they provide food eternally for the divine descendants for with choice offerings from the divine descendant we raise our words of praise.

[10] Before the presence of the mighty *kami* that dwell in the openings of the mountains[321] we humbly speak. Making bold to utter the sacred names of Asuka, Iware, Osaka, Hatsuse, Unebi, and Miminashi, we dare to cut the trunks and branches of great trees and small trees that sprout and grow in the farther mountains and the nearer mountains. And we come up bearing the wood therefrom that we may undertake to build a new and splendid august dwelling for the divine descendant, in which he may rest sheltered from the gaze of heaven and from the blazing sun. May the *kami* vouchsafe that the land in all directions be calmed to a peaceful land. With choice offerings from the divine descendant of heaven we raise our words of praise.

[11] Before the presence of the water-dividing *kami* we humbly speak. We make bold to utter the sacred names of Yoshino, Uda, Tsuge, Katsuragi,[322] as we humbly raise our words of praise. Let the mighty *kami* vouchsafe to us a crop of long-eared grain, of vigorous grain, in the late-ripening harvest of rice, and we shall offer up to the mighty *kami* the first-fruits in countless myriads of grains, the grain and the liquid made from it, filling the offering jars to the brims, and setting up the rows of full-bellied jars, we shall offer up our words of praise. If there be any left over, may it grace the table of the divine descendant for the august morning food and the august evening food, that he may partake of it for eternity. As in partaking his august cheeks become ruddy,[323] so shall we bring the choice offerings from the divine descendant as we raise our words of praise, and let all those present hearken hereunto.

[12] We turn now and ask the Imbe, their frail shoulders bound with potent sleeve-ties,[324] to consecrate the offerings that are here prepared, and ask the divine chiefs and all priests to humbly receive these offerings, and making no error, to bear them up and present them [to the *kami*].

---

[321] *Yamanokuchi* (*yamaguchi*) 山口 are the mouths or entrances of the mountains whence pour forth the waters to bless the land and irrigate the rice paddies. These are also the names of local *kami* dwelling in those mountains. Offerings to the *yamanokuchi* deities are prescribed in the *E-S*, Bk I, under *Toshigoi* Festival.

[322] *Mikumari* (*mikomari*) 水分 deities were those who controlled the streams used for irrigation, the most vital part of rice culture. These are also contained in the regulations for *Toshigoi* offerings, *E-S*, Bk I.

[323] Although *akani-no-ho* has been interpreted to mean 'grain the color of red earth'. But both Kaneko and Uda take *ho* to mean 'cheek'. *Aka-ni* is red clay, used for coloring as well as for pottery.

[324] Here, with the expression *koto-waite* 辞別 the address shifts from *kami* to the participants themselves. The *futo-dasuki* 太多須支 has been translated 'potent sleeve-ties' to get the force of the adjective *futo*, which is one of those words of magical import. Sleeve-ties (*tasuki* or *yūda-suki*, see n. 233) are used to tie back the sleeves when preparing sacred food or offerings. *Futo* is a word which is used to induce magical effect—here, to increase the potency and effect of offerings presented to the *kami*.

## [2]

### *Kasuga Festival*[325]

BY THE august decree of the Sovereign, in great awe, we humbly speak in the awesome presence of the four mighty *kami*, Take-mikazuchi-no-mikoto who resides in Kashima, Iwainushi-no-mikoto who resides in Katori, Ame-no-koyane-no-mikoto and Himegami, who reside in Hiraoka,[326] thus: In the manner in which the mighty *kami* have ordained, we have planted firmly the pillars of the shrine in the rocks deep under Mt Mikasa of Kasuga. The crossed beams thereof reach toward the heavens, offering a shelter from the gaze of heaven and from the blazing sun. And in it we have prepared[327] and offered these treasures for the *kami*: august mirror, august sword, august bow, august spear, and august horse; and for sacred raiment, we offer up bright cloth, shining cloth, soft cloth, and coarse cloth. And we place in rows the first-fruits sent in tribute from the provinces in all directions as offerings: the products of the blue sea, things wide of fin and narrow of fin, seaweeds from the deep and seaweeds of the shore, and even unto the sweet herbs and the bitter herbs from mountain and moor. Let the offering jars be filled with sake to their brims, yea, let the bellies of the rows of jars be full, and let all manner of goods be heaped up like a range of hills.

Let the surname, clan-rank-title, Court Rank, and position of those who are divine chiefs be made known.[328] May the choice great offerings which we present be pleasing offerings, be abundant offerings, and may they be received in tranquillity and pleasure. So we pray as we raise our words of praise to the four mighty *kami*. Since we serve thus by our worship, we pray that now and in the future our Sovereign may reign in his palace in peace and tranquillity and be blessed with a prosperous reign. May it be firm as solid rock, eternal as enduring rock, and be caused to flourish. May all the princes and court nobles of all the families from each locality who have participated and served here be at peace. May the August Sovereign flourish in his palace more than the trees and plants which grow, for

---

[325] The *Kasuga* Festival, according to the first book of *E-S*, was of the 'small' category. It was celebrated at Kasuga Jinja in Sounokami District, Yamato Prov., on the first monkey day (上申) of the 2nd and 11th months each year. The Kasuga Jinja was built to enshrine the ancestral and *uji* deities of the Fujiwara Uji.

[326] After the founding of the Kasuga Jinja, purportedly in the reign of Empress Gemmyō (708–14), the ancestral *kami* of the Nakatomi Family—of which the Fujiwara were a branch—were moved to Kasuga. These were Ame-no-koyane-no-mikoto and his consort Himegami.

Also, the *ujigami* of the Fujiwara were moved to Kasuga: namely, Take-mikazuchi-no-kami from Kashima Jingū in Hitachi Province, and Iwainushi-no-mikoto (who is identified with Futsunushi-no-kami of the myths) from Katori Jingū in Shimōsa (Shimotsufusa) Province.

[327] 'Prepared', or fitted, means that the mirror has its container, the sword its scabbard, the bow its arrows, the spear a shield, and the horse its saddle.

[328] The surname is *na* 名, the clan-rank title is *kabane* 姓, the Court Rank is *kurai* 位, and the government position or office is *tsukasa* 官.

a reign that prospers, thus we pray as we humbly raise our words of praise.
(This is used likewise for the *norito* at Ooharano and Hiraoka Shrines.)[329]

## [3]

### Hirose no Oomi Festival[330]

AT THE confluence of the streams of Hirose we raise our words of praise. We
make bold to utter the sacred name of Waka-uka-no-me-no-mikoto,[331] who grants
to us august food. Before this mighty *kami* we humbly raise our words of praise,
bearing the choice offerings from the divine descendant. With imperial princes
and court nobles as bearers of the offerings, we raise our words of praise that all
ye chiefs of shrines and priests may hear, so say we.

The choice offerings we present are for divine raiment: bright cloth, shining
cloth, soft cloth and coarse, five kinds of goods, shields, spears, and horses. Let
the sake fill the offering jars to the brim, yea, let the full-bellied offering jars be
arrayed in rows. We bring fine hulled rice and coarse unhulled rice, and, of things
dwelling in the mountains, those with soft fur and those with coarse fur;[332] of
things that grow in the meadows of the great moors, sweet herbs and bitter herbs;
of things that live in the blue sea-plain, things wide of fin and narrow of fin, even
unto the seaweeds of the deep and seaweeds of the shore. We heap these up high
and offer them as we speak our words humbly before the presence of the mighty
*kami*. The offerings which we thus present, may they be pleasing offerings, bountiful offerings; may the *kami* receive them with peaceful and tranquil heart, we
pray. May the food be eternally partaken of by the divine descendant who rules
us, and his cheeks become ruddy as he partakes. Starting with the sacred fields
of the mighty *kami*, the people under heaven[333] till the sacred late-ripening rice
for the imperial princes, princesses, and the court nobles; up to their elbows in
the churning water of the rice paddies, and up to their thighs, they work the

[329] The statement shows that the same *norito*
was to be recited at the festival of Ooharano
Shrine, where were enshrined the same four
deities as at Kasuga (the four venerated as
*ujigami* by the Fujiwara), and where it was held
on the 'first hare day of the 2nd month, and on the
middle rat day of the 11th month' (*E-S*, Bk I).
It was also to be used for the festival to the four
*kami* enshrined at Hiraoka in Kawachi Province
celebrated on the first monkey day of the 2nd
and 11th months (*E-S*, Bk I).

[330] The festival is *Hirose no Oomi (Ooimi)
no matsuri*, celebrated at the Hirose Shrine
located in former Hirose District (now Kita-
Katsuragi-gun), at the confluence of the Saho,
Hatsuse, and Asuka rivers, which unite to water
the Yamato plain. In the *Nihongi*, the reign of
Temmu Tennō, it says that the sovereign sent
messengers 'to worship the Oho-imi Deity at
Kawawa in Hirose'.

[331] Aston calls the Waka-uka-hime deity 'the

young-food-lady' (*Nihongi*, II, 328). In the myths,
Uka-no-mitama (the Spirit of Food) was created
from the breath of Izanagi, the male of the
creator-gods (ibid. I, p. 22). The *waka* in her
name means 'young' or 'fresh'; *uka* (or *uga, uke*,
etc.) means 'food'; *me* is 'female'. This goddess is
also known as Uketsu-hime or Miketsu-hime,
and at Ise Watarai Shrine as Toyouke-no-kami.

[332] The expression 'of soft fur and coarse fur'
has led some scholars to think it means birds
and beasts, and others to think it means different
kinds of beasts. Mabuchi in the *Norito-kō* takes
it to mean the feathers of birds and the coarse
hair of beasts; Tsugita interprets soft fur as that
of little animals and coarse fur as that of large
animals.

[333] 'The people' is the expression '*ame-no shita
no ōmutakara*' 天下公民, lit. 'the great treasure
beneath heaven'; or *ta-kara* may mean 'workers
in the rice paddies' 田族 (Kaneko, p. 85).

late-ripening harvest of rice. Let the mighty *kami* vouchsafe to us long ears of grain, and we shall heap up the first-fruits of the crop in liquid and in grain, like a range of hills, as offerings in the autumn festival; thus do we humbly speak before the presence of the mighty *kami*.

Before the presence of the mighty *kami* who dwell in the openings of the mountains in the six august districts in Yamato,[334] we bring the choice offerings from the divine descendant who rules us: offerings of bright cloth, shining cloth, soft cloth, and coarse cloth, and five kinds of goods, even unto shields and spears. As we present these offerings, so may we receive the waters which ye send down the hills and valleys from the openings of the many mountains governed by these mighty *kami*, and may it be sweet water. May the people under heaven who till the paddies of late-ripening rice not be smitten by fierce winds or angry waters.[335] May ye divinities vouchsafe this to us and we shall offer up the first-fruits in liquid and in grain, and filling the offering jars to the brim and lining up the full-bellied jars in rows, we shall heap up the offerings like a range of hills. Now let all imperial princes, princesses, nobles of the court, the host of officials, and chiefs and men and women of the six august districts[336] who are gathered here in this year, in this——month and——day[373] come humbly, and bowing their necks low like the cormorant in obeisance before the presence of the mighty *kami*, at this moment of the majestic and brilliant dawning of the morning light humbly raise the words of praise; oh, hearken, all ye chiefs of shrines and all ye priests, to what we utter.

[4]

*Tatsuta Wind Gods Festival*[338]

*Ritual*

BEFORE the presence of the mighty *kami* of Tatsuta we humbly raise our words of

---

[334] At this point the address shifts from the goddess Waka-uka-no-me-no-mikoto of the Hirose Shrine to the *kami* of the six imperial (or august) districts and the *yamanokuchi* deities of water supply.

[335] Or, evil winds and rough waters—*ashiki kaze, araki mizu*—such as strike in the typhoon season, often destroying the rice which ripens in the late summer.

[336] *Tone* were chiefs of households, but here they are officers attached to the districts producing food for the Imperial Table. They are local officials as opposed to Court officials, and appear to be supervisors of the men and women who work the paddies and fields of the six imperial districts.

[337] When the festival is held in spring, the words 'Fourth month, fourth day' are supplied; when held in summer, 'seventh month, fourth day' are supplied.

[338] According to the Register of Deities (*Jimmyō-chō*) of Bks IX and X, below, there are two deities enshrined in the main shrine at Tatsuta.

Both are 'principal deities' (*myōjin* 名神) and are 'major' (*dai* 大). They are titled Ame-no-mihashira and Kuni-no-mihashira, lit. 'Divine Pillar of Heaven' and 'Divine Pillar of Earth', between which the winds are supported. In a second shrine at the same site are dwelling Tatsuta-hiko and Tatsuta-hime, male and female divinities of the locality. According to H. Aida, these two are identifiable with Shinatsu-hiko and Shinatobe-no-mikoto of mythology. See *Chūkai yōrō-ryō*, p. 344. They are found in the *Nihongi*, where *shinaga*, from which their names derive, is interpreted to mean 'long of breath'. Worship of the gods of the winds is mentioned in the *Nihongi* in the 4th, 5th, 6th, and 10th years of Temmu Tennō's reign; also in Empress Jitō's reign, especially in times of drought. See Aston, *Nihongi*, II, pp. 328, 331. The birth of the wind god is described in the creation myth of Izanagi and Izanami, and the wind god is also referred to in the Jingū Kōgō legend (Aston, op. cit. I, pp. 22, 230).

praise. Once the divine descendant who ruled the great land of Yamato, the great country of many islands,[339] did partake of the august eternal food, and his cheeks grew ruddy as he partook of the five grains[340] and the fruit of the crops tilled by the people under heaven. But when these did not grow unto the least blade, when they failed to ripen for not just one year or two, but for many years, the divine descendant decreed that the will of the *kami* must be made known from divination by many wise men and women as to which *kami* had ordered the harm to befall. But the divination by the wise ones did not reveal which of the *kami* had willed it. And the divine descendant declared: 'We have not forgotten any of the *kami* of heaven and earth and have omitted none in raising to them our words of praise. If the crops which the people under heaven are tilling do not grow, let the *kami* who bring harm to them reveal that it was their will and make an oath to us.[342] And thereupon the divine descendant envisioned a great dream: 'When the crops which are tilled by the people under heaven encounter fierce winds and angry waters, when they are harmed and grow not, it is because of Ame-no-mihashira and Kuni-no-mihashira.' Thus their august names were made known. 'If you present here before us offerings of divine raiment: bright cloth, shining cloth, soft cloth, and coarse cloth, five kinds of goods, shields, spears, august horse and saddle and all manner of offerings, and if you set up our august abode situated where the light of the morning sun shines and the light of the evening sun casts its shadows,[343] in the little moor of Tatsuno in Tatsuta, here is our august abode located. If ye raise up words of praise in our presence, the crops which the people under heaven till and work, from the five grains to the very least blade of grass, ye shall know that they all will grow and be made to prosper.'

[339] The expression *shiki-shima* in the *norito* is a fixed epithet for the land of Japan. *Ooyashima kuni* is another poetic epithet, meaning 'Great Eight-Island Country' (or, 'Great Many-Island Country'). In the Izanagi and Izanami creation story, the latter gives birth to eight different islands, which stand for the principal islands of the archipelago. See Aston, I, 16.

[340] The *itsukusa no tanatsu-mono*, or *itsutsu no tanatsu-mono*, may mean five kinds of things from seeds (*tane no mono*). The traditional 'five cereals' of China were (according to the *Chou li*, and other sources): Glutenous millet, panicled millet, hemp, wheat, and beans, or, according to Mencius, rice, both millets, wheat and pulse, and so forth. The traditional Japanese five grains were: rice, wheat, millet, soybeans (*daizu*), and red beans (*azuki*). See Tsugita, p. 174.

[341] *Monoshiri-bito*, lit. 'knowers of things' in this context, may, since they are credited with performing divination (*uragoto* or *uranai*), be the *urabe* diviners whose role in preparations for festivals is essential. The origin of the root *ura* is obscure, but one theory (advanced by Nishimura Shinji 西村眞次) is that it derives from the Tungusic *ula*, the word for deer. Since the favored method of determining the divine will of the *kami* was by examining the cracks and delineations in the heated scapula of deer, this is a possible explanation of *ura-goto, uranai, uramu, ura-hame* and other terms related to the functions of the *urabe*. See J. Tsugita, p. 175.

[342] *Ukehi* is *renyōkei* (conjunctive) of *uke(f)u*, to swear an oath—a means of soliciting divine approval or a divine judgment. In the *Kojiki* the Storm God Susano-o-no-mikoto says, 'Let us swear oaths and bear children', which Philippi interprets to mean, 'Let us judge who is in the right by producing offspring' (Philippi, *Kojiki*, p. 75).

[343] The *honsha*, or main shrine building, faces the east to receive the light of the morning sun. A parallel passage is found in the *Kojiki* in the story of the Heavenly Grandson, Ninigi-no-mikoto, descending from heaven to the land of Himuka (Hyūga) in Kyushu: 'a land where the morning sun shines directly, a land where the rays of the evening sun are brilliant' (Philippi, op. cit. p. 141).

In this place in which the mighty *kami* make known their words of instruction, here where the pillars of their august abode are fixed, here in the presence of the mighty *kami* we raise our words of praise as we humbly present the choice offerings from the divine descendant. The princes and the ministers who act as messengers raise their words of praise. In the presence of the mighty *kami* let the chiefs of shrines and all the priests hearken unto the words which are handed down to them.

The choice offerings which we present here[344] are of divine raiment for the male god: of bright cloth, shining cloth, soft cloth, and coarse cloth, and five kinds of things: shields, spears, august horse fitted with august saddle, and all manner of offerings. And to the goddess we present: for her divine raiment, a thread holder, a golden spindle, a golden reel, bright cloth, shining cloth, soft cloth, coarse cloth, five kinds of things; an august horse fitted with august saddle, and all manner of offerings. Let the sacred sake fill the offering jars to the brim, let the full-bellied jars be lined up, let polished rice and whole-grain rice, let the creatures who live in the mountains soft of fur and coarse of fur, and of the things which grow in the plains of the great moors, the sweet herbs, the bitter herbs, and the things that live in the blue sea-plain, those wide of fin and narrow of fin, even unto the seaweeds of the deep and the seaweeds of the shore—let them be heaped up like a range of hills. Yea, these choice offerings which we present, may they be pleasing offerings, plentiful offerings, and may they make glad and peaceful the divine hearts of the mighty *kami*. May the crops which the people under heaven till and work not encounter fierce winds or angry waters; if the mighty *kami* vouchsafe to let them grow and be caused to prosper, we shall fill the offering jars to the brim with the first-fruits of the grain, and the full-bellied jars shall be arrayed in rows. As liquid and as grain we shall offer up hundreds, yea, thousands of ears of rice placed here for the autumn festival. Thus all of the princes, princesses, the nobles, and the host of officials, and even unto the chiefs and the men and women of the six august districts of Yamato, in the fourth (or the 7th) month of this year gather together to worship. Bending our necks low like the cormorants, at this the brilliant and majestic dawning of the morning light, we raise the words of praise as we offer the choice offerings from the divine descendant; and receiving them the chiefs of shrines and priests shall not be remiss in presenting them, according to divine command. Hearken all ye unto what we say.

---

[344] It does appear that this second set of offerings is being presented at the auxiliary shrine (*sessha*) in which the pair, Tatsuta-hiko and Tatsuta-hime, are enshrined.

## [5]

### *Festival of Hirano*[345]

BY THE divine decree of the divine descendants of heaven, we humbly speak before the awesome presence of the great and mighty *kami* whom we have humbly worshiped ever since he resided in the place of Imaki,[346] saying, As thou, great and mighty *kami*, hast commanded us, we have raised upon the foundation rocks the potent pillars of thy shrine. The crossed gable-boards reach toward the Plain of High Heaven, for this is the dwelling place of the great and mighty *kami*, sheltered from the gaze of heaven and the blazing sun.

Let the council of *kami* affairs determine the office, Court Rank, clan-title, and name of the chief of the shrine.[347] The treasures which we offer to thee are arrayed here: the august bow, august sword, august mirror, bells, silk umbrella, and august horse;[348] and for divine raiment, bright cloth, shining cloth, soft cloth, and coarse cloth we have prepared and do present. And from the provinces all around tribute of first-fruits are brought and arrayed here. Let the august sake fill the offering jars and the full-bellied jars be arrayed in rows. We humbly offer up the things from mountains and moors: sweet herbs and bitter herbs; and from the blue sea-plain: creatures wide of fin, creatures narrow of fin, even unto the seaweeds of the deep and seaweeds of the shore; all manner of things we heap up high like a range of hills. May the choice, great offerings which we pres-

[345] The Hirano Shrine, located in Kadono District, Yamashiro Province, enshrined four deities: Imaki-no-kami, Kudo-no-kami, Furuseki-no-kami, and Himegami, all principal deities (*myōjin*) and major (*dai*). (See Bk IX, below.) Himegami is an *aidono kami*, meaning one who is worshiped in the same shrine building with another *kami*. Why the invocation to Imaki-no-kami is separated from the next *norito*, which is addressed to Kudo-no-kami and Furuseki-no-kami, is not explained. Evidently separate worship services were held for the different kami, at the occasions of the celebrating of the *Tsukinami* and *Niiname* festivals. The transcription Furuaki apparently arose from the use of 開 instead of 關 as a short form of *seki* 關. Furuseki 古關 appears in the Kujō-ke MS of *E-S*, and in the *Montoku jitsuroku* and other texts. Tsugita, pp. 202–3. Three entirely different theories have grown up concerning the identities of these four deities. One is that they are hearth gods related to the fires and stoves in the Imperial Palace. Another is that they are the *ujigami* of certain noble families: the Imaki-no-kami an *ujigami* of the Minamoto Family, Kudo the *ujigami* of the Taira Family, Furuseki an *ujigami* of the Takashina Uji, and Himegami that of the Ooe

Uji. A third theory is that all four of these *kami* were ancestral *kami* of the mother of Kammu Tennō, who was descended from Shumō (Tobo), the first King of Paekche! See *Shoku-nihongi*, Enryaku 4th year, vol. XL. The signs point to this shrine having been founded in the Heian period. In the first Bk of *E-S*, in the description of the Hirano Festival, participation of the Yamato Uji and Ooe Uji is mentioned.

[346] Imaki was the name of the place where the mother of Kammu Tennō had her palace, in Tamura, Yamato Province. The name is thought to mean 'now come' (今來), alluding to the presence of immigrants or naturalized persons from Paekche (Kudara). See Tsugita, p. 199. In this particular passage the use of 'awesome', . . . *no hiro-mae* (rather than the usual *on-mae*), may be an indication of a higher rank of *kami*, because this *kami* was the ancestral *kami* of the emperor's in-laws.

[347] The chief of this shrine was a member of the Nakatomi clan. See *E-S*, Bk I: '. . . the Nakatomi who is chief of the shrine comes forward and recites the ritual.' Bock, *E-S*, (I), p. 77.

[348] As in other passages in the *norito*, the mention of bows implies also arrows; the horse is also presumed to be saddled.

ent be peacefully received, may the reign of our Sovereign be firm as solid rock, eternal as enduring rock, we pray, and may it be a prosperous and happy reign, may it last through countless ages; thus we pray as we raise our words of praise.

Moreover we humbly speak in behalf of the Imperial Princes, Princesses,[349] Court Chieftains, and the host of officials who are gathered here to worship; safeguard us with protection at night and protection by day, we pray. May the court of our Sovereign flourish like magnificent trees that grow ever taller, ever broader, we humbly pray as we raise our words of praise.

### [6]

### [Festival to] The Deities Kudo and Furuseki[350]

BY THE divine decree of the divine descendants of heaven, we have come to humbly worship before the shrines of Kudo and Furuseki. We make bold to speak in the awesome presence of these mighty *kami* whom we serve. As the great and mighty *kami* have commanded us, we have raised upon the foundation rocks the potent columns of these shrines. Their crossed gable-boards reach toward the Plain of High Heaven and they are sheltered from the gaze of heaven and the blazing sun. Let the office, Court Rank, clan-title, and name of the chief of the shrine be told. The treasures which we offer to the *kami* are arrayed here: the august bows, august swords, august mirror, bells, silk umbrella, and august horse. And for divine raiment, bright cloth, shining cloth, soft cloth, and coarse cloth we have prepared and do present. From provinces all around initial tribute goods are brought and arrayed here. Let the august sake fill the offering jars to the brim and let the full-bellied jars be arrayed in rows. We humbly offer up things from the mountains and moors: sweet herbs and bitter herbs; and from the blue sea-plain: creatures wide of fin and narrow of fin, even unto the seaweeds of the deep and the seaweeds of the shore; all manner of things we heap high like a range of hills. May the choice, great offerings which we present be peacefully received. May the reign of our Sovereign be firm as solid rock, eternal as enduring rock, we pray, and may it be a prosperous and happy reign; may it last through countless ages, thus we pray as we raise our words of praise.

Moreover, we humbly speak in behalf of the imperial princes, princesses, court chieftains, and the host of officials gathered here to worship; safeguard us with protection at night and protection by day, we pray. May the court of our Sovereign flourish like magnificent trees which grow ever taller and ever broader, we humbly pray as we raise our words of praise.

---

[349] As elsewhere when this phrase is used, the text says 'Imperial Princes and other princes' but implicit in this are 'Imperial Princesses and other princesses'.

[350] This is connected with Hirano Shrine. See n. 345 above.

[7]

### *Tsukinami Festival*[351]
### *(in the 6th month and the 12th month)*

[1]   All ye shrine chiefs and all ye priests assembled here, hearken unto the words which we speak.

[2]   We humbly speak in the presence of all the mighty ancestral gods and goddesses who augustly abide in the Plain of High Heaven, before the many *kami* enshrined in heaven and earth, we raise our words of praise. We humbly present as offerings for the monthly festival of the sixth month [or the 12th month] bright cloth, shining cloth, soft cloth, and coarse cloth. At this moment of the majestic and brilliant dawning of the morning light, we humbly raise our words of praise.

[3]   Before the mighty *kami* to whom the great Sacred Maidens offer words of praise, we utter the hallowed names of Kami-musubi, Takami-musubi, Iku-musubi, Taru-musubi, Tamatsume-musubi, Oomiya-no-me, Miketsu-no-kami and Kotoshironushi, to whom we offer our words of praise. May this age of the divine descendant be an everlasting age, as firm as solid rock, eternal as enduring rock; that it may flourish and be a happy reign, we present the choice offerings from the divine descendant of heaven together with our words of praise for our mighty ancestral gods and goddesses.

[4]   Before the presence of the mighty *kami* to whom the Igasuri Sacred Maidens offer their words of praise, we make bold to utter the hallowed names of Ikui, Sakui, Tsunagai, Asuha, and Haigi, and offer to them our words of praise. On the bed of rock beneath the ground the pillars of the shrines to these mighty *kami* are rooted. Toward the Plain of High Heaven the crossed gable-boards reach up, as we humbly serve and worship at the sacred dwelling of the divine descendant of heaven. May it be sheltered from the gaze of heaven and from the blazing sun. That ye grant from it the lands in all directions may be governed and made peaceful lands, tranquil lands, we offer up the choice offerings from the divine descendant of heaven together with our words of praise.

[5]   Before the presence of the mighty *kami* to whom the Mikado Sacred Maidens raise their words of praise, we make bold to utter the hallowed names of Kushi-iwamado-no-mikoto and Toyo-iwamado-no-mikoto and offer to them our words of praise. May they defend with strength like a mass of ponderous rock the gates of the four directions, and open the gates in the morning and close the gates in the evening. If things to be shunned come from below, let them protect

---

[351] The exact title is *Minazuki no Tsukinami* 六月月次 (Monthly Festival in the Waterless Month). Perhaps this festival at one time was celebrated every month, but in the period of the *E-S* it was celebrated once in six months: on the 11th day of the 6th month and the 11th day of the 12th month. The purpose of this festival is almost identical with that of the *Toshigoi*: to pray for security for the nation, for the success of the rice crop, and for abundant harvest. The text of this *norito* is also identical with that of the *Toshigoi* except for the third section of the *Toshigoi*, which is addressed to Mitoshi-no-kami. According to *E-S*, Bk I, this festival was held to worship 304 *kami*, who were all 'major' and were presented with offerings from the *Jingi-kan* (i.e. the government) placed on top of the offering tables. Presentations were made at 198 shrines.

below. If things to be shunned come from above, let them protect above. May they watch by night and watch by day, we pray, as with choice offerings from the divine descendant of heaven we offer up our words of praise.

[6] Before the presence of the mighty *kami* to whom the Ikushima Sacred Maidens offer words of praise, we make bold to utter the hallowed names of Ikukuni and Tarukuni and offer to them our words of praise. In all the many lands far and wide over which the mighty *kami* hold sway, to the uttermost corners whither creeping creatures may crawl, and as far as the salt foam of flood tides reaches, may the narrow places be made wide and the steep places be made level, and may there be no escaping of water in the lands far and wide. Let the mighty *kami* vouchsafe this to us, as with the choice offerings from the divine descendant of heaven we now raise our words of praise.

[7] And turning now, before the mighty presence of Amaterasu-ō-mikami who abides in Ise we make bold to say: In all the lands through which this mighty *kami* clearly sees, as far as the heavens stretch above, and as far as the ground stretches beneath, to the uttermost heights of clouds in the blue, to the limits reached by the white clouds a-massing, to the uttermost reaches of the plain of the blue sea, on which with pole and helm never dry the prows of ships do ply; yea, on the great ocean where sail heavy-laden ships, and on the land routes where ropes are pulled taut over loads of tribute cargo, may the mighty goddess vouchsafe to the divine descendant that treading over rough rocks and roots of trees as far as horses can travel, the narrow places may be made wide and the steep places level, and may the distant countries send tribute pulled by dozens of hawsers. If the great ancestral goddess grant us this, before the presence of the great ancestral goddess we shall heap up our tribute of first-fruits like unto a range of hills, and if any be left over, may the divine descendant partake thereof. Moreover, may the reign of the divine descendant be an everlasting reign and may it be firm as solid rock, eternal as enduring rock, we pray, and that it may flourish and be a happy reign, we present the choice offerings from the divine descendant of heaven together with our words of praise to our mighty ancestral gods and goddesses.

[8] Before the presence of the mighty *kami* who dwell in the august districts we humbly speak. We make bold to utter the hallowed names of Takechi, Katsuragi, To-ochi, Shiki, Yamanobe, and Sou. As we come humbly bearing the sweet herbs and bitter herbs that grow in these six districts, may the *kami* vouchsafe that they provide food eternally for the divine descendants of heaven; for with choice offerings from the divine descendant of heaven we offer up our words of praise.

[9] Before the presence of the mighty *kami* who dwell in the openings of the mountains we humbly speak. We make bold to utter the hallowed names of Asuka, Iware, Osaka, Hatsuse, Unebi, and Miminashi. We dare to cut the trunks and branches of the great trees and small trees that sprout and grow in the farther mountains and the nearer mountains. We come up bearing the wood therefrom that we may undertake to build a new and splendid august dwelling for the divine descendant of heaven, in which he may rest sheltered from the gaze of heaven and from the blazing sun. May the *kami* vouchsafe that the land in all directions

be a peaceful land, a tranquil land. With choice offerings from the divine descendant of heaven we raise our words of praise.

[10] Before the presence of the mighty *kami* residing in the water divides we humbly speak. We make bold to utter the hallowed names of Yoshino, Uda, Tsuge, and Katsuragi, as we humbly raise our words of praise. Let the mighty *kami* vouchsafe to us a crop of long-eared grain, of vigorous grain, in the late-ripening harvest of rice, and we shall offer up to the mighty *kami* the first-fruits of the myriad grains. The grain and liquid made from it filling the offering jars to the brims, the full-bellied jars arrayed in rows shall we offer up together with our words of praise. If there be any left over, may it grace the table of the divine descendant for the august morning food and the august evening food, that he may partake thereof for eternity. As in partaking of it his august cheeks become ruddy, so shall we bring the choice offerings of the divine descendant as we raise our words of praise. Let all those present hearken thereunto.

[11] We turn now and request the Imbe, their frail shoulders bound with potent sleeve-ties, to consecrate and purify the offerings that are here prepared, and we ask the chiefs of shrines and all priests humbly to take these offerings, and making no error, bear them up and present them unto the *kami*.

## [8]

[The *Ootono-hogai*, or Luck-wishing of the Palace, was both a regular festival and an occasional one. Procedures for this appear in the Annual Festivals of Book II of the *Engi-shiki*, for it was performed before and after the festivals of *Jinkonjiki* (Sacred Food Ritual) and *Niiname* (First-Fruits). It also preceded the *Daijō-sai* (Great Food Festival of the Enthronement). In the third book of *Engi-shiki* it appears as an extraordinary festival celebrated when the Imperial Palace was moved to a new building, or whenever the selection of a princess to be consecrated to the Ise Shrines, or the Kamo Shrines, was completed. In the latter cases the palace to serve as residence for the princess each time had to be consecrated. The *Ootono-hogai* consisted of exorcizing all defilements and impurities from the Imperial Palace, likewise the consort's palace, the Heir Apparent's Palace and, on occasion, the princesses' palaces. It addresses itself to the deities who are worshiped within the Palace and who were its special protectors: Yabune Kukunochi-no-mikoto, Yabune Toyouke-no-mikoto, and Oomiya-no-me-no-mikoto. The text which follows was recited by a member of the Imbe.]

### *Ootono-hogai*[352]

AFTER the divine command of the mighty ancestral gods and goddesses who abide

---

[352] The *Ootono-hogai*, lit. 'Blessing of the Great Hall', was performed to purify and consecrate the palace of the sovereign or of his consort, the Heir Apparent, the Princess to Ise, the Princess to Kamo, and so forth. The verb *hogu*, to bless or bring good fortune to, is related to *hoga(f)u*, to bring luck, and *kotohogu*, to bless with words, to flourish, and is similar in meaning. Tsugita, p. 214.

in the Plain of High Heaven and who caused the Heavenly Grandson to sit exalted upon the throne of heaven, we raise aloft the divine imperial emblems, the mirror and sword,[353] as we pronounce these words of blessing.[354] Ye have decreed that our August Sovereign, the supernal divine descendant, seated on the throne of heaven, maintain the heavenly light succession[355] for endless autumns, yea, for a thousand times ten thousand autumns, and that he rule the country of rich rice-ears growing from the abundant reedy plains of the land of many islands[356] in peace and tranquillity.[357] Relying on the heavenly command which was given after the divine discussion, which was spoken by the rocks,[358] the trees, and even unto the least blade of grass, he descended to the earth to rule the land under heaven.[359] And for the august dwelling of the divine descendant who carries on the heavenly succession, the sacred axes of the Imbe are being taken to cut the trees growing in the great and the narrow gorges of the mountain recesses, leaving the stumps and branches for the worship of the mountain gods to take the trunks themselves, and, using the sacred spades,[360] they will raise up sacred pillars of a splendid dwelling for the divine descendant, sheltered from the gaze of heaven and from the blazing sun. O, ye Yabune deities,[361] using the miraculous auspicious words, we pray that ye may bring good fortune and pacify this house.

To the limits of the bedrock beneath the ground of this great palace, let not the coupling ropes[362] nor any crawling creatures below cause harm. And above, as far as clouds amass in the blue, let no harm come from defilement by flying

---

[353] Here the heavenly emblems are called 'amatsu-shirushi'. These refer to the *yata-kagami* and the *kusanagi* sword, regalia of the imperial succession. As was the case in Bk VII, the third of the three sacred emblems, the divine curved jewels, are not included here. The *Kojiki*, however, mentions all three in the story of Ninigi-no-mikoto. Philippi, p. 139. See nn. 267, 268, and 269 above.

[354] *Kotohogi*, 'words of blessing,' is the ritual or formula for bringing good fortune; it is equivalent to *sakahogai*, according to the gloss here. *Kotohogi* is the archaic form of the *kotobuki* of present-day Japanese.

[355] Some believe that the expression 'amatsu-hitsugi' ('heavenly sun lineage', 'heavenly light succession', or possibly 'heavenly fire succession') may refer to an actual function of the sovereign in keeping perpetually burning a sacred fire for the worship of those *kami* who were ancestors of the Imperial House. Hence the sovereign became 'prince of the fire-succession' (*hitsugi no miko*), and the imperial dignity, *amatsu-hitsugi*.

[356] These are euphonious epithets for the land of Yamato. See n. 339 above. *Toyo-ashiwara* ('abundant reedy plains') is thought to describe the natural condition of the country before it was developed for rice culture. The *ashi* is a common plant with jointed stalk that grows in moist places. The rich rice-ears are *mizu-ho*: *mizu*, splendid, good, beautiful; and *ho*, grain (of rice).

[357] Gloss says that in the ancient language *shiroshimesu* means 'deign to rule', etc.

[358] *Iwa-ne* is said to mean the rocks below; for *ne* in this use parallels are: *ya-ne*, 'roof', and 'ha-ne', wings. On the other hand, *iwao* means 'rocks above', or 'rocks rising up'. This passage appears again in the *Ooharae-no-kotoba* (no. 10), and *Tataru-kami* (no. 25), below. The ancient belief was that the rocks, trees, and plants had the power of speech.

[359] The subject of this phrase is the Heavenly Grandson, Ninigi-no-mikoto, who was sent by the *kami* in heaven to rule the land of Yamato.

[360] The Imbe Uji by their own tradition were responsible for the building of the Palace and hence were charged with overseeing the ceremonial cutting of wood from the forest with the taboo axe, *imi-ono*, and the ceremony of digging for the foundations with the taboo spade, *imi-suki*. See n. 168. As for the house tradition, see n. 292, above.

[361] The two Yabune deities are revered as indwelling *kami* of the Palace. See n. 367, below.

[362] As the gloss explains, the *tsuna-ne* are the joining ropes which tie the crossbeams to the uprights in this building, built without nails.

birds.[363] May there be no moving or creaking of the firmly fastened pillars, cross-beams, rafters, doors, or windows; may there be no loosening of the knots in ropes that bind together, let not thatching reeds come loose,[364] nor floor-boards squeak.[365] Let not the night attendants make disturbance nor fail in their duty.[366] We make bold to utter the august names of the *kami* who in peace and tranquillity protect this thine abode—Yabune Kukunochi-no-mikoto (the spirit of the wood) and Yabune Toyouke-hime-no-mikoto (the spirit of the rice, otherwise called Uka-no-mitama)[367] and raise to them our praises. That they may make the reign of our divine descendant as firm as hard rock, enduring as the solid rock, that it may be a prosperous reign, a reign of plenty, a lengthy reign, and that it may flourish, let the sacred jewel-makers[368] consecrate and make pure for presentation the splendid myriad long strands of curved jewels.[369] And placing them on bright soft cloth and shining soft cloth, the Imbe of *sukune* rank,[370] his frail shoulders bound with the potent sleeve-ties, shall offer them up. In uttering the propitiatory words of congratulation, if there should be any carelessness, we pray that the divinities Kamu-naobi-no-mikoto and Oo-naobi-no-mikoto may vouchsafe to make our prayers sound rightly and our offerings correct,[371] we humbly say.

[363] What appears to mean 'blood dropping from heaven', *ame no chidari*, has been given various interpretations. One comes from the Chinese belief that such birds as goatsuckers dripped blood while in flight. Motoori in this connection cites a song of Oojin Tennō where the phrase '*momo chidari*' occurs, which Philippi translates 'of the myriad leaves'. Other interpretations are that noxious droppings from birds are apt to fall into a chimney opening or smoke window of a dwelling and contaminate the stove inside.

[364] The reading here for 草 is *kaya*, miscanthus, although actually it is generic for any thatching material, which could also be *susuki* 薄, pampas, *karukaya* 萱, *Anthistiria arguens*, *chigaya* 茅, *Imperata arundinacea*, or *ashi* 葦, reeds.

[365] *Mi-yuka-tsuhi* describes the joining or dovetailing of boards in this construction in which no nails were used.

[366] *Ya-me* or *yo-me* means either 'night-eye' (night watch) or 'night-female'; if the latter, it could mean ladies-in-waiting who attend the Imperial Family. The word *isusuki* is believed to mean 'wake up and be agitated'; *itsutsushiki* seems to mean 'without harm', or else 'without fear of apparitions'.

[367] The glosses explain the roles of these two *kami*: the tree-spirit, *ko-no-mitama*, and the rice-spirit, *ine-no-mitama*. The etymology of Yabune may be: *ya*, a dwelling; and *fune*, a receptacle. The element *kuku*, according to Tsugita, means 'stem' or 'trunk' (*kuki*), while *chi* in the

names of *kami* refers to divine power or divine virtue. In the Izanagi creation myth the creator gods give birth to the 'tree deity', Kukunochi-no-kami. See Philippi, *Kojiki*, 7: 8, p. 56. The food goddess (Ooketsu-hime, Waka-uka-mitama, or Ukemochi-no-kami, Toyouke-no-kami, etc.) in this role is protector of life within the Palace. Not only is she goddess of food and of cereals, but even of the rice-straw used to thatch the Palace roof. See J. Tsugita, op. cit. pp. 233–4.

[368] *Imi-tamazukuri*, for their name suggests that these jewel-makers are a branch of the Imbe Uji. See n. 292, above.

[369] *Yasaka-ni* means to be of 'great length'; the *mifuki-tama* are probably equivalent to *mihogi* (*tama*), meaning jewels of august felicitation. The *mifuki-tama* are mentioned in the description of the festival held when the Local Chieftain of Izumo came up to Court, in *E-S*, Bk III, extraordinary festivals.

[370] The name of the member of the Imbe Uji of *sukune* rank who recites this ritual is inserted here.

[371] The two *kami* referred to appear in the *Kojiki* account of the god Izanagi returning from the nether world and having to cleanse himself from the pollution he had suffered: 'in order to rectify these evils, there came into existence the deity Kamu-napobi-no-kami; next, Opo-napobi-no-kami...' Philippi, *Kojiki* (11:15), p. 69; *naobi* (*napobi*) means 'corrective working' (ibid. p. 546).

Turning now we speak and make bold to utter the august name of Oomiya-no-me-no-mikoto, who defends the dwelling of our divine descendant, judging the merit of persons who enter and exit thence, and deigns to remonstrate with and mollify those *kami* who are agitated and unruly. Let those who serve the august morning food and the august evening food to the divine descendant, the scarf-wearing[372] palace ladies and sleeve-tied palace chefs, make no slip of the hand or slip of the foot. Let all imperial princes and princesses and all other princes, ministers, and the host of officials, without asserting their own wills, and with no evil purpose or sullied mind, proceed unto this palace and serve in this palace. If there be any misdeed or accident, let it be rectified to the eye and the ear. That they may serve in peace and tranquillity, we humbly raise our words of praise uttering thine august name, Oomiya-no-me-no-mikoto.

## [9]

[The Festival of the August Gates, *Mikado-matsuri* (or *Mikado-hogai*) was the luck-wishing for the gates of the palace and was held immediately after the service of luck-wishing for the palace, the *Ootono-hogai*. Like the latter, it was held as a regular twice-yearly festival, according to Book I of the *Engi-shiki*, and then was held on special occasions when a new palace was to be dedicated. This luck-wishing for the gates was also the prerogative of the Imbe Uji, and a member of that clan recited this ritual addressed to the indwelling *kami* of the gates which are the entrances to the palace compound. These *kami*, Kushi-iwamado and Toyo-iwamado, were also invoked in the *Toshigoi* Festival as the deities whose worship was conducted by the Mikado Sacred Maidens of the palace. There is no introductory invocation, since this followed the celebration of the luck-wishing for the palace as a whole.]

### *Mikado-matsuri*[373]

WE MAKE bold to utter the hallowed names of Kushi-iwamado and Toyo-iwamado, who as they reside in the august gates, inner and outer, on all sides, defend the palace like a magic-working mound of rock. Vouchsafe, we pray, that no hateful or disturbing things enter on the four sides or at the four corners; and that there be no sinister encounter nor speaking together with those known as heavenly, evil-working *kami*. If such things should come from above, protect above, we pray; if such things should come from below, protect below, we pray. Waylay and ward them off; exorcise and drive them out; expel them with words. Open the gates in the morning, and in the evening close the august gates. Inquire the names of those persons who come up and enter the palace, and of those who withdraw and go

---

[372] 'Scarf-wearing' probably refers to the *uneme* ladies who waited upon the sovereign. Quiver bearers and sword wearers were his personal bodyguards, whose formal name was *konoe* (Inner Palace Guards).

[373] In the first book of *E-S* the Festival of the Gates is prescribed to be held regularly in the 4th and 12th months. For the names of the Gate Gods, see n. 313, above.

out from it.[374] If there be any misdeed or accident, let it be rectified to the eye and to the ear by the deities Kamunaobi and Oonaobi. Let them who serve the divine descendant do so peacefully and tranquilly as we humbly raise our words of praise to the hallowed names of Toyo-iwamado-no-mikoto and Kushi-iwamado-no-mikoto. Thus humbly we speak.

## [10]

[Twice a year the Court, the ministers, and the host of officials assembled at the Suzaku Gate of the Imperial Palace to participate in the ceremonial of driving out all impurities and defilements. This was the *ōharae* of the last day of the sixth and the twelfth months, respectively. In the *jingi-ryō* (of the Yōrō Code) was stated: 'At all times, at the Great Purification on the last day of the 6th and 12th months, the Nakatomi offer up the purificatory offerings (*harae-nusa*), the *fubitobe* of Yamato and Kawachi offer up swords. The *harae-kotoba* is recited. That done, the host of officials, men and women, gather together at the purification place and the diviners (*urabe*) perform the exorcism. . . .' In the *Shoku-nihongi* history however, the entry for Taihō 2, 12th month, says the *ōharae* was omitted but the *fubitobe* of Yamato and Kawachi performed exorcism as usual.[375]

In the *Engi-shiki*, Book I, the requirements for offerings for the Great Purification[376] are listed, followed by the statement: 'For the above, before the monkey hour on the last day, the host of officials from Princes-of-the-Blood and on down assemble at the Suzaku Gate, and the Diviners recite the ritual. (See the *Gishiki* for this matter.)'[377] But the *jōgan-gishiki* says: 'That done, the Nakatomi go to their kneeling-place and recite the *norito*.' An added gloss says 'beforehand the imperial decree (*semmyō*) is read'—so possibly the *urabe* recited this *semmyō* and the Oonakatomi the main ritual, the *ōharae-kotoba*.[378] The *urabe* were charged with the performance of imitative magic which would bring about the expulsion of all forms of defilement and pollution from all persons present, and from the nation's people as a whole.]

---

[374] This function of examining those who come and go through the palace gates was actually the responsibility of the *emon-fu,* Outer Palace Guards (n. 244 above). See the function of Oomiya-no-me-no-mikoto in the preceding ritual.

[375] *Shoku-nihongi,* Taihō 2 (A.D. 702), 12th month.

[376] *Minazuki no tsugomori no ōharae* 六月之晦 大祓, the great driving out on the last day of the waterless month (repeated in the 12th month). The derivation of *tsugomori* is *tsuki-komori,* the darkening, or ending, of the month. This semi-annual grand exorcism had its precedent in ancient China, for it says in the *Chou li*, in *ch'un-kuan* 春官 sec.: 'The female shamans have charge

of the yearly seasonal driving-out and ceremonial bathing' (a medicinal bath into which fragrant herbs had been put). Tsugita, p. 260. And again: 'female priests have charge of the seasonal prayers and sacrifices to ward off calamity' (loc. cit.).

[377] The list of offerings to be prepared includes items some of which are mentioned in the ritual: the gold ornamented swords, the gilt and silvered effigies onto which defilements were symbolically removed from the persons being cleansed of impurities; other swords and ceremonial weapons, bows, arrows, mattocks, symbolic foodstuffs, salt, water, ceremonial cloth and hemp, and, finally, six horses. *E-S*, Bk I.

[378] Kaneko, pp. 431–2.

## Ritual of Great Purification

O, ALL ye assembled imperial princes and princesses, ye other princes, ministers, and all the host of officials, hearken unto the words which we pronounce. Commencing with His Sovereign Majesty's scarf-decked attendants, quiver-bearing attendants, and sword-wearing attendants, yea, all the multitude of attendants,[379] from all of these and from the many persons of all the different offices, let the varieties of offenses unwittingly or wilfully committed[380] be driven out, in this great driving-out of the last day of the sixth month [or twelfth month] of this year; let them all be driven out and washed away, hearken ye all unto these words.

At the command of the mighty ancestral gods and goddesses divinely abiding in the Plain of High Heaven, the many myriad *kami* were divinely gathered together to discuss and plan, and by their words entrusted to the divine descendant[381] the country of rich rice-ears growing in the abundant reedy plains as a pleasant land to rule in peace.

Lest there be any unruly *kami*[382] in the midst of the land entrusted to him, the *kami* asked and inquired why they were thus, and caused them to be divinely cleansed and purged. The words of questioning from rocks and trees, and even the least blade of grass, were ended. Leaving the worthy throne of heaven, parting asunder the many-layered heavenly clouds, with awesome parting, he descended from heaven to the land entrusted to him.

In the land in the center of all lands which was entrusted to him, the land of Yamato where the sun shines high, a pleasant land, the columns of his palace are auspiciously planted, the crossed gable-boards reaching up toward heaven. Here is built the splendid, august dwelling-place of the divine descendant, sheltered from the gaze of heaven and from the blazing sun. In the pleasant land which he rules in tranquillity, from the many people who by divine grace are born into it, may the countless offenses unwittingly or wilfully committed be purged; beginning with the heavenly offenses (breaking down the paddy dikes, filling in irrigation ditches, opening the sluice-gates, double planting, setting up stakes, flaying alive, flaying backwards, cursing with excrement, and many such, these are designated as heavenly offenses)[383] and then earthly offenses—defilement due

---

[379] See n. 372 above concerning the personal attendants of the sovereign.

[380] *Ayamachi okashikemu* is equivalent to modern *ayamattari okashitari*. *Ayamu* is to incur offense by inadvertence, while *okasu* is to commit a crime, or incur defilement by deliberate acts.

[381] Again in this passage the title Sume-mima-no-mikoto refers to the Heavenly Grandson of the myths. See n. 303, above.

[382] Unruly *kami* are *araburu kamitachi*. Starting with Ookuninushi-no-mikoto, *kami* were sent down by command of Amaterasu-ō-mikami to wrest the land from unruly terrestrial *kami*. Philippi, *Kojiki*, pp. 129 ff.

[383] The seven so-called 'heavenly' transgressions (*tsumi*) were enumerated in the myth of

Susano-o-no-mikoto (the Storm God), who broke down the ridges in the rice paddies, filled in irrigation ditches, opened sluice gates, put stakes between the rows of rice. See *Kojiki*, pp. 79–80. The setting up of stakes, *kushisashi*, has been explained as either (1) changing boundaries to steal a neighbor's rice, (2) planting sharp bamboos which are hidden and will cut the farmer's feet, or, (3) by putting in prohibited articles, bringing an evil curse upon the paddies. The skinning of a live animal was taboo because of bloodshed offensive to the *kami*; the skinning from head to tail (rather than tail to head) was a reversal and was taboo, the defiling with excrement was also a form of evil magic (*kuso-to*, 'dung curse').

to cutting live flesh, cutting dead flesh; due to vitiligo, due to excrescences; defilement due to intercourse with one's own mother, or one's own daughter, due to cohabiting with a woman and then her daughter by previous marriage, or from cohabiting with a girl and then her mother; defilement due to copulation with an animal, due to attack from creeping things, due to calamity from the *kami* on high, or from birds overhead, due to having caused death to livestock or other evil magic—let all these defilements be purged.[384]

And when these are purged, by the divine ceremonial, let the Oonakatomi[385] take the sacred branches[386] and, cutting off the thick ends, cutting away the leaf ends, lay them upon the many offering-tables in ample numbers.[387] Let them gather and cut the stalks of thatching reeds and, cutting off the thick ends, clipping the leaf ends, divide them finely, needle-like, and recite the solemn liturgy of the heavenly magic formula.[388] When he has thus recited, may the heavenly *kami* push open the worthy doors of heaven, and part with an awesome parting the many-layered heavenly clouds. May the terrestrial *kami* ascend to the summits of the high mountains and summits of the hills and may they clear away the mists from the high mountains and the mists from the hills.

If they vouchsafe to do this, commencing with the august palace of the divine descendant, throughout all the lands, let every last offense—just as the winds of the boundless skies blow away the many-layered clouds of heaven, just as the morning wind blows to dispel the mists of the morning and the evening wind blows to dispel the winds of the evening; just as at the harbor's edge[389] by letting loose its prow and letting loose its stern a big ship is put afloat on the broad plain of the sea; and just as the long, young branches are cut from the tree trunk with

---

[384] Ceremonial defilement resulted from cutting live flesh (blood caused defilement) or dead flesh (death caused pollution). Skin diseases were thought to result from witchcraft. The taboos on sexual relations prohibited a man from having relations with his mother, his daughter, the daughter of his wife, or the mother of his wife, as stated. Nothing is said here about relations between siblings, though intercourse between children of the same mother was prohibited. The Great Exorcism performed after the death of Chūai Tennō makes collective mention of 'upper and lower incestuous marriages'. See Philippi, *Kojiki*, pp. 259-60. Afflictions from *kami* above may include accidents from thunder and lightning, misfortunes believed caused by heavenly bodies or *tengu* monsters. See Aston, *Nihongi*, I, pp. 307-8, where the sudden death of a concubine of Richū Tennō is attributed to a 'divine curse'. Defilement might be caused by droppings from birds, or ill luck from predatory birds or flying goblins. The 'bringing down of beasts', *chiku-taoshi*, meant the killing of domestic animals by a person bearing a grudge who invoked an evil *kami* or evil magic upon them for purposes

of revenge. Evil magic or a curse is *majimono*.

[385] The adjective 'great' added to the surname Nakatomi was an honorary addition in the beginning, but eventually was the surname of the branch of that *uji* associated with performing the highest religious ceremonies, particularly those to Amaterasu-ō-mikami, ancestral *kami* of the Imperial House. The Nakatomi claimed Ame-no-koyane-no-mikoto as their divine ancestor.

[386] The sacred branches, *amatsu kanagi*, are a kind of wand used for exorcising defilement. It is not known exactly what tree is meant, but commentaries say it is the branch of a small tree, cut to a certain size.

[387] The expression is: *chikura no oikikura ni oki-tarawashite*—'placing them plenteously upon the thousand-fold offering-tables' (i.e. the tables or stands upon which expiatory offerings for the *kami* are placed).

[388] *Amatsu norito no futo-noritogoto*, lit., 'the potent words for casting the spell of the heavenly formula'.

[389] *Minato-be*, 'at the edge of the river mouth', or 'at the sea-straits', or 'at the harbor'.

the tempered blade of a sharp sickle—so let the offenses be driven out and be purged so that none remain. From the tops of the high mountains, from the tops of the hills, in the waters which tumble into churning rivers, may the *kami* called Seoritsu-hime,[390] who dwells in the mainstream of swift rivers, carry them out to the broad sea-plain. When they are carried away thus, over the myriad routes of the tides, may the *kami* called Haya-akitsu-hime,[391] who dwells in the currents of the wild tides, swirl them about and swallow them up.[392] When they are thus swallowed up may the *kami* called Ibukido-nushi,[393] who dwells in the place of blowing air, blow them out and away from the country beneath, from the nether regions.[394] When they are thus blown away from the country beneath and from the nether regions, may the *kami* called Haya-sasura-hime carry them and as she wanders about dissipate them.[395] When they are thus dissipated, commencing with all the people of the various offices serving the Court of the Sovereign, from this day forth in all regions under heaven, may the offenses and defilements disappear. Let the creatures in heaven lend their ears, as the horses are led forward.[396] On this the last day of the sixth [or the twelfth] month of this year, at the great driving out, at the setting of the sun, we humbly pray that Ye cause the driving out and cleansing of all, so say we. And let the *urabe* of the four provinces carry these and withdraw to the stream of the great river[397] and cast them all out, so we pray.[398]

[11]

[In the *jingi-ryō* of the Yōrō Code, it says: 'At all times, on the last day of the 6th month and the 12th month, at the Great Purification, the *fubitobe* of Yamato and

---

[390] The name of the goddess is composed of: *se*, shallows or rapids; *ori* from *oru*, to drop or descend; *tsu* the possessive particle; and *hime*, princess.

[391] According to the *Kojiki*, the deities of the sea-straits or harbors were Haya-akitsu-hiko and Haya-akitsu-hime, a pair whose names contain the elements: *haya*, swift, and *aki*, bright or clear, which have the propitious effect of being cleansing agents. The two deities were offspring of Izanagi and Izanami. See Philippi, *Kojiki*, p. 55.

[392] Here *kaka-nomu* is an onomatopoeia for the sound of swallowing, gulping, or drinking up.

[393] The name of the deity is composed of: *i*, breath or air; *fuki* (*buki*) from *fuku*, to blow; *to*, a door or portal; and *nushi*, lord. Thus he is 'Lord of the Portal of Blowing Air', the portal being that through which defilements and impurities were blown down into the nether regions.

[394] The *ne-no-kuni* and *soko-no-kuni* are thought to mean the same thing: the land underneath, and are also synonymous with *shitatsu-kuni*, a

term which appeared in the ritual for the *Hoshizume* Festival.

[395] The name is made up of: *haya*, swift; *sasura(f)u*, to wander about; and *hime*, princess or goddess. Thus 'wandering about' is a play on her name. Motoori has identified her with Suseri-bime of the myths.

[396] The requirements for presentation at this festival include six expiatory horses, *harae-uma*, which are to carry away all defilements. The horse, because of its pointed, erect ears, was thought to be alert to every sound around it. This is why mention of the horse is associated with petitioning the *kami* to lend their august ears closely to the invocations and prayers.

[397] That is, great river of the capital—either the Kamo or the Katsura is intended.

[398] As the *urabe* diviners perform exorcism, the defilements and impurities are driven out of the persons present, by means of the metaphors, formulas, and imitative magic, into the effigies. Then the *urabe* depart the Palace precinct and throw the dolls into the river.

Kawachi[399] offer up the sword of exorcism and recite the words of exorcism.'
In procedures for annual festivals in Book I of the *Engi-shiki* the list of requirements for the Great Purification (*ōharae*) include, among other things: '2 swords
ornamented with gold, 2 each of gilded and silvered effigies (the foregoing are
kept by the recorders of Yamato and Kawachi)'. There are also six black-lacquered
swords, bows, arrows, mattocks, deerskins, antlers and other items, and, finally,
six horses. The instructions say that . . . 'before the monkey hour on the last day
[of the month], the host of officials from Prince-of-the-Blood and on down assemble at the Suzaku Gate, and the Diviners recite the ritual.' The recorders (*fubitobe*)
themselves gather in the forbidden courtyard of the palace. They present the
swords and the effigies successively to the Sovereign. He in turn breathes his
honorable breath upon these objects in order to transfer to them any defilement,
pollution, or misfortune, and thus to symbolically cleanse himself and the Court
of any offenses to the *kami*. This ceremony takes place before the recitation of the
*ōharae no kotoba*, the ritual of exorcism for the Great Purification, no. 10 above.
Why the *fubitobe* used this Taoist charm, which they recited in Chinese pronunciation, may be explained by their personal history as scholars in Chinese at the
Court. The language of this ritual is altogether a contrast to the archaic Yamato
language of the other *norito*.]

### The Charm Recited by the Yamato no Fumi no Imike-be
### When Presenting Swords (Duplicated by the Fubitobe of Kawachi)[400]

WE humbly beseech the Supreme Ruler of Heaven,[401] the (Six) Great Lords of
the Three Terraces,[402] the sun, the moon, the stars, and planets, the hosts of gods

---

[399] Also written *fumi-be, fumibito,* or *fumibito-be,* these were the official scholars or recorders. In the beginning they were scribes who wrote in Chinese, and eventually, since their occupation was hereditary, it became the name of their *uji* or clan. According to the *Shinsen shōjiroku,* a gene-alogy of important clans in the Nara period, they were descended from immigrants. The *gakuryō*(law concerning learning) of the Yōrō Civil Code says: 'At all times, scholars [*dai-gakusei*] are children of 5th Court Rank and above, as well as the Scholars of East and West. . . .' The *Ryō-no-gige* explains that the latter live to the left and to the right of the imperial precinct, and hence are called 'east' and 'west'. Those who lived in Yamato Prov. were the '*Yamato no fumi no atae*' 倭文値, and those who lived in Kafuchi (Kawachi) were '*Kafuchi no fumi no obito*' 河內文首, thus including also their *kabane,* or clan-rank title (*atae, obito*). When Temmu Tennō revised the *kabane* system to reduce the number to eight *kabane,* these *uji* received the *imiki* rank, thus becoming '*Yamato no fumi no imiki-be*' and

'*Kawachi no fumi no imiki-be*', respectively.

[400] The title of this incantation reads: *Yamato no fumi no imiki-be no tachi wo tatematsuru no toki no zu (Kafuchi no fumi-be kore wo junzuru),* in which *zu* is the name for the actual charm which appears at the end. We can imagine the symbolic gestures of the recorders as they cast out evil influences into the 'silver effigies', thus removing them from the Court. The use of effigies in ex-orcism was practiced in pre-historic times. Such tiny figures made of stone, wood, iron, and clay, have been unearthed all over Japan at sacred sites. See S. Koyama, 'Shintō ni okeru ikon hassei no genryū', *Jimbun kagaku kenkyū,* 1971: 6.

[401] By this conventional Chinese expression is understood the supreme ancestral *kami* of the line of sovereigns.

[402] The 'three terraces' were the three pairs of bright stars in Ursa Major, which to the Chinese symbolized in the heavens the three chief Minis-ters of State, the *san kung* 三公.

in eight directions,[403] the arbiters of human destiny and the keepers of records,[404] the Father King of the East on the left, the Mother Queen of the West on the right,[405] the five rulers of the five directions,[406] the four climates of the four seasons, as we humbly present these silver effigies, we beseech ye, free us from calamities. As we humbly present the golden sword, we beseech ye, prolong the reign of our Sovereign. We pronounce the charm: To the East as far as Fusō,[407] to the West as far as Yu-yen,[408] to the south as far as the burning tropics, to the north as far as the arctic,[409] to a thousand cities, a hundred countries, let the eternal reign extend! Banzai! Banzai!

## [12]

### The Pacification of Fire[410]

### Ritual

BY THE divine command of the mighty ancestral gods and goddesses abiding in the Plain of High Heaven, the divine descendant rules in peace and tranquillity the land of rich rice-ears growing in the abundant reedy plains. Ever since the time he was entrusted with the land under heaven, the solemn liturgy of the heavenly magic formula has been repeated. When the two deities Izanagi-no-mikoto and Izanami-no-mikoto were united as husband and wife[411] they propagated the many lands and the many islands that make up the Country of Many Islands, they propagated the myriads of deities, and when she gave birth to her last child, it was Homusubi-no-kami, the Fire God, in doing which her parts were burned

[403] This expression includes the Taoist deities of the four cardinal directions and the four intermediate directions, and could be interpreted to mean the *kami* residing in all parts of heaven and earth.

[404] This is the Taoist belief in stars which oversee human behavior and control the fate and happiness of humans according to their good or bad actions. The keeper of registers keeps the names and records of human beings.

[405] The reference to left and right is to positions when facing south (as does the sovereign). The East King Father controls *yang* 陽 and the West Queen Mother controls *yin* 陰, the opposing forces in the universe. See Kaneko, p. 165.

[406] This could refer to the five legendary emperors of China, but more likely it alludes to the five ethereal gods of Taoism who control the seasons.

[407] Fusō 扶桑 was an old Chinese name for Japan.

[408] Yu-yen 虞淵 in Chinese lore was the place where the sun set.

[409] The name used is 'weak waters' 弱水, for the body of water believed to surround the northern regions—like the *ōkeanos* of the Greeks,

the great river supposed to encompass the earth.

[410] The *Hoshizume*, or *Hishizume*, Festival was the propitiation or subduing of fire; also called *Chinka-sai* (鎮火祭). The *Ryō-no-shuge* states that it was held at the four outside corners of the Palace precinct, where the *urabe* diviners and others conduct ceremonies to pacify or subdue— that is, prevent—fires. The festival took place after the conclusion of the Great Purification (*ōharae*) ceremonies on the last night of the 6th and 12th months, or else on a propitious day during each of those months. In the house tradition of the Urabe Uji, the secret magic for the controlling of fire was handed down. Part of the ceremonies included the kindling of fires out of doors and the extinguishing of the fires by means of salt and water. See Tsugita, p. 334.

[411] *Imose* 妹妋 may mean either 'husband and wife', or 'brother and sister'. The myth of the births of the myriad deities, culminating in the birth of the fire god, duplicates the tale told in the *Kojiki* and *Nihongi* (see Philippi, *Kojiki*, pp. 55 ff. and Aston, *Nihongi* I, pp. 21 ff). This gives the impression that this particular *norito* was of later composition than that of the chronicles.

and she withdrew to the rock-tomb.[412] She spake, saying: 'For seven nights and seven days you must not look upon me, O my spouse!' Before the time ran out, he perceived that she was in hiding and looked upon her who had become burned in giving birth to the Fire God. When this occurred, the goddess declared: 'Though I told him not to look upon me, my spouse did so and caused me shame'; and further spake she, 'O my spouse, thou shalt rule the upper regions, and I shall rule the nether regions.' And she concealed herself in the rock; she went as far as the flat slope to Hades,[413] while thinking: 'I have given birth to a child of evil heart in the upper regions which my spouse is ruling.' So she returned and gave birth to four more kinds of children. She gave birth to the Water Spirit, to the gourd, to the water lily, and to the Earth Goddess, Haniyama-hime.[414] And then she spake, saying: 'When the offspring of evil heart becomes unruly let the Water God by means of the gourd, and let the Earth Goddess by means of the water lily, subdue him!'

Therefore, if we raise our words of praise may [that god] not cause destruction in the palace of the divine descendant. To this end we prepare offerings of bright cloth, shining cloth, soft cloth, and coarse cloth, and five kinds of goods, and of things that live in the blue sea-plain, creatures wide of fin and narrow of fin, even unto the seaweeds of the deep and the seaweeds of the shore. Let the sacred sake fill the offering jars to the brims, let the full-bellied jars be arrayed in rows; even unto rice in whole grain and polished grain, we heap up our offerings like unto a range of hills, and using these words of the solemn liturgy of the heavenly magic formula, we offer up our words of praise.

## [13]

### *The Banquet of the Roads*[415]

[According to *Engi-shiki* Book I, the *Michiae* festival was held annually in the sixth

---

[412] The phrase *iwa-kakurimashite*, 'concealing herself in the rock', seems to suggest her being entombed in a rock-chamber type of tomb such as we know were used for nobility in the tumulus mound period. It is a way of saying that she died. The story also implies that she was resurrected from this death.

[413] *Yomi no hirasaka* is the broad pass to the nether world. Aston, *Nihongi*, I, p. 25, translates as 'Even Pass of Yomi'.

[414] The text says *mizu-no-kami* (kami of water), *hisago* (gourd), *kawana* (a kind of water lily growing in rivers; according to Brinkley, *Nupher japonicum*), and Haniyama-hime (Clay-hill Princess). According to this *norito*, as atonement for having created the destructive fire god, Izanami has produced four means of quelling or subduing fire. Whether the water plant was an apotropaic device for exorcising fire, or whether because it was laden with much moisture it was useful in extinguishing fire, is not clear. The

*Kojiki* and *Nihongi* give slightly different versions of this part of the creation myth, but both include a water goddess (Mizuna-no-me, or Mizuha-no-me) and a goddess of clay or earth. Philippi, *Kojiki* (Ch. 7), p. 58; Aston, *Nihongi*, I, p. 21.

[415] The *Michia(h)e* Festival, or Banquet of the Road, was held annually for the purpose of warding off evils, disease, and misfortune by preventing their entrance into the capital. It was held after the fire-subduing, but held at the perimeter of the capital as a regular occurrence to offer a feast (*mi-ahe*) to the protector-gods, in order to prevent misfortune and pestilence from coming in. It is closely related to the extraordinary festivals for protection in advance of the entry of foreign visitors to the capital, and for the festivals of Sae-no-kami 障神, a deity who blocks evil spirits at the boundary and who is identical with Kunado. Another was the *yosumi no sakai no matsuri*, the festival of the boundaries.

month (and twelfth month) at the four corners of the capital. Its purpose was to waylay evil spirits or evil-working *kami*, and prevent them from entering the capital by any of its roads. The three *kami* who were feted and feasted in order to invoke their protection against those evil *kami* of epidemic and disease, were Yachimata-hiko, Yachimata-hime, and Kunado, who were deities of roads and boundaries.[416] The festival was closely related to the Festival to Deities of Epidemic at the four corners of the Palace precinct and at ten places on the boundaries of the Inner Provinces, as well as festivals to deities enroute when foreign guests arrive at the capital, all of which are treated in Book III of the *Engi-shiki*, in the 'Extraordinary Festivals'. The purpose of all these was to prevent evils, misfortunes, diseases, or epidemics from abroad from coming into the capital. Another festival, the *Goryō-e*, which is celebrated to ward off epidemic, is said to have arisen in the Jōgan period when great numbers of people, from princes and princesses on down to farmers, were stricken with an epidemic disease—perhaps diphtheria or influenza—and a special shrine was built to appease the *kami*. The development of the *Goryō-e* may account for the eventual decline and abandonment of the *Michiae no matsuri*.]

### *Ritual*

HAVING commenced in the Plain of High Heaven by the command of the divine descendant, we raise these words of praise before the mighty *kami*, who as if by means of a powerful mass of rock, blocked off the great crossroads. Thus we humbly speak. Making bold to utter the hallowed names of Yachimata-hiko and Yachimata-hime and Kunado, we raise our words of praise to them. We beseech that if things of evil intent that are hateful arise from the country beneath, from the nether regions, let there be no contact with them, let there be no speaking with them. If they should pass below, protect us below, if they should pass above, protect us above; protect us by night, protect us by day, we humbly beseech ye. For we bring as offerings to be consecrated unto ye: bright cloth, shining cloth, soft cloth, and coarse cloth. Let the sake fill the offering jars to the brims, and let the full-bellied jars be arrayed in rows as we offer the rice in liquid and in grain, and offer creatures that live in mountain and moor, those soft of fur and those coarse of fur; of things that live in the blue sea-plain, those broad of fin and

---

[416] Yachimata-hime and Yachimata-hiko were a pair of deities who guarded the crossroads, or, as their names say, 'road fork'. *Ya* is a decorative or euphonious prefix; *chi* is road; *mata*, a fork or crotch. They are undoubtedly a pair of phallic deities who protect travelers from the harms and perils of the trip. Kunado is a deity who obstructs evil spirits. The name is made up of *ku*, from the verb to come; *na*, the negative; and *to* (*do*), place. According to mythology, a deity named Yachimata was born when Izanagi came back from the nether world and had to perform purification; in the process of his casting off his trousers this *kami* came into existence. Philippi, *Kojiki*, p. 69. The myths mention Funado (or Kunado) in the episode when Izanagi threw down his stick and said: 'Come no further.' This is an etiological explanation of the name. See Aston, *Nihongi*, I, p. 25. In the *Kojiki* this deity was called Tsukitatsu-funado-no-kami. See Philippi, op. cit. p. 68. Yachimata-hiko, Yachimata-hime, and Kunado were collectively called Sae-no-kami, meaning the *kami* who ward off disaster and disease. Tsugita, *Norito shinkō*, p. 354.

those narrow of fin, even unto the seaweeds of the deep and the seaweeds of the shore; these choice offerings we heap up like a range of hills, praying that ye may be pleased to receive them. May we close off the many crossroads as with a magic mound of rocks, may the divine descendant be blessed with a reign as firm as hard rock, as enduring as everlasting rock, and may his reign be a prosperous and happy one, we pray. Moreover, we pray that the imperial princes and princesses, the princes, ministers, the host of officials, and even all the people under heaven may be blessed in peace, as the members of the *Jingi-kan*,[417] reciting this solemn liturgy of the heavenly magic formula, raise to ye their words of praise.

## [14]

### *The Great New Food Festival*[418]

O ALL ye assembled divine chiefs and priests hearken unto us as we say: By the divine command of the mighty ancestral gods and goddesses abiding in the Plain of High Heaven, we humbly speak before the presence of the mighty *kami* who dwell in heaven and earth. On this day of the hare in the eleventh month of this year, of the heavenly food, the food partaken eternally over the ages, the divine food partaken of by the divine descendant, may the mighty *kami* consent to partake thereof with him.[419] May his reign be a prosperous and happy one, lasting five hundred, yea, a thousand autumns in peace and tranquillity. With resplendent brightness may he glow as he partakes,[420] the divine descendant, whose choice offerings we prepare for presentation: the bright cloth, shining cloth, soft cloth, and coarse cloth; at this moment of the majestic and resplendent rising of the morning sun, we raise our words of praise.

Turning now, we ask the Imbe whose frail shoulders are bound with the potent sleeve-ties to consecrate the offerings that are here prepared; and let the divine chiefs and priests humbly receive them and, making no error, raise them up in presentation to the *kami*.[421]

---

[417] Specifically, for this *norito*, members of the Nakatomi.

[418] In Bk VII this ritual was referred to as the *Amatsu kami no yogoto* (Blessing of the Heavenly Kami); see n. 266. It is believed this ritual was used both for the annual New Food Festival (*Niiname* or *Shinjō-sai*) and the Great Food Festival of the Enthronement (*Senso Daijō-sai*). More than two centuries after the completion of the *E-S*, a greatly expanded version was in use. Known as the *Nakatomi no yogoto*, the text was recorded in the journal of the Great Minister of the Left, Fujiwara no Yorinaga, as having been recited at the enthronement ceremonies of Konoe Tennō in 1142 (Kōji 1, 11th month), by the Asst. Chief of the *Jingi-kan*, Oonakatomi *ason* Kiyochika. See Kaneko, op. cit. p. 288.

[419] The honorific expression, *ahi-uzunohi matsurite*, signifies the intimate agreement on the part of the *kami* to deign to participate in this sacramental feast.

[420] This unique poetic figure, '*toyono akari ni akari*' is a kind of hyperbole thought to be equivalent to that passage in the *norito* for the *Toshigoi* and *Tsukinami* festivals which says: *akani no ho nimo* 'with cheeks becoming ruddy . . .' (as he drinks the sacred sake at the divine repast).

[421] This phrase, which also appears at the end of the ritual for the *Toshigoi*, clearly shows that the Nakatomi recites the ritual, that the Imbe have charge of the making of offerings, and that assistance is given by the deity chiefs (*kannushi*) and by the priests who take the offerings to be presented at their respective local shrines.

[15]

### Festival for the Pacification of
### August Imperial Spirits[422]

[The following is the *norito* recited by the Nakatomi in the sacred courtyard (Sai-in) of the *Jingi-kan* in the 12th month when worshipping the collective august spirits of the sovereign, which in the 11th-month ceremonies of the *Mitama-shizume no matsuri* (*Chinkon-sai*) were pacified and subdued.[423] These ceremonies grew out of what the ancients believed concerning the separation of the spirits from the material body, from which they from time to time emigrated. The collective august spirits—the turbulent spirit (*ara-mitama*), the benign spirit (*nigi-mitama*), the joyous spirit (*saki-mitama*), and the wondrous or miraculous spirit (*kashi-mitama*)—were all to be invited to refrain from wandering and come to harmonious rest within the august person of the sovereign.[424]

In the *Mitama-shizume* ceremonies in the 11th month the sovereign and his consort (on the middle tiger day) and the heir apparent (on the serpent day) participated in the spirit-quieting festival. They gathered with *Jingi-kan* officials and members of the Court in the Ministry of the Imperial Household to worship the eight *kami* who protect the Imperial Household. The continuation of this calming and integrating of august spirits on a lucky day in the following month moved to the Sai-in of the *Jingi-kan*, where the Nakatomi officials conduct the service. This comprised the ceremony of consecrating the three articles of divine raiment (*miso*) which represented the august spirits of the three personages

---

[422] The full title is '*Mitama iwaito ni shizume matsuri*'—'Festival to Pacify the August Spirits in (or with) *iwaito*'. There are differing interpretations of *iwaito* (or *iwaido*). One is that it is a place within the *Jingi-kan* were the ceremony of calming the divine spirits is held. Tsugita supports this view, basing it on a passage in the *Sandai jitsuroku*, vol. 4, for Jōgan 2 (A.D. 860) which speaks of it taking place 'within the *Jingi-kan*, in the Sai-in', as though it were a building in the sacred courtyard. Tsugita, p. 387. The other interpretation is that *iwai*, from *iwa(f)u*, means 'consecrating' or 'tabooing', and *to* is a magical spell (as in *norito*, *kusoto*, etc.). See T. Uda, *Norito jiten*.

[423] Detailed requirements for the *Mitama-shizume* and for the *Iwaido* Festival and the procedures for both are given under the 11th and 12th months, respectively, in the Annual Festivals, *E-S*, Bk II.

[424] Tsugita gives the following interpretations of the four kinds of divine spirits. The turbulent spirit, *ara-mitama*, relates to the active side of life, imbuing one with valor, enterprise, and action. (A reference to this spirit comes in the

legend of Empress Jingū, when she led the campaigns against Korea. Aston, *Nihongi*, I, p. 229: 'A gentle spirit will attach itself to the Empress's person, and keep watch over her life; a rough spirit will form the vanguard and be a guide to the squadron.') The benign, gentle spirit, *nigi-mitama*, represents the passive side of life and the continuance of life. The *saki-mitama*, the process or agent which brings happiness or contentment, is responsible for preserving a man's life. And the *kushi-mitama* is the source of intellectual activity. The latter two are sometimes used in place of *nigi-mitama*, as they are regarded as two facets of the benign spirit.

In the myth concerning Ohonamochi-no-kami (offspring of Susano-o-no-mikoto), the *Nihongi* relates that 'a Divine radiance illuminated the sea and ... something ... floated towards him and said: "Were I not here, how couldst thou subdue this land?" and the god asked, '"Then who art thou?" It replied ... "I am thy guardian spirit, the wondrous spirit" [*kushi-mitama*].' Aston, I, 61. This is an example of a deity meeting his own spirit as it wandered. See also R. Ponsonby-Fane, *Divine Spirits of Shintō and the Hirota Jinja*.

(sovereign, consort, and heir apparent), as well as the sacred thong of bark-cloth which had been tied during the *tamashizume* ceremonies by the Nakatomi priests to symbolize the binding together of the august spirits of the sovereign. The divine raiment is dedicated in the *norito*, but the tying of the bark-cloth is not mentioned herein.]

## Ritual

BY THE divine command of the mighty ancestral gods and goddesses abiding in the Plain of High Heaven, the divine descendant made the land of rich rice-ears growing in the abundant reedy plains a peaceful country. The columns of his palace are auspiciously set in the bedrock beneath, its crossed gable-boards reaching up toward the Plain of High Heaven; as it is sheltered from the gaze of heaven and from the blazing sun, we offer up our words of praise. We have prepared to offer here divine raiment in upper and lower garments, and present him choice offerings of bright cloth, shining cloth, soft cloth, and coarse cloth, and five kinds of goods. Let the sacred sake fill the offering jars to the brim and let the full-bellied jars be arrayed in rows. Of things from the mountains and moors, we offer sweet herbs and bitter herbs; of things from the blue sea-plain, creatures wide of fin and narrow of fin, even unto seaweeds of the deep and seaweeds of the shore, placing them heaped up like a range of hills. These choice offerings we pray ye to accept as pleasant offerings and bountiful, and grant that our Sovereign may be blessed with an enduring reign, an everlasting reign; grant him a prosperous and happy reign, we pray. Commencing with the 12th month of this year, and continuing till the 12th month of the next year, may (these spirits) tranquilly dwell in their dwelling-place,[425] thus we pray on the (such and such) day of the 12th month of this year.

## Rituals for Use at the Grand Shrines of Ise

[The nine *norito* which follow were composed to be recited by the master-of-ceremonies (whether the messenger from the Court or the superintendent of the Shrines) at festivals held respectively at the Inner Shrine (*naikū*) of Amaterasu-ō-mikami, the Sun Goddess, and the Outer Shrine (*gekū*) of Toyouke-no-kami, the Food Goddess. The procedures for festivals held at the Grand Shrines are contained in Book IV of the *Engi-shiki*, and those at which the Consecrated Imperial Princess specifically took part are contained in Book V.]

## [16]

### Ritual for Use at Toshigoi Festival in 2nd Month
### and Tsukinami Festival in the 6th Month and 12th Month

ACCORDING to the august command of the Sovereign, on the upper reaches of the

---

[425] The *mimashi-dokoro* 御座所 refers to the residing place of the august spirits in the Hall of Eight Deities, Hasshin-den, in the *Jingi-kan*. See n. 309 above.

Isuzu at Uji in Watarai, we raise our words of praise (at the shrine)[426] set firmly on the bedrock beneath, and before the lofty presence of the Great Goddess[427] humbly do we speak. To present the customary great offerings for this *Toshigoi* in the second month (or, at the *Tsukinami* festival, 'for this *Tsukinami* festival in the sixth month') as Imperial Messenger I, (of such-and such name, rank, and position), do humbly raise up and present these offerings in accordance with the august command and purpose. Thus humbly I speak.

[17]

*Ritual for the Same Festivals at the Toyouke Shrine*

ACCORDING to the august command of the Sovereign, we humbly speak before the presence of the mighty Toyouke-no-kami,[428] to whom we raise words of praise (at the shrine) set upon the bedrock neath the plain of Yamada in Watarai. To present the customary great offerings for the *Toshigoi* in this second month (or, 'for the *Tsukinami* in this sixth month'), as Imperial Messenger I, (of such-and-such name, rank, and position), do humbly raise up and present these offerings in accordance with the august command and purpose. Thus humbly I speak.

[18]

*Ritual for Festival of Deity Raiment in the 4th Month*[429]

AT Uji in Watarai on the upper reaches of the Isuzu, where the columns of the great shrine are auspiciously set and its crossed gable-boards reach up toward the Plain of High Heaven, we raise our words of praise and speak before the mighty presence of Amaterasu-ō-mikami. Members of the Hatori and Omi perform their customary presentation of the august raiment woven out of soft fibers and coarse fibers. And we announce that the same are offered at the Shrine of Aramatsuri.[430] (*Negi* and *uchindo* respond: 'Ooh!')[431]

---

[426] 'At the shrine' . . . is supplied here because of the implication of what follows. In the next passage the phrase 'at the shrine' is included in the text.

[427] This is addressed to the 'Great Goddess', Amaterasu-ō-mikami, and the adjective *great* is used in respect to her presence: '. . . *no oho-mae*'. Other *kami* are not so addressed. See the rituals for *Toshigoi* and *Tsukinami* above, as regards Amaterasu-ō-mikami.

[428] She is called Toyouke-no-sumegami here, but in *E-S*, Bk IV, she is called Toyouke-no-ōkami.

[429] The *Kammiso* 神衣 Festival was held at the Ise Shrines in the 4th (*uzuki*, 'rainy month') and the 9th (*nagatsuki*, 'long month'), and the

procedures for this festival are given in Bk IV of *E-S*. The Superintendent of the Grand Shrines (*dajingūji*) conducts the ceremonies and reads the ritual.

[430] The Aramatsuri-no-miya is one of the separate shrines (*bekkū*) of the Shrine of the Great Deity (Amaterasu-ō-mikami) and enshrined the turbulent spirit, *ara-mitama*, of the Great Deity.

[431] For *negi*, see n. 74, above. The *uchindo* (*uchibito*), 'penetrants', were shrine officials serving under the *negi* whose special duties were to prepare offerings and foods to be presented to the *kami*. They were divided into classifications of *ko-uchindo* and *ō-uchindo* (lesser and greater penetrants).

[19]

### *Tsukinami Festival of the Sixth Month*[432]
### *(Repeated in the Twelfth Month)*

AT Uji in Watarai on the upper reaches of the Isuzu, the columns of the great shrine are auspiciously set and the crossed gable-boards reach up toward the Plain of High Heaven. Before the mighty presence of Amaterasu-ō-mikami raising our words of praise, we make bold to pronounce the solemn liturgy of the heavenly magic formula, and we enjoin all shrine chiefs and *mono-imi* and others to hearken unto it.[433] (*Negi, uchindo,* and all respond: 'Ooh!')

According to the divine command of the Sovereign, we pray thee to grant that his august life be a long-lasting life; that his reign, like a great magical heap of rocks, be everlasting, yea, that it be as firm as the solid rock; may his reign be a prosperous and happy reign. Bring blessing upon the imperial children who are born.[434] May the host of officials of all the offices of government and all people even unto the common people of the land in all directions under heaven be caused to grow and furnish the five cereals in flourishing abundance; may thou protect, bless, and make them prosper, we pray.

From the members of deity households[435] of the three districts[436] and of many places in many provinces[437] who purvey tribute goods of silk thread, as well as the consecrated august sake and august foods, these offerings are heaped up in plenty like unto a range of hills. Let the Oonakatomi, bearing before him the potent ornamented *sakaki* branch,[438] lead (the procession) on this 17th day of the sixth month of this year, at the moment of the majestic and brilliant dawning of the morning light, and all ye shrine chiefs, *mono-imi,* and other participants hearken unto the praises which we offer up. (Shrine chiefs together respond 'Ooh!') At

---

[432] The reason the *Tsukinami* Festival appears with two different *norito* is that two sets of rituals were recited at this festival—the first was the imperial message recited by the Nakatomi official who was the envoy from the Court (no. 16, above); and the second is this one, which followed and was recited by the Superintendent of the Grand Shrines.

[433] Even though *kannushi* and *mono-imi* are the only ones mentioned here by name, undoubtedly all the sacerdotal groups are being addressed. The *negi* and *uchindo* are required to make the responses. The *mono-imi* are child abstainers attached to the Great Shrine. They assisted the *uchindo* in the tasks of preparing offerings, of brewing light and dark sake, burning salt, etc. They were attended by their fathers. According to *E-S,* Bk V, there were at least nine *mono-imi* (in the text a gloss says 8 girls and one boy) plus their fathers. Also, at the Kasuga Shrine, at least one *mono-imi* is mentioned among the staff. *E-S,*

Bk I.

[434] *Aremasu miko-tashi. Aru* has two meanings: 'to appear' (*arawareru*) and 'to be born' (*umaru*). Tsugita, p. 401.

[435] Members of *kambe* 神戸 (*shinko*), the deity households that furnished sustenance to the shrines. (To be distinguished from the *kamutomo,* also pronounced *kambe,* who were officials of the *Jingi-kan*). See n. 7 above.

[436] These were the three deity districts (*shingun* 神郡), Take, Watarai, and Iino, whose deity households supported the Grand Shrine of Ise.

[437] Other localities which purveyed to the Grand Shrines were in the provinces of Ise, Iga, Owari, Oomi and Tōtoumi, and Mikawa, as designated in *E-S,* Bk IV.

[438] This is the *futo-tamagushi*. The term is made up of *futo,* potent, auspicious; *tama,* jeweled, or ornate; *kushi,* a stick. It is a branch of the sacred *sakaki* hung with streamers of bark-cloth.

the Aramatsuri Shrine and at the Tsukiyomi Shrine we present offerings and speak the same words.[439] (Shrine chiefs again respond: 'Ooh!')

[20]

*Festival of First-Fruits to the Deities in the Ninth Month*[440]

ACCORDING to the august command of the divine descendant, on the upper reaches of the Isuzu in Watarai in Ise, humbly raising our words of praise before the mighty presence of Amaterasu-ō-mikami, we present the customary great offerings for the Deity First-Fruits in the ninth month, the Prince (of such-and-such rank and position) and the Nakatomi (of such-and-such name, rank, and position) serving as (imperial) messengers. While the Imbe, their frail shoulders bound with the potent sleeve-ties, consecrate and raise aloft and present them, we make these offerings in accordance with the august command and purpose. Thus humbly we speak.

[21]

*For the Same Festival at the Toyouke Shrine*

ACCORDING to the august command of the divine descendant, before the presence of the mighty *kami* to whom we raise our words of praise on the plain of Yamada in Watarai, we humbly speak. To present the customary great offerings for the Deity First-Fruits, the Prince (of such-and-such rank and position) and the Nakatomi (of such-and-such name, rank, and position) serve as (imperial) messengers, while the Imbe, their frail shoulders bound with the potent sleeve-ties, consecrate and raise aloft and present them. We make these offerings in accordance with the august command and purpose. Thus humbly we speak.

[22]

*For the Same Festival of First-Fruits to the Deities*[441]

ON THE upper reaches of the Isuzu at Uji in Watarai, where the columns of the

---

[439] For Aramatsuri-no-miya, see n. 430, above. The Tsukiyomi-no-miya is the shrine to the Moon Deity. According to the *E-S*, Bk IV, both the Moon Deity and his turbulent spirit (*ara-mitama*) were enshrined in the Tsukiyomi Shrine.

[440] According to the *Ryō-no-gige*, 'on the day of the *Kammiso* Festival the Imperial Messenger conducts this...' i.e. the *Kanname* or Deity First-Fruits Festival. Thus it appears both the Deity Raiment and the Deity First-Fruits were held on the same day of the 9th month, but on consecutive days at the two Grand Shrines. In the *E-S*, Bk IV, the *Kanname* Festival is held at the Watarai (i.e. Toyouke) Shrine on the 16th day of the 9th month, and at the Shrine of the Great Deity (Amaterasu-ō-mikami) on the 17th day.

[441] A *norito* to be recited at the same festival as the two foregoing. The first one for the *Kanname* Festival was recited by the Nakatomi official who was Imperial Messenger for the occasion, but this one by the Superintendent of the Grand Shrines, the *daijingūji*. Similarly to the ritual for the *Tsukinami* Festival in the 6th and 12th months, this one is recited by the Superintendent to the *kannushi* (shrine or deity chiefs) and the *mono-imi* and other shrine functionaries. It was likely paraphrased for use at the Toyouke Shrine.

great shrine are auspiciously set and the crossed gable-boards reach up toward the Plain of High Heaven, we raise our words of praise before the mighty presence of Amaterasu-ō-mikami, and humbly recite the solemn liturgy of the heavenly magic ritual. Hearken ye unto it all ye shrine chiefs, *mono-imi*, and others, we humbly say. (*Negi, uchindo*, etc. respond 'Ooh!')

According to the command of the divine descendant, we pray that his august life may be a long life, and like unto a magical heap of rocks may his reign be like enduring rock, like everlasting rock; may his reign be a prosperous and happy reign, and bring blessing upon the imperial children who are born. Let all the host of officials and even down to the common people of the land under heaven long and peacefully be protected, be blessed, and made happy. And may the various people of the deity households of the three districts and the many localities in the many provinces, who customarily offer the consecrated august sake and august foods and the first-fruits of the rice to the *kami*[442] in a thousand and five-hundred fold, let them heap up these offerings like a range of hills. As the Oona-katomi raises before him the potent ornamented *sakaki* branch, at the brilliant and majestic dawning of the morning light, let all the shrine chiefs, *mono-imi*, and all, hearken as we pronounce the solemn liturgy of the heavenly magic ritual. Thus humbly we speak. (*Negi, uchindo*, etc. respond: 'Ooh!')

At the Aramatsuri-no-miya and the Tsukiyomi-no-miya the same words are pronounced and offerings made. (Shrine chiefs make the response: 'Ooh!')


[23]

*At the Time the Consecrated Imperial Princess First Participates*[443]

WHEN THE offerings of first-fruits to the *kami* have been made and the ritual has been recited, the following words are spoken:

And turning now, we humbly speak, saying, according to established custom, the Consecrated Imperial Princess, after three years of abstinence and purification, has been appointed to serve as sacred handmaiden [to the Great Goddess].[444] O, do thou grant that the divine descendant, together with heaven and earth, sun and moon, may have a reign as firm as solid rock, eternal as enduring rock, and may he rule in peace and tranquillity. And may she serve as divine handmaiden

---

[442] *Kakejikara*, 'hung up tax', was the first rice-ears harvested and placed upon the shrine fence.

[443] *Itsuki-no-hime-miko wo irematsuru no toki.* Itsuki-no-hime-miko (or Itsuki-no-miya) is the Imperial Princess consecrated to serve the Great Deity (Amaterasu-ō-mikami) at the Grand Shrine. This institution of Princess to the Ise Shrines is the subject of *E-S*, Bk V. This *norito* is recited by the Nakatomi official at the Festival of First-Fruits in the year when the Princess entered her sacred residence in proximity to the Great Shrine and participated for the first time in festivals at the shrines. This is recited at the time offerings of deity food are presented to the *kami*.

[444] *Mitsueshiro* is an epithet for the Imperial Princess, coming from: *mi* (honorific); *tsue*, a cane or staff; and *shiro*, a likeness or substitute for something.

with the Oonakatomi to carry out the command as he mediates with the wondrous spear the divine relation.[445] Most reverently and respectfully do we pronounce these words.

[24]

### Ritual for the Removal of the Shrine of the Great Deity
### (Duplicated for the Toyouke Shrine)[446]

ACCORDING to the august command of the divine descendant in the mighty presence of the mighty Ancestral Goddess, we humbly speak. Since by established ancient custom the Great Shrine is to be removed once in twenty years, the 54 different kinds of august ceremonial articles, and the 21 deity treasures are to be prepared, to be cleansed, purified, and consecrated, I the Controller[447] (name, clan-title rank, Court Rank, and position), having been sent as Imperial Messenger to take charge of these matters, humbly do now pronounce these words of dedication and worship.

[25]

### Ritual to Dispel a Malevolent Kami[448]

ACCORDING to the divine command of the *kami* who abide in the Plain of High Heaven, the mighty ancestral gods and goddesses who commenced the world caused the many myriad *kami* to gather together in the Meeting Place of High Heaven, and after the divine discussion and debate, they caused the divine descendant to make the land of rich rice-ears growing in the abundant reedy plains a pleasant land and peaceful. Leaving the worthy throne of heaven, he parted with a majestic

---

[445] The spear is used as part of the ceremony. The sentence is: *Ikashi hoko no nakatori mochite,* in which *ikashi* means awesome, auspicious; *hoko,* spear; *nakatori,* taking in the middle; *mochite,* holding or grasping. A similar passage occurs in the *Nihongi*: 'Ye, the Ministers sent to me by the Oho-omi [Soga no emishi], are men who have always addressed the sovereign as it were holding the sacred spear by the middle.' Aston, *Nihongi,* II, p. 161. (In the record of Jomei Tennō, but spoken by Suiko Tennō).

[446] *Oo-mikami-no-miya utsushi-matsuru no norito.* The removal of the Great Shrines took place every twentieth year (after the reign of Empress Jitō) in a ceremony called the *sengū.* New buildings were erected and the sacred treasures and paraphernalia put into the new buildings during nocturnal ceremonies. This is treated in *E-S,* Bk IV. The *hatatase,* twenty-years unit, may be a survival of a use in prehistoric times of a base of twenty in calculations. This *norito* was recited

by the Nakatomi official from the *Jingi-kan* who presided at the Shrine removal ceremonies.

[447] *Benkan,* a controller who was of 5th Rank or higher, a chief ritualist (*sakan*) of the *Jingi-kan,* other officials of the *Dajō-kan* and *Jingi-kan,* girl attendants, maidservants, messengers, and 63 workmen or artisans are listed as conducting the making of sacred treasures and articles to furnish the new shrines.

[448] *Tataru-kami wo utsushi-yaru.* There is no mention in the *E-S* of a festival (*matsuri*) for driving away malevolent *kami.* According to Suzuki Shigetane, this ceremony and its ritual would have been used in connection with festivals to the Kantoki-no-kami (gods of thunder), the Yachimata road-fork deities, and the deities of epidemics, as are found in the procedures for extraordinary festivals in the *E-S,* Bk III. *Tatari* (from the verb *tataru,* to malign, to put a curse on) is the substantive meaning 'curse' or 'evil spell'.

parting the many-layered clouds of the heavens, and at the time he was delegated to descend from heaven, the *kami* debated which one should be despatched the first, to overcome and divinely purge the unruly *kami* from the land of rich rice-ears. All the many *kami*, as they weighed the matter, said they would despatch Ame-no-ho-hi-no-mikoto to overcome them.[449] As it was, he did not report back. Secondly, they despatched Take-mikuma-no-mikoto.[450] In obedience to his father, he made no report back. Next they despatched Ame-no-waka-hiko, and he made no report. Owing to calamity from birds which fly overhead, he lost his life in the place where he lay.[451] Whereupon the *kami* in heaven again discussed and debated and then sent down from heaven two *kami*: Futsunushi-no-mikoto and Take-mikazuchi-no-mikoto, who divinely expelled and forced all the unruly *kami* into submission.[452] Then the words of questioning from rocks and trees and even unto the least blade of grass were brought to an end, and they sent down from heaven the divine descendant and entrusted the land unto him.

Thus it was he was sent down from heaven to the land in the center of all lands, and he made the land of Yamato where the sun shines on high a pleasant land. Beneath it the columns of the palace were auspiciously set in the bedrock and its crossed gable-boards reached up toward the Plain of High Heaven, sheltered from heaven's gaze and from the blazing sun, in the land which the divine descendant was to rule as a pleasant and peaceful land. May the mighty *kami* who abide in heavenly abodes have no discord nor be angry, may they be aware of the heavenly appearance of *kami* as it was in the beginning in the Plain of High Heaven. May they be rectified by the grace of Kamu-naobi and Oo-naobi[453] and from this place may they go out and away to pure places of the mountains and rivers where they may clearly see in all directions; may they make those their own dwelling-places, and to this end we offer up offerings of bright cloth, shining cloth, soft cloth, and coarse cloth, and also for the purpose of revealing their brightness (we

[449] According to the *Kojiki*, Ame-no-ho-hi-no-mikoto was the ancestor of the *kuni-no-miyatsuko* (local chieftain) of Izumo. See Philippi, *Kojiki* (Ch. 15), pp. 77–8; also see n. 458 below.

[450] Take-mikuma-no-mikoto appears in the following passage in the *Nihongi*: 'Taka-mi-musubi no Mikoto . . . made Ama-no-ho-hi no Mikoto to go and subdue them. This Deity, however, curried favour with Oho-na-mochi no Mikoto, and three years passed without his making any report. Therefore his son Oho-se-ihi no Mikuma no ushi (also called Take-mikuma no ushi) was sent.' Aston, I, p. 64.

[451] Ame-no-waka-hiko ('Heavenly young prince') was killed when the arrow he shot into a pheasant (or a person) sent to spy on him, turned back on him. See Philippi, *Kojiki*, pp. 123 ff. Also, Aston, *Nihongi* I, pp. 65–6.

[452] Futsunushi-no-kami is revered as ancestor of the Fujiwara Uji and worshiped in the Kasuga Shrine. The story of his creation is found in the Izanagi myth. Aston, *Nihongi*, I, p. 23. Take-mikazuchi was also ancestral *kami* of the Fujiwara, and the story of his creation is in the same myth. The story of these two *kami* descending from heaven and arriving at Inasa in Izumo is related in the *Nihongi* (Aston, I, p. 68). According to the *Kojiki* account, the two *kami* who descended to rule the Central Land of Reed Plains were Ame-no-toribune-no-kami and Take-mikazuchi, the former being the name to represent the sacred boat which Take-mikazuchi-no-kami sailed in to reach Inasa Beach in Izumo. Philippi, *Kojiki*, pp. 129–30.

[453] Kamu-naobi and Oo-naobi are the 'rectifying *kami*'. See n. 371, above.

offer) mirrors; for their amusement (we offer) jewels; for hitting the mark (we offer) bow and arrows; for cutting down (we offer) swords; and for riding forth, august horses. Let the sacred sake fill the offering-jars to the brims, let the full-bellied jars be arrayed in rows; (we offer) polished rice and unpolished grain;[454] of things that dwell in the mountains, creatures soft of fur, creatures coarse of fur; of things that grow in the great moors and plains, sweet herbs and bitter herbs; of things that live in the blue plain of the sea, creatures wide of fin and narrow of fin, even unto seaweeds of the deep and seaweeds of the shore; we heap up all these offerings in abundance on offering tables like unto a range of hills. Let the august hearts of the mighty *kami*, in their serenity, peacefully receive the pleasant offerings, the plentiful offerings which we present; and may there be nothing malevolent, nothing violent; may they withdraw to the broad, pure places in mountains and rivers, and may they in divine manner be calmed, thus we raise our words of praise, humbly speaking.[455]

[26]

*For Presenting Offerings at the Time of Despatching*
*an Envoy to China*[456]

ACCORDING to the august decree of the divine descendant, before the presence of the mighty *kami* of Suminoe[457] to whom we raise our words of praise, humbly I speak: For the despatch of envoys unto the Great T'ang, on account of having no mooring, embarkation was to be from Harima Province. While (His Majesty) pondered sending abroad these envoys, relying upon the words of command of the mighty *kami*, he learned from them the wisdom of how to construct the ship's mooring, and after its having been constructed, he rejoiced and was glad. In thanksgiving for this event, I, (so-and-so, of such-and-such clan-rank-title, Court Rank, and position), do bear and present these offerings; so humbly do I speak.

---

[454] *Yone ni mo kahi ni mo*—'in rice and in grain'—is taken to mean light and dark rice: polished and unpolished grains of rice.

[455] Although malevolent and evil-working, these *kami* are appeased in the most respectful manner in order to soothe their wrath, and are implored to betake themselves away from the populated areas.

[456] The title for this is: *Morokoshi ni tsukai wo tsukawasu toki mitegura wo tatematsuru*. During the Asuka period (reign of Empress Suiko) embassies began to be sent to T'ang China at the beginning of that empire. During the Nara and Heian periods many embassies were sent, and priests, scholars, and students went in considerable numbers to travel and study in China. The characters are 'Great T'ang', but the reading is *Morokoshi*—an archaic name for China.

[457] Suminoe is the name for the great shrine which later is called Sumiyoshi. The Suminoe-no-ōkami was a trinity of *kami*, known as Uwa-tsutsu-no-o, Naka-tsutsu-no-o and Soko-tsutsu-no-o, who are believed to be gods of war, associated with the expansion of the Yamato people. Suminoe is believed to mean 'pure stream'. The fourth *kami* reverenced at this shrine is said to be the deification of the legendary Empress Jingū, who conducted a great campaign against Korea. See Yamane, *The Naniwa Courts and the Sumiyoshi Shrine*, pp. 12, 22, 23.

## [27]

### Laudatory Ritual to the Kami Offered by the
### Local Chieftain of Izumo[458]

THOUGH many days have passed by, on this fortunate and auspicious day I, (name and rank), the Local Chieftain of Izumo Province, most reverently do address myself (to those present). Fearing to put into words the name of the incarnate *kami*, we pray that the august reign of the mighty Sovereign who rules the Great Country of Many Islands may be a fortunate and everlasting reign.[459]

In the green-mantled mountains of Izumo, the pillars of the august dwelling[460] are auspiciously set upon the bedrock beneath, the crossed gable-boards reach upward toward the Plain of High Heaven. It is here we worship first of all the two *kami* who were beloved offspring of Izanagi, our ancestral *kami*: Kushimikeno-no-mikoto, the great god of Kumano, and Oonamochi-no-mikoto, who built the land, and all the other mighty *kami* who abide in the 186 shrines of Izumo.[461]

I, (so-and-so), binding the potent sleeve-ties around my frail shoulders and tying the sacred bark-cloth into a sacred chaplet worn on my head,[462] in my purified hut I cut and spread out the virgin wild grasses to sit on;[463] with the sacred jars

---

[458] The title is: *Izumo no kuni no miyatsuko no kamu-yogoto*, in which *kuni-no-miyatsuko* is an archaic *kabane* for the local magnate who administered an entire *kuni*, or province, of the pre-Taika divisions. Later this title became the name of the position of 'local chieftain'. Strictly speaking, after the Taika Reform (A.D. 645–6) this local position was superseded by the *kuni-no-tsukasa*, or governor of the province under the new administrative divisions. When a new local chieftain took office, it was the custom for him to come up to the capital and participate in ceremonies at which this *norito* was recited. From the description of this ceremony in *E-S*, Bk III, it is plain to see that the *kuni-no-miyatsuko* still had the hereditary title and function, even though the governor of Izumo Province also participated. A ceremony of investiture of the *kuni-no-miyatsuko* of Izumo, and probably also the *kuni-no-miyatsuko* of Kii Province, was held in the *Dajō-kan* at the capital, as is recounted in the *Jōgan-gishiki*. It appears from the *E-S* procedures for this event that the function of the *kuni-no-miyatsuko* of Izumo was primarily religious (at least after the time of Kōtoku Tennō in the Taika era. He performed abstinence and religious austerity for the period of a year between visits to the Yamato Court. When he came up to the Court it was to receive sacred emblems from the sovereign and to present offerings to the *kami* and to recite this laudatory ritual.

[459] A gloss adds that for subsequent good wishes to the sovereign, the incarnate *kami*, these words may be added: 'Tenaga no ō-miyo to iwai nochi to nasete'—('may His long and mighty reign have blessing succeeding to blessing').

[460] The Great Shrine of Izumo (Izumo-no-ōyashiro) enshrining Oonamochi-no-kami. Kizuki was the earlier name for the area which after Taika became Izumo District of Izumo Province. Kushimikeno, great god of Kumano, was revered as ancestral deity of the grandees of Izumo (Izumo no *omi*) in Ou District, Izumo Prov.

[461] In Book X of *E-S* (below) a list of 187 shrines in Izumo Province appears, while the *Izumo fudoki* gave a total of 399 shrines, of which 184 were *kansha* and 215 were not under the authority of the *Jingi-kan*. See M. Y. Aoki, *Izumo fudoki*, p. 80.

[462] The sentence, '*Itsu nusa no wo musubi, ame no mikage kagafurite*', would seem to mean that purified bark-cloth strands were tied into a head-covering in order to protect the worshiper from the concentration of divinity or from the 'gaze of heaven'. In the translation of the *Nihongi* there is a passage that says: 'An ornamental chaplet was offered at the Palace of temporary interment. This was called Mikage'. Aston, II, p. 385. This is no doubt the same thing as the *yū-kazura* of other ceremonies. *Yū*, which means 'bark-cloth', has the same sound as *yū*, 'tabooed' or 'purified'.

[463] The word *itsu*, meaning 'taboo' or 'sacred', is used for the *mushiro* seat-mat of woven grass; and the hut is called *itsu no maya*, 'the taboo dwelling'.

blackened on the bottom, and heavenly brewing jars at hand,[464] I served in the sacred shrine in abstinence and purification; so that now, at the moment of the majestic and brilliant dawning of the morning light I offer up the favorable report in the form of auspicious words of this laudatory ritual to the *kami*; so humbly do I speak.

When those ancestral *kami* of High Heaven, Takami-musubi and Kamu-musubi-no-mikoto, yielded the Great Country of Many Islands to the divine descendant, the distant ancestor of the nobles of Izumo, Ame-no-ho-hi-no-mikoto,[465] was sent to inquire the condition of the land. He pushed asunder the many-layered clouds of heaven, and, flying through the heaven and over the land, he viewed all the lands under heaven and brought back an answer, saying: 'The land of rich rice-ears growing in the reedy plains in the daytime buzzes with flies as in early summer, and in the nighttime there are *kami* who shine like fire-pots. Everywhere sounds from the rocks, the tree-stumps and the bubbles of foam on blue waters are heard as they talk in this restless land.[466] Nevertheless, I shall calm and pacify it, and I shall cause the divine descendant to rule it as a pleasant and peaceful country.' So spake he.

His divine offspring, Ame-no-hina-dori-no-mikoto, together with Futsunushi-no-mikoto, was despatched and sent down from heaven. These two drove out and pacified the unruly *kami*, and calmed with flattery the Great Kami who made the land, and caused him to give up the visible and material things of the Great Country of Many Islands. Whereupon, Oonamochi-no-mikoto spake, saying: 'Let the divine descendant dwell in the pacified country of Yamato.' And he instilled his own benign spirit into a many-spanned mirror[467] to which he gave the august name Yamato no Oomononushi-kushi-mikatama-no-mikoto, which he caused to dwell in the divine woods of Mt Miwa in Yamato.[468] His august off-

[464] The sacred jars for cooking (*itsu-he*) become blackened (*kuromashi*) over the fire. The sacredness of the brewing of sacramental sake is apparent in this passage, and the strict taboo of a life in an 'abstinence hut' marks the chieftain of Izumo as a religious figure of prime importance. A parallel has been seen in the establishment of an abstinence hut by Yamato-hime in the legend concerning the worship of Amaterasu at Ise.

[465] According to the 15th chapter of the *Kojiki*, Ame-no-ho-hi-no-mikoto begat Take-hira-tori-no-mikoto, who was the ancestor of the *kuni-no-miyatsuko* of Izumo and the *miyatsuko* of other provinces as well. See Philippi, *Kojiki*, p. 78. The Ame-no-hina-dori-no-mikoto may be an alternate name for Take-hira-tori-no-mikoto.

[466] See Aston, *Nihongi*, I, 64: 'But in that Land there were numerous Deities which shone with a lustre like that of fireflies, and evil Deities which buzzed like flies. There were also trees

and herbs all of which could speak.'

[467] *Ya-ata kagami* means a mirror of eight, or of many, spans in perimeter. The belief was prevalent in ancient times that a *kami* dwelt in the mirror.

[468] In this passage, the deity Oonamochi of Izumo accounts for the transfer of his worship to Yamato-no-kuni, where he is revered as Oomononushi-kushi-mikatama enshrined as Oo-miwa-no-kami in the sacred hill of Oomiwa. At Mt Miwa the hill itself is the *kami* and object of worship. Although it is listed in Bk IX as a *jinja* (in Shikinokami District, Yamato), it had no shrine building. Other localities which have 'shrines' but no building are the Takimatsuri Jinja, an auxiliary of the Shrine of the Great Deity in Ise, the Kanasana Jinja in Kotama District, Musashi Province, and the forbidden enclosure of the Kami Suwa Shrine of Shinano. See M. Nishitsunoi, *Kodai saishi to bungaku*, p. 282.

spring, Ajisuki-taka-hikone-no-mikoto, was made to dwell in the divine woods of Kamo in Katsuragi,[469] and the august spirit of Kotoshironushi-no-mikoto was made to dwell in Unade,[470] the august spirit of Kayanarumi-no-mikoto to dwell in the divine woods of Asuka[471]—all of them worshipped as protector *kami* and placed nigh to the divine descendant, while he himself dwells peacefully in the shrine of Kizuki, rich in cinnabar.[472]

Hereupon the mighty ancestral gods and goddesses announced by august decree: 'May thou, Ame-no-ho-hi-no-mikoto, grant the Sovereign a long, august reign; may it be blest as solid rock, may it be as everlasting rock, may it flourish and be a prosperous reign.' Thus their divine command has been handed successively down until now at this moment of the brilliant and majestic dawning of the morning light, I offer up the divine treasures to praise the *kami* as tokens of reverence to the *kami* and tokens of reverence from the nobles, thus humbly I speak.

Like the white beads[473] may your august locks grow white with longevity; like the red beads, may your august countenance grow ruddy; like the clear blue beads, may your image be blest, may they ensure you long-continuing rule over the Great Country of Many Isles as an incarnate *kami*. May the august sword with broadly tempered blade[474] ensure the mighty and enduring reign of the great sovereign. May the hooves of the forefeet of the august white horse[475] and the hooves of his hindfeet tamp down the upper stones for the posts of the inner and outer palace gates, and may they pack down the posts into the bedrock below. May thy reign be exalted as the ears of the august horse prick up when he is alerted. Like the live tribute of white swans[476] for your enjoyment and like the colored hempen cloth, may your august heart remain steadfast. Like the rejuvenating springs which bubble up on that bank of an ancient river, and on this bank, may you abide ever wise and youthful. As the water of ponds may be turned back to

[469] In *E-S* Bk IX it says: 'four principal deities worshiped in Takakamo, Ajisuki-taka-hikone-no mikoto Shrine' located in Takakamo, Katsuragi-mura, Katsuraginokami District, Yamato Province.

[470] Bk IX lists 'Takechi-miagata ni masu Kamo no Kotoshironushi', a major deity.

[471] This deity and shrine are not mentioned elsewhere, and evidently are not among those registered with the central government.

[472] *Yaoni* (八百丹) is a fixed epithet (*makura-kotoba*) of the Kizuki Shrine. It appears to mean 'abundant red-earth', as *ni* 丹 usually referred to the red clay which yielded cinnabar, a valuable natural pigment.

[473] The passage in *E-S*, Bk III, describing this ceremony speaks of *mifuki-dama* to be presented by the Izumo chieftain at Court. *Mifuki* is analogous to *mi-hogi*, meaning 'august fortune-bringing'. Here the expression is *mihogi no kamu-takara*—'august fortune-bringing deity treasures',

therewith described as talismanic beads in three symbolic colors (perhaps *magatama*, the sacred 'curved jewels' of prehistoric times).

[474] The ceremonial sword presented here by the Izumo *kuni-no-miyatsuko* to the Yamato sovereign could be interpreted as symbolic of the acknowledgement of the supremacy of Yamato over the local magnate of Izumo in a time before recorded history. The Court also bestows a sword upon the *kuni-no-miyatsuko* among the 'congratulatory gifts' (*oisachi-mono*) upon his investiture, perhaps commemorating the concluding of a treaty between the two great chieftains.

[475] The description in *E-S*, Bk III, mentions a roan horse with white eyeballs (*samitsukige uma*).

[476] Among the 'congratulatory gifts' were also 'two white swans perched on the eaves' (*E-S*, Bk III). As to migrating swans frequenting Izumo, see M. Y. Aoki, *Izumo fudoki*, p. 64.

flow uphill, may your youth return and be renewed. As a clear mirror is made clearer by polishing,[477] so may your majesty view the entire land under heaven, and as an incarnate *kami* together with heaven, earth, sun, and moon, may you rule the Great Country of Many Isles in peace and tranquillity. To this end we offer up divine treasures of good auspices which are tokens of reverence for the *kami* and tokens of reverence from the nobles. Most reverently and respectfully I offer these words of blessing for the laudation of the *kami* who are our ancestral *kami*; thus humbly I speak.

*    *    *    *    *

End of Book Eight of the *Engi-shiki*
   Enchō 5th Year, 12th Month, 26th Day
      [Same signatures as at end of Book Six]

---

[477] The mirror is called '*masohi no ō-mikagami*' ('great, august mirror of purity')—*masohi* being equivalent to the adjectives *maso* and *masumi*, used for mirrors in the *Man'yōshū*; and again, *masumi no kagami* in the *Nihongi*. Tsugita, op. cit. p. 514.

# Chapter Four

## INTRODUCTION TO BOOKS NINE AND TEN

I F T H E *Jimmyō-cho* (or *Shimmei-chō*) were in truth what its title says—a register of names of deities—we would be fortunate indeed, for our knowledge of the officially endorsed pantheon of Nara and early Heian would be vastly enriched. The fact is, however, that this is a register of the official shrines throughout the country by province (*kuni*) and district (*kōri*), and the shrine name often gives us no clue either to the *kami* enshrined therein or to the origin or affiliation of the shrine.

The shrines of today are known to proclaim their antiquity by asserting that they are '*shikinai-sha*', or 'shrines within the *shiki*' (i.e. shrines listed in the *Engi-shiki*). But the claim does not authenticate their continued existence as a shrine at the particular site ever since the Heian period. Over the thousand years since the completion of the *Engi-shiki*, the ravages of war and other forces have caused many a small shrine to disappear, and others to be destroyed and rebuilt at another site; local boundaries have been altered; new cults have arisen to replace old. Then in the Meiji period the worship at many small shrines was forcibly merged with that of larger shrines in order to reduce the total number in the government-supported system.

The Meiji period attempts to restore the ancient government system of shrines resulted in the compilation of a work called *Tokusen jimmyō-chō*, a reconstruction of the old system, based not only upon the *Engi-shiki* list but also upon post-Heian sources. It is arranged according to the old provincial and district divisions rather than the new prefectural divisions introduced during Meiji. While it is tempting to annotate the *Engi-shiki* list of shrines with information from *Tokusen jimmyō-chō* and from other recent publications concerning shrines, we must scrupulously avoid reading into the *Engi-shiki* text any interpretations or traditions which belong to later ages. To corroborate or interpret the text, sources from Nara and early Heian must be used, and these yield only sporadic references to shrines and festivals. The available evidence from these sources has scarcely been compiled, and profound studies of the shrine system and of individual shrines up to the time of completion of the *Engi-shiki* have not yet been carried out. As indicated by Prof. K. Shiga, who has begun research on *shikinai-sha*, no comprehensive study of the relation of the system of shrines to the ancient society has as yet been undertaken.[478]

---

[478] *Shikinai-sha no kenkyū*, pp. 1–3. Shiga's in-depth study of individual shrines of the ancient system commenced with this volume on the Sai-kaidō (including present Kyushu and Iki and Tsushima Islands) and Nankaidō, but much remains to be uncovered concerning the nature of shrines and shrine worship up to the Heian period, especially as regards smaller shrines.

Hence we must regard the lists in the *Jimmyō-chō* of the *Engi-shiki* as indicative of the shrine system supported by the central government and provincial government during the Nara and Heian periods (eighth, ninth, and early tenth centuries), and probably neither earlier nor later than that span. Some additional information about the shrines is found here and there in the Six National Histories (*Rikkoku-shi*), the *Kōtaijingū-gishikichō*, the *Izumo fudoki*, the *Kogoshūi*, the *Ruijū-kokushi* and *Ruijū-sandaikyaku*, and lesser works of the ninth century, but very little is said about shrines outside the Inner Provinces, Ise, and Izumo.

It is possible to view this long list of 2,861 shrines throughout the country by groups or types. The list begins with the 36 deities worshiped within the Imperial Palace. These *kami* are mentioned elsewhere in the first eight books of the *Engi-shiki* and all of them are directly connected to the Imperial Household. Secondly, there are the shrines related to prominent families (*uji*) in close association with the Imperial Court. Outside of the Palace, the Ise and Watarai Shrines belonged to the Imperial House, while the shrines of the family next in importance to the Imperial Family, the Fujiwara Uji, had its deities enshrined at Kasuga Jinja and also at the Hiraoka, Ooharano, Katori, and Kashima Shrines. The Kamo Uji had founded the Kamo Shrines, the Hata Uji the Matsuno-o Shrine. The Naka-tomi Uji, of which the Fujiwara were an offshoot, shared the latter's identity with their shrines, but were also the Court ritualists supervising all Court-related ceremonies. The Imbe Uji claimed to be the official builders of the Palace and of shrines, and their family shrines are found in various provinces.[479]

Another type are shrines to *kami* of natural phenomena; these are ubiquitous. We find that most *kami* are local and not only dwell in a certain locality but are also the possessors of that locality. They not only influence the destinies of the human beings in the locality but also are owners of its soil, its air, its flora, and its waters. Although the deities of sun, moon, wind, storm, and lightning were looked up to and worshiped in their celestial habitat, they were nevertheless given an earthly dwelling where their spirit could reside and be worshiped in a shrine.

The most numerous category of shrines relates to various *kami* of water: of bubbling springs (*yu*), of drinking water (*i*), of rivers, lakes, harbors, rain, irrigation, and the ocean. Of shrines to *kami* of drinking-water wells—besides those which were in the Imperial Palace—we find Ooi and Iwai in Yamashiro Province; Hata-mikai, Mii, and Itsui in Yamato; four *i* in Izumi Province; Ite, Izumi, Ishiri, and Ooi in Ise; Sakai, Asai (2), and Ite in Owari, and countless others. There are enshrinements of the deity of water: Oomizukami, as well as Minushi in Yamashiro and Sanuki; in Oomi there are shrines to Mio and Oomizuwake; and elsewhere there are Shimizu ('clear-water') and Imizu shrines. Those to bubbling water include Amayu-kawata in Kawachi, Yu Shrine in Settsu, Yuta in Watarai in Ise, two Yu and a Yu-no-ishi in Mutsu. Among the *kami* of rivers is the one worshiped at Kawa-ai Jinja in Shinano. As for deities of the sea and seafarers—popularly, the great gods of Sumiyoshi are thought to be sea gods (although

---

[479] See Katō and Hoshino, *Kogoshūi*, pp. 31, 47.

there is another interpretation), as are those of Sumiyoshi shrine of Tsushima, the Watatsumi Shrines on the same island, and the Ooyosami deities.

Of thunder and lightning deities, the most prominent is Wake-ikazuchi-no-mikoto of the Upper Kamo Shrine, Hono-ikazuchi (believed to be the same deity as the foregoing) and Naru-ikazuchi in Yamato; Hono-ikazuchi in Nawa District, Kōzuke Province; Hyakuraku deities in Iwami; and other Ikazuchi shrines in Echizen, Tajima, and Tsushima, not to mention Narukami Shrine in Kii and Inahikari in Izumi. There is also a thunder god, Narukami, worshiped in the Imperial Palace Water Office.

We have already seen that Izumo Province had its regional deity—Oonamochi (also called Ookuninushi, or Ookunitama of Izumo), who created that land. So also other regions had their regional patron deity, and we find in almost every province a shrine to the Ookunitama or Great Spirit of the Land of that province.

We find the frequent occurrence of shrines called Niu (丹生), which literally seems to mean 'cinnabar-producing'; here probably was venerated a goddess of earth which yielded the red soil (see n. 472 above). *Hani* in a name refers to a deity of clay or earth. In another category are shrines named for an occupational group; significantly, there are Mononobe Shrines in all parts of the country founded by the *be* (occupational group) of armorers, or by the families of that name wherever they were settled (see n. 218). We find a total of 14 Shidori (Shitsuori) Shrines in 12 different provinces, which indicates that the occupational groups engaged in weaving this kind of hempen cloth were scattered throughout the land.[480] There are quite a number of shrines titled Hyōsu (兵主); this is believed to be a military deity and is sometimes identified with Susano-o-no-mikoto, the storm god of the myths.

Shrines with mythological deities in their names are found everywhere. There are ten shrines to Amaterasu (or the variant Amateru), the Sun Goddess, in addition to the Shrine of the Great Deity in Ise. There are Izanagi-Izanami shrines in Awa, Awaji, and Ise. Besides the Oonamochi Shrine in Izumo there are shrines to that deity in Yamato, Noto, and Harima provinces. The so-called Great Gods of Kumano, originally enshrined in the location in Ou District of Izumo, were also enshrined in Oomi, Tamba, and Shinano, as well as in the present great shrines in Kii (Wakayama Pref.).

Very few shrines at the time of compilation of the *Engi-shiki* reflect the syncretic movement which already had progressed. Shinto deities identified with Buddhist *bodhisattva* became more numerous as time went on, but in this list we find only the Hachiman Daibosatsu Usa-no-miya in Usa District, Buzen Province; the Hachiman Daibosatsu Hakosaki-no-miya in Naka District, Chikuzen; a Yakushi Bosatsu in Kashima District, Hitachi; and a Kokubunji Hyakuraku in Iwami Province. There doubtless were many other enshrinements of *suijaku* deities, even though not recorded in the *Engi-shiki*.

---

[480] A detailed study of these shrines appears in S. Koyama, 'Shitsuori-be no kōkogakuteki kōsatsu', in *Jōdai bunka*, no. 38, Oct. 1969, pp. 14–25.

At the beginning of Book IX we learn that the whole system embraces 3,132 *kami* (celestial and terrestrial) enshrined in 2,861 shrines. They extend from the Shigarewake Jinja in Suwa District, Mutsu Province, in the north (near the present city of Morioka) to the Yaku Jinja in Oosumi Province, Kyushu, in the south; they vary in size from the huge complex of the Grand Shrines of Ise to the minutest local shrine in a humble hamlet. Of the total, there were 492 major (*dai*) and 2,640 minor (*shō*) shrines (strictly speaking, it is the *kami* which are accorded the designation 'major' or 'minor'). To all the *kami* of these shrines, presentations were made at the annual *Toshigoi* Festival in the 2nd month marking the commencement of the agricultural year. Of the 'major' shrines, 304 received offerings from the central government known as *kampei* ('official offerings') which were to be placed on top of offering-tables in the shrines. In addition, 433 'minor' shrines received government offerings which were to be placed *below* the offering-tables (because of lesser rank). The other included 188 'major' shrines which received offerings from the provincial government (*kokuhei*) to be placed on top of offering-tables, and a total of 2,207 'minor' shrines which received provincial official offerings presented below the offering-tables.

Besides the 'major' and 'minor' designation, *kami* of primary importance are labeled *myōjin* (also pronounced *meishin*). These prominent *kami* appear to have emerged from primeval folk worship and acquired pre-eminence because they were believed to be efficacious in answering prayers of the people. As the shrines became systematized into a government-sponsored scheme, some of these local cults received national recognition and classification. There are a total of 285 *myōjin* in the list. The name of a shrine in which more than one deity is worshiped is followed by a number which signifies the number of deities. Thus, in the Inner Shrine of Ise (the Shrine of the Great Deity) three *kami* are enshrined; in the Minushi Shrine in Kuze District, Yamato, ten deities are enshrined. Such additional *kami* are called *aidono no kami* (jointly residing *kami*) and are auxiliary to the main *kami*.

It is difficult to determine what led to a shrine's becoming a registered shrine in the government system, while many other shrines were left out (the so-called *shikigai-sha*). Certainly some shrines rose in importance as seats of flourishing popular cults, others on account of their geographical situation or the physical features of the land. But the chief criterion for selection of important shrines and 'major' deities seems to have been their connection with the Court. How and when the list came into being is not clear. But the *Shoku-nihongi* and the *Kogoshūi* do make mention of a list of government shrines in the Taihō era (701–10). The first compilation of government-registered shrines throughout the land is reported to have been made in the Tempyō era (reign of Shōmu Tennō, 724–49). In this connection, Imbe no Hironari complains in the *Kogoshūi* that the compilation was done under supervision of the Nakatomi Uji and that all the shrines associated with that family (and hence the Fujiwara Uji) were included in the list, while shrines not related to that family were excluded.[481]

---

[481] *Shoku-nihongi*, III. Katō and Hoshino, op. cit. pp. 44–5.

The text of the *Engi-shiki* which was preserved in the keeping of the Urabe Family through the centuries enjoyed considerable care regarding interpretation of the list of shrines. In his epigraph to this ms., dated Kambun 7 (1667), Matsu-shita Kenrin (1637–1703) comments on his long labors in analyzing and correcting the erroneous readings of shrine names. His diligent research and careful emendations are very significant for modern scholars in regard to transcription of the list of shrines. (Nevertheless many alternate readings for these old names still exist.) Also, in the late Tokugawa period Ban Nobutomo (1775–1846) did an encyclopedic study of the Heian shrine system, including all references to the shrines contained in works of the Nara and Heian periods as well as in the text of the *Engi-shiki*. This work, *Jimmyō-chō kōshō*, and his studies on shrines, *Jinja shikō*, are indispensable for study of the shrine system and the pantheon of *kami* of that bygone age.

The plan of Books IX and X and an index to the list, by circuit and province, is found in Appendix II, below.

# BOOK NINE

## REGISTER OF DEITIES (A)

## THE PALACE, THE CAPITAL, THE INNER
## PROVINCES, THE TŌKAIDŌ

3,132  *kami* of Heaven and Earth [enshrined in]
 2,861 shrines, in which 271 *kami* are worshiped jointly[482]
 492 are major *kami* [including]:
   304 (for whom *Toshigoi*, *Tsukinami*, and *Niiname* Festivals are celebrated
    with government offerings presented on top of the tables;[483] of these,
    71 *kami* are also worshiped at the *Ainame* Festival)
   188 (for whom *Toshigoi* is celebrated with provincial offerings)[484]
 2,640 are minor *kami*
   433 (for whom *Toshigoi* is celebrated with government offerings presented
    below the tables)
   2,207 (for whom *Toshigoi* is celebrated with provincial offerings)

36  *kami* worshiped in the Imperial Palace[485]
 23 are worshiped in the Sai-in of the *Jingi-kan* by Sacred Maidens (all are major;
   *Tsukinami* and *Niiname*)
 8 *kami* worshiped by Sacred Maidens (all major; *Tsukinami*, *Niiname*; these
   are likewise worshiped in palaces of the Consort and Heir Apparent)

| | |
|---|---|
| Kami-musubi-no-kami | Takami-musubi-no-kami |
| Tamaru-musubi-no-kami | Iku-musubi-no-kami |
| Taru-musubi-no-kami | Oomiya-no-me-no-kami |
| Miketsu-no-kami | Kotoshironushi-no-kami[486] |

---

[482] *Kami* are enumerated by the auxiliary *za* 座, and additional *kami* worshiped in the same shrine as the main deity are enumerated by *zen* 前.

[483] *Kampei* 官幣 means 'official offerings', and a shrine so designated received offerings for the *kami* sent out from the *Jingi-kan* in the capital. If *Tsukinami* or *Niiname* or *Ainame* festivals were celebrated for a *kami* in addition to the *Toshigoi*, it is so indicated each time.

[484] These shrines are called *kokuhei* 國幣 and are those which receive offerings distributed by the provincial (*kuni*) governments.

[485] Within the Imperial Palace precinct (*kyūchū* 宮中) are included the *kami* who were worshiped in the Sai-in, or sacred courtyard of the *Jingi-kan*, and another thirteen under the supervision of the Ministry of the Imperial Household.

[486] These are the so-called '*musubi* deities', the eight *kami* of the *Jingi-kan*. See n. 309 above.

5 *kami* worshiped by the Igasuri Sacred Maidens (all major; *Tsukinami, Niiname*)

| | |
|---|---|
| Ikui-no-kami | Sakui-no-kami |
| Tsunagai-no-kami | Haigi-no-kami |
| Asuha-no-kami[487] | |

8 *kami* worshiped by the Mikado Sacred Maidens (all major; *Tsukinami, Niiname*)

Kushi-iwamado-no-kami (1 in each of the four gates)

Toyo-iwamado-no-kami (1 in each of the four gates)[488]

2 *kami* worshiped by the Ikushima Sacred Maidens (both major; *Tsukinami, Niiname*)

Ikushima-no-kami                Tarushima-no-kami[489]

3 *kami* worshiped in the Imperial Household Ministry (principal deities;[490] all major; *Tsukinami, Niiname*)

[1 in] Sono Shrine                2 in Kara Shrine

3 *kami* of the Palace Table Office (all minor)

| | |
|---|---|
| Miketsu Shrine | Hono-ikazuchi Shrine |
| Takabe Shrine | |

6 *kami* of the Imperial Sake Office[491] (4 major, 2 minor)

Oomiya-no-me Shrine—4 (all major; *Tsukinami, Niiname*)

Sakadono Shrine—2 (both minor)

Sakamitsu-o-no-kami            Sakamitsu-me-no-kami

1 *kami* of the Water Office (minor)

Narukami (Naru-ikazuchi) Shrine

3 *kami* of the Capital (all major)

2 in shrines in Nijō, Left Capital (both: *Tsukinami, Niiname, Ainame*)

Futonoto-no-mikoto-no-kami (main shrines: Futonoto Shrines in Souno-kami Dist., Yamato Prov., and Shimo(tsu)agata Dist., Tsushima Prov.)

---

[487] This set of *kami* of the water-supply and grounds of the Palace are directly invoked in the ritual for the *Toshigoi* Festival. See n. 310 above.

[488] The ritual for the Festival of the August Gates (*Mikado-matsuri*) is no. 9 in Bk VIII of *E-S*, translated above. See n. 313.

[489] In the ritual for the *Toshigoi* and *Tsukinami* festivals, the *kami* whose worship is conducted by the Ikushima Sacred Maidens are invoked as: 'Ikukuni and Tarukuni'. The names given here are equivalent to those, since *shima* meant 'land', just as *kuni* did. The *Kogoshūi* says that the Ikushima-no-kami are the Spirits of the entire land. See Katō and Hoshino, op. cit. p. 34, and p. 70, n. 61.

[490] The principal deities, or *myōjin* (名神 or 明神), were the outstanding *kami* who had demonstrated extraordinary powers. They were feted in the *Myōjin-matsuri*, a festival held on special occasions. The list comprising 285 *myōjin* shrines is given in *E-S*, Bk III, on the Extraordinary Festivals (*rinji-sai*).

[491] The importance of sake and the sacredness of its brewing and its use, were second only to that of rice, from which it was made. The deities of sake brewing were worshiped whenever and wherever the facilities for fermentation were set up within the Palace, or for festivals away from the Palace, as in the case of the *Daijō-sai*, when a special building for the purpose was erected.

Kushimachi-no-mikoto-no-kami (main shrine: Ama-no-kaguyama ni masu Kushima-no-mikoto, To-ochi Dist., Yamato Prov.)[492]

1 *kami* dwelling in Shijō in the Left Capital (*Tsukinami, Niiname*): Hayafusa-no-kami

658 *kami* in the Five Inner Provinces *(Kinai)* 231 major; 427 minor
YAMASHIRO Province—122

 53 Major (all *Tsukinami, Niiname*; 11 of them also *Ainame*)
 69 Minor (all receive government offerings)
 *Otokuni District*—19 (5 major; 14 minor)
  Hatsukashi ni masu Takami-musubi-no-kami (major; *Tsukinami, Niiname*)
  Ooi Shrine     Yodo Shrine
  Ishitsukuri Shrine
  Otokuni no Hono-ikazuchi Shrine[493]
  Mitani Shrine    Hashirita Shrine
  Mukae Shrine    Kuninaka Shrine
  Mamuta Shrine   Ootoshi Shrine
  Kamukawa Shrine  Iwai Shrine
  Suhara Shrine    Kuga Shrine
  Irino Shrine     Okura Shrine
  Yoritamate-matsurikitaru-sakatoke Shrine (principal deity, major; *Tsukinami, Niiname*; former name: Yamasaki Shrine)
  Kamutari Shrine
 *Kadono District*—20 (14 major; 6 minor)
  Tsukiyomi Shrine of Kadono (principal deity, major; *Tsukinami, Niiname*)
  Konoshima ni masu Amateru-mimusubi (principal deity; major; *Tsukinami, Ainame, Niiname*)
  Ochikawa Shrine   Ato Shrine
  Matsuno-o Shrine—2 (both principal deities, major; *Tsukinami, Ainame, Niiname*)[494]
  Fukagawa Shrine   Ochikawa-mikami Shrine
  Ichii-tani Shrine
  Four *kami* of Hirano (all principal deities, major; *Tsukinami, Niiname*)[495]
  Mume-no-miya—4 (all principal deities; major; *Tsukinami, Niiname*)
  Amatsu-iwato-wakewaka-hime Shrine (principal deity, major; *Tsukinami, Niiname*)

---

[492] These entries regarding the two *kami* of the Left Capital are virtually the only ones which relate for us certain shrines to their original or parent shrine. If more such relations were recorded, we would be able to determine the relative antiquity of shrines, as well as the movement of the worship of certain *kami* from one locality to another.

[493] Although written Oo-ikazuchi 大雷 here, editors have emended this to correlate with Hono-ikazuchi (火雷) listed in Uchi District, Yamato Province.

[494] Matsuno-o Shrine, founded in the eighth century, was the *ujigami* shrine of the Hata Uji. Procedures for its annual festival are given in *E-S*, Bk I. Another Matsuno-o Shrine appears in Kawada District, Tamba Province.

[495] For the deities of Hirano, see n. 345 above.

Tomo-uji Shrine (major; *Tsukinami, Niiname*)

Oosake 大酒 (formerly written 大辟)

*Otagi District*—21 (8 major; 13 minor)

Kamo-no-wakeikazuchi Shrine (principal deity, major; *Tsukinami, Ainame, Niiname*) (the Upper Shrine)

Izumo-no-inoe Shrine (major; *Tsukinami, Ainame, Niiname*)

Kamo-no-mioya Shrine—2 (both principal deities; major; *Tsukinami, Ainame, Niiname*) (the Lower Shrine)

Izumo-no-takano Shrine          Kamo-no-yamanokuchi Shrine[496]

Kamo-no-hani Shrine

Ono Shrine—2 (mattocks, quivers)[497]

Kuga Shrine                      Mato Shrine

Suwa Shrine                      Itata Shrine

Kifune Shrine

Kamo-no-kawa-ai ni masu Kosoyake Shrine (principal deity, major; *Tsukinami, Ainame, Niiname*)

Kamo-no-okamoto Shrine          Oota Shrine

Mii Shrine                       Ooshiba Shrine

Takahashi Shrine

Katayama-no-miko Shrine (major; *Tsukinami, Ainame, Niiname*)

*Kii District*—8 (3 major; 5 minor)

Mimoro Shrine

Inari Shrine—3 (all principal deities, major; *Tsukinami, Niiname*)

Oomukura Shrine

Asukata Shrine (also called Kaki-no-moto)

Mahataki Shrine—2

*Uji District*—10 (5 major; 5 minor)

Uji Shrine—2 (mattocks, quivers)

Himukai Shrine

Kowata Shrine—3 (all principal deities, major; *Tsukinami, Niiname*)

Ama-no-hohi-no-mikoto Shrine

Uji-no-ochikata Shrine (mattocks, quivers)

Yamashina Shrine—2 (both principal deities, major; *Tsukinami, Niiname*)

*Kuze District*—24 (11 major; 13 minor)

Iwata Shrine (major; *Tsukinami, Niiname*)

Minushi Shrine—10 (all major; *Tsukinami, Niiname; Ainame* celebrated for Minushi no Amateru-mitama-no-kami and Minushi no Yamashiro no Ookunitama)

---

[496] Concerning the *yamanokuchi* shrines, see n. 321 above.

[497] One must consult the first book of the *E-S* for the precise lists of items to be presented to the *kami* at the *Toshigoi, Tsukinami, Ainame,* and *Niiname* festivals. For reasons not explained, additional offerings of quivers (*yanagui*) and mattocks (*kuwa*) have been added to the names of certain shrines in this list. Votive offerings usually included farm implements and ceremonial weapons.

Arami Shrine                        Sakuri (Sakuha) Shrine—3
Mito Shrine—3                       Asakura (Asamuku) Shrine
Iseta Shrine—3 (mattocks, quivers)
Ookura Shrine
Muroki Shrine
*Tsutsuki District*—14 (3 major; 11 minor)
Kabai-no-tsuki Shrine (major; *Tsukinami, Niiname*)
Suchi Shrine
Tsukiyomi Shrine (major; *Tsukinami, Niiname*)
Kuioka Shrine (mattock, quiver)
Taka Shrine (mattocks, quivers) Uchi Shrine—2
Awa Shrine                          Tanakurahiko Shrine
Sakakono Shrine                     Sakaya Shrine
Kamunabi Shrine                     Amatsukami Shrine
Kunitsukami Shrine
*Sakaraka District*—6 (4 major; 2 minor)
Hafusono Shrine                     Waki ni masu Amenofukime Shrine
Kamuhara no Takeinada-hime Shrine
Sakaraka Shrine
Okada-no-kamo Shrine (major; *Tsukinami, Niiname*)
Okada-no-kunitsukami Shrine (major; *Tsukinami, Niiname*)
YAMATO Province—286
   128 Major (all: *Tsukinami, Niiname*; 38 of them also *Ainame*)
   158 Minor (all receive *kampei*)
*Sounokami District*—37 (9 major; 28 minor)
Naru-ikazuchi Shrine              Izakawa-no-ōkami-no-miko—3
Saoka Shrine—8                    Izakawa-no-awa
Unatari no Takami-musubi Shrine (major; *Tsukinami, Niiname*)
Wani no Akasaka-hiko Shrine (major; *Tsukinami, Niiname*)
Anafuki Shrine                    Wani-no-shimo Shrine—2
Nara-no-tsuhiko Shrine (mattocks and quivers)
Kamuhata Shrine                   Takahashi Shrine
Futonoto Shrine (major; *Tsukinami, Niiname*)
Iefuse Shrine                     Ooyamato-himukai Shrine
Yagyū-no-yamanokuchi Shrine (major; *Tsukinami, Niiname*)
Kasuga Shrine                     Himeta Shrine
The four *kami* worshiped at Kasuga (all principal deities, major; *Tsukinami, Niiname*)[498]
Akaho Shrine                      Shimada Shrine
Misaki-no-morihara-iwatachi-no-mikoto Shrine

[498] Kasuga Jinja, founded by the Fujiwara Uji in the 8th century to enshrine its *ujigami* in the Nara capital, was of great importance. Its festival Procedures are given in *E-S*, Bk I, and the ritual for the festival is the second one in Bk VIII.

Amenoiwasui Shrine               Iotachi Shrine
Amenoiwatachi Shrine
*Sounoshimo District*—10 (4 major; 6 minor)
  Yata no Kushitamahiko Shrine—2 (both major; *Tsukinami, Niiname*)
  Sou no Miagata (major; *Tsukinami, Niiname*)
  Sugatahime Shrine—2 (mattocks; quivers)
  Saki Shrine                    Sugawara Shrine
  Tomi Shrine                    Sugata Shrine
  Izanagi Shrine (major; *Tsukinami, Niiname*)
*Heguri District*—20 (12 major; 8 minor)
  Tatsuta ni masu Ame-no-mihashira-kuni-no-mihashira Shrine—2 (both
    principal deities, major; *Tsukinami, Niiname*)
  Tatsutahiko and Tatsutahime Shrine—2
  Ikoma ni masu Ikomatsuhiko Shrine—2 (both major; *Tsukinami, Niiname*)
  Heguri no Iwatoko Shrine (major; *Tsukinami, Niiname*)
  Ikoma-no-yamanokuchi Shrine
  Five *kami* of Heguri Shrine (all major; *Tsukinami, Niiname*)
  Kudo Shrine
  Heguri ni masu Ki-no-uji Shrine (principal deities, major; *Tsukinami,
    Niiname*)
  Inoe (Ikami) Shrine            Funayama Shrine
  Mikushi Shrine                 Kamuoka Shrine
  Unkanji ni masu Naramoto Shrine
*Hirose District*—5 (one major; 4 minor)
  Hirose ni masu Waka-ukanome-no-mikoto Shrine (principal deity, major;
    *Tsukinami, Niiname*)
  Sanuki Shrine                  Kushitamahime-no-mikoto Shrine
  Hono-ikazuchi-no-mikoto Shrine
  Ue Shrine
*Katsuraginokami District*—17 (12 major; 5 minor)
  Shimotsukamo-yaekotoshironushi-no-mikoto Shrine—2 (principal deities,
    major; *Tsukinami, Ainame, Niiname*)
  Katsuragi no Mitoshi Shrine (principal deity, major; *Tsukinami, Niiname*)
  Katsuragi ni masu Hitokotonushi Shrine (principal deity, major; *Tsuki-
    nami, Ainame, Niiname*)
  Tata Shrine (mattocks, quivers)
  Nagara Shrine (mattocks, quivers)
  Kose-no-yamanokuchi Shrine
  Katsuragi-no-mikumari Shrine (principal deity, major; *Tsukinami, Nii-
    name*)[499]

[499] *Mikumari* ('water-dividing') deities are listed in Bks I, III, and VIII (in the *norito* for the *Toshigoi* and *Tsukinami* festivals), and here in Yamato Province. There are but four shrines: at Yoshino, Uda, Katsuragi, and Tsuge (also pron. Tsuke or Chikkei). See n. 322 above.

Kamo-no-yamanokuchi Shrine

Takamahiko Shrine (principal deity, major; *Tsukinami, Ainame, Niiname*)

Katsuragi no Ooe Shrine

Ooanamochi Shrine

Ookura-no-hime Shrine

Takakamo no Ajisuki-taka-hikone-no-mikoto Shrine—4 (all principal deities; major; *Tsukinami, Ainame, Niiname*)

*Katsuraginoshimo District*—18 (13 major; 5 minor)

Katsuragi no Shidori ni masu Ame-no-hazuchi-no-mikoto Shrine (major; *Tsukinami, Niiname*)

Kataoka Shrine (principal deity; major; *Tsukinami, Niiname*)

Nagao Shrine (major; *Tsukinami, Niiname*)

Iwazono ni masu Takutsutama Shrine—2 (both major; *Tsukinami, Niiname*)

Tsukita ni masu Hitokotoneko Shrine (major; *Tsukinami, Niiname*)

Kanamura Shrine (major; *Tsukinami, Niiname*)

Katsuragi no Miagata (Miyagata) Shrine (major; *Tsukinami, Niiname*)

Fukamizo Shrine

Hohata Shrine (principal deity; major; *Tsukinami, Niiname*)

Shitsumi Shrine                    Izanagi Shrine

Taimatsuhiko Shrine—2              Taima-no-yamanokuchi Shrine

Oosaka-no-yamanokuchi Shrine (major; *Tsukinami, Niiname*)

Katsuragi no Futakami Shrine—2 (major; *Tsukinami, Niiname*)

*Oshinomi District*—3 (2 major, one minor)

Ishi Shrine

Katsuragi ni masu Hono-ikazuchi Shrine—2 (both principal; major; *Tsukinami, Ainame, Niiname*)

*Uchi District*—11 (all minor)

Uchi Shrine                  Atahime Shrine

Araki Shrine                 Niukawa Shrine

Futami Shrine                Miyasaki no Narukami Shrine

Hono-ikazuchi Shrine         Takama-no-kishino Shrine

Ochisoma Shrine              Takama-no-yamasatao Shrine

Hito-ose Shrine

*Yoshino District*—10 (5 major, 5 minor)

Yoshino-no-mikumari Shrine (major; *Tsukinami, Niiname*)

Yoshino-no-yamanokuchi Shrine (major; *Tsukinami, Niiname*)

Oonamochi Shrine (principal deity, major; *Tsukinami, Ainame, Niiname*)

Niu-no-kawakami Shrine (principal deity, major; *Tsukinami, Niiname*)

Kane-no-mitake Shrine (principal deity, major; *Tsukinami, Ainame, Niiname*)

Takahoko Shrine              Kawakami-no-kashio Shrine (mattocks)

Iwata Shrine                 Haho (Namiho) Shrine (mattocks)

Hahime (Namihime) Shrine

*Uda District*—17 (one major, 16 minor)

Uda-no-mikumari Shrine (major; *Tsukinami, Niiname*)

Aki Shrine (mattocks and quivers)

Kadomori Shrine (mattock, quiver)

Niu Shrine (mattock, quiver)

Mitsue Shrine                    Mukumoto Shrine

Takatsuno Shrine—2 (mattocks, quivers)

Yatakarasu Shrine (mattock, quiver)

Misosakahime-no-mikoto Shrine (or Umasakahime-no-mikoto)

Mii Shrine                       Okada-no-ohata-no-mikoto Shrine

Miwa-no-miko-mimusubime-no-mikoto Shrine

Sakurami Shrine                  Tsuruginushi Shrine

Murō-no-ryūketsu Shrine          Tsukanaki Shrine

*Shikinokami District*—35 (15 major, 20 minor)

Oomiwa no Oomononushi Shrine (principal deity, major; *Tsukinami, Ainame, Niiname*)

Miwa ni masu Himukai Shrine (major; *Tsukinami, Niiname*)

Anashi ni masu Hyōsu Shrine (principal deity, major; *Tsukinami, Ainame, Niiname*)

Makimuku ni masu Wakamitama Shrine (major; *Tsukinami, Ainame, Niiname*)

Osata ni masu Amateru-mitama Shrine (major; *Tsukinami, Ainame, Niiname*)

Shiki no Miyagata Shrine (major; *Tsukinami, Niiname*)

Sai ni masu Ookami-no-aramitama Shrine—5 (mattocks, quivers)

Osaka-no-ikune Shrine (major; *Tsukinami, Niiname*)

Ha(tsu)se-no-yamanokuchi Shrine (major; *Tsukinami, Niiname*)

Osaka-no-yamanokuchi Shrine (major; *Tsukinami, Niiname*)

Tomi Shrine                      Eguri Shrine

Minakuchi Shrine

Kuwauchi Shrine—2 (mattocks, quivers)

Hikita Shrine—2 (mattocks, quivers)

Uda-no-yorita Shrine             Tamatsura Shrine

Izanagi Shrine                   Tsunakoshi Shrine

Toshishiro Shrine                Anashi no Oohyōsu Shrine

Wakasakura Shrine                Nabekura Shrine

Takaya-abe Shrine—3 (principal deities, major; *Tsukinami, Niiname*)

Munakata Shrine—3 (principal deities, major; *Tsukinami, Niiname*)[500]

*Shikinoshimo District*—17 (3 major, 14 minor)

Muraya ni masu Mifutsuhime Shrine (major; *Tsukinami, Ainame, Niiname*)

Ike no Asakiriyokokihatahime Shrine (major; *Tsukinami, Ainame, Niiname*)

Kagamitsukuri ni masu Amateru-mitama Shrine (major; *Tsukinami, Niiname*)

Chishiro Shrine

---

[500] See also the 'major' Munakata Shrine in Munakata District, Chikuzen Province, and 'minor' Munakata Shrines in other localities.

Kitashita Shrine—2 (mattocks, quivers)

Yamato-onchi Shrine (mattock, quiver)

Himekuha Shrine

Hatori Shrine—2 (mattocks, quivers)

Futsu Shrine (mattock, quiver)    Itoi Shrine (quiver)

Muraya Shrine—2    Kagamitsukuri-ita Shrine

Kagamitsukuri-make Shrine    Kususumi Shrine

*Takechi District*—54 (33 major, 21 minor)

Takechi-miagata ni masu Kamo no Kotoshironushi Shrine (major; *Tsukinami, Niiname*)

Four *kami* of Asuka Shrine (all principal *kami*, major; *Tsukinami, Ainame, Niiname*)

Soga no Sogatsuhiko Shrine—2 (both major; *Tsukinami, Niiname*)

Asuka-no-yamanokuchi Shrine (major; *Tsukinami, Niiname*)

Four *kami* of Amagashi (all major; *Tsukinami, Ainame, Niiname*)

Inashiro (Toshishiro) Shrine (major; *Tsukinami, Niiname*)

Musa Shrine (major; *Tsukinami, Niiname*)

Unebi-no-yamanokuchi Shrine (major; *Tsukinami, Niiname*)

Takechi no Miagata Shrine (principal deity, major; *Tsukinami, Niiname*)

Kose-no-yama ni masu Iwakurahiko Shrine

Sagi-no-su Shrine (quiver)

Karokomura Shrine—2 (both major; *Tsukinami, Niiname*)

Ame-no-takechi Shrine (major; *Tsukinami, Niiname*)

Haruta Shrine (mattock, quiver)

Futotama-no-mikoto Shrine—4 (all principal deities, major; *Tsukinami, Niiname*)

Kushitama-no-mikoto Shrine—4 (all major; *Tsukinami, Niiname*)

Kayanarumi-no-mikoto Shrine

Asuka-no-kawakami no Usatakihime-no-mikoto Shrine

Higashi-ōtanihime-no-mikoto Shrine

Kuretsuhiko Shrine

Kawamata Shrine—3 (all major; *Tsukinami, Niiname*)

Ketsuwaki Shrine    Ootoshi Shrine—2

Hata Shrine (mattock, quiver)    Mitoshi Shrine (mattock, quiver)

Omiashi Shrine

Torisaka Shrine—2 (mattock, quiver)

Taki-no-moto Shrine    Kosetsuhiko-no-mikoto Shrine

Amatsu-iwatowake Shrine

Hatamikai Shrine (major; *Tsukinami, Niiname*)

Kume no Miagata Shrine—3

Ibukuikazuchi-naruikazuchi-yoshino Ookuzumitama Shrine—2 (both principal deities, major; *Tsukinami, Niiname*)

*To-ochi District*—19 (11 major, 8 minor)

Oo-no-mishiritsuhiko Shrine—2 (both principal deities, major; *Tsukinami, Ainame, Niiname*)

To-ochi no Miagata Shrine (major; *Tsukinami, Niiname*)
Mehara no Takami-musubi Shrine—2 (both major; *Tsukinami, Niiname*)
Iware-no-yamanokuchi Shrine (major; *Tsukinami, Niiname*)
Unebi-no-takehaniyasu Shrine (major; *Tsukinami, Niiname*)
Miminashi-no-yamanokuchi Shrine (major)
Taketa Shrine
Sakato Shrine (mattock, quiver)
Kobe Shrine—2 (both major; *Tsukinami, Niiname*)
Unebi-tsutamoto Shrine (mattock, quiver)
Ama-no-kaguyama ni masu Kushima-no-mikoto Shrine (major; *Tsukinami,*
    *Niiname*; formerly named Oomatonochi-no-kami)
Miko-no-kami-no-mikoto Shrine    Himemiko-no-mikoto Shrine
Omori-no-kami-no-mikoto Shrine  Yatsuki-no-kami-no-mikoto Shrine
    (the four preceding are the *ōyashiro-no-miko-no-kami*)
Shitai (Orii) Shrine
*Yamanobe District*—13 (7 major, 6 minor)
Ooyamato no Ookunitama Shrine—3 (all principal deities, major; *Tsuki-*
    *nami, Ainame, Niiname*)
Isonokami-no-furu-no-mitama Shrine (principal deity, major; *Tsukinami,*
    *Ainame, Niiname*)
Tsuge-no-mikumari Shrine (major; *Tsukinami, Niiname*)
Yama-no-be no Miagata Shrine (major; *Tsukinami, Niiname*)
Shirotsutsumi Shrine              Yatsuki Shrine
Tsuge-no-yamanokuchi Shrine (major; *Tsukinami, Niiname*)
Hafurita Shrine                   Isonokami-ichi Shrine
Shimobe Shrine                    Izumo-takeo Shrine

KAWACHI Province—113
23 Major (all *Tsukinami, Niiname*; of these *Ainame* is held for eight)
90 Minor (all *kampei*)
*Ishikawa District*—9 (all minor)
Kanko Shrine (mattock, quiver)  Shinaga Shrine
Take-mikumari Shrine            Ooge-no-okami Shrine
Mikukuru-no-mitama Shrine       Sabi Shrine
Kanko-sabi Shrine              Isuka Shrine
Kamonarahita Shrine
*Furuchi District*—2 (both minor)
Tokari Shrine                  Takaya Shrine
*Asukabe District*—5 (3 major, 2 minor)
Morimoto Shrine—2 (both principal deities, major; *Tsukinami, Niiname*)
Asukabe Shrine (principal deity, major; *Tsukinami, Niiname*)
Hakutahiko Shrine (mattock)    Hakutahime Shrine (mattock)
*Oogata District*—11 (all minor)
Amayukawata Shrine             Sukunakawata Shrine
Kanayamahiko Shrine            Kanayamahime Shrine
Takuhiko Shrine                Takuhime Shrine

Ookoma Shrine                Wakayamatohiko-no-mikoto Shrine
Wakayamatohime-no-mikoto Shrine (mattock)
Iwagami (Ishigami) Shrine      Tokoyokihime Shrine

*Takayasu District*—10 (4 major, 6 minor)
  Omuchi Shrine—2 (both principal deities, major; *Tsukinami, Ainame, Niiname*)
  Tsufukumi Shrine
  Amaterasu-ō-mikami-takakura Shrine—2 (both major; *Tsukinami, Niiname*; formerly called Kasugabe-no-kami)
  Tama-no-oya Shrine      Mioya Shrine
  Kamo Shrine            Samatado Shrine
  Kasugabe no yashiro ni masu Miko Shrine

*Kawachi District*—10 (4 major, 6 minor)
  Hiraoka Shrine—4 (principal deities; major; *Tsukinami, Ainame, Niiname*)
  Tsuhara Shrine      Kajinashi Shrine (mattock)
  Ootsu Shrine        Kurihara Shrine (mattock)
  Iwakiri-no-tsurugiya-no-mikoto Shrine—2

*Sarara District*—6 (one major, 5 minor)
  Suhama Shrine (mattock, quiver)
  Mitsukue Shrine
  Takamiya Shrine (major; *Tsukinami, Niiname*)
  Tsuhoko Shrine
  Takamiya-no-ōmori-no-mioya Shrine
  Kunaka Shrine

*Mamuta District*—5 (all minor)
  Tsutsumine Shrine
  Tsushimabe Shrine (mattock, quiver)
  Hosoya Shrine      Takase Shrine
  Okami Shrine

*Katano District*—2 (both minor)
  Katano Shrine (mattock, quiver) Kususumi Shrine (mattock)

*Wakae District*—22 (2 major; 20 minor)
  Sakai Shrine—2      Yatsukuri (Yahagi) Shrine
  Wakae-no-kagami Shrine
  Mino-no-agatanushi Shrine—2 (mattocks, quivers)
  Iwata Shrine—3      Kawamata Shrine (mattock, quiver)
  Yuge Shrine—2 (both major; *Tsukinami, Ainame, Niiname*)
  Tsurumishima Shrine (mattock) Nagara Shrine (mattock)
  Okibe Shrine        Mito (Iyato) Shrine
  Uba Shrine          Shibukawa Shrine—2
  Kurusu Shrine      Katsura Shrine
  Nakamura Shrine

*Shibukawa District*—6 (all minor)
  Kamo-takata Shrine     Yokono Shrine
  Hamukoso Shrine      Michibe Shrine

Koma Shrine                          Tsurumi Shrine
*Shiki District*—14 (6 major, 8 minor)
  Shikiagatanushi Shrine (major; *Tsukinami, Niiname*)
  Nagano Shrine                       Shiki Shrine
  Kuroda Shrine
  Makimoto (Kusumoto) Shrine—3 (mattocks, quivers)
  Shiki-no-nagayoshi Shrine—2 (both major; *Tsukinami, Niiname*)
  Tomohayashi-no-uji Shrine
  (Shiki-no-)Karakuni Shrine
  Masamune Shrine—3 (all major; *Tsukinami, Niiname*)
*Tajihi District*—11 (3 major, 8 minor)
  Tajihi Shrine                       Amamikoso Shrine (mattock, quiver)
  Sayamatsutsumi Shrine (major; *Tsukinami, Niiname*)
  Ootsu Shrine—3 (mattocks, quivers)
  Sayama Shrine (major; *Tsukinami, Niiname*)
  Sugau Shrine (major; *Tsukinami, Niiname*)
  Sakaya Shrine                       Ichimoto Shrine (mattock, quiver)
  Tai Shrine
IZUMI Province—62
  1   Major (*Tsukinami, Niiname*)
  61  Minor (all *kampei*)
*Ootori District*—24 (1 major, 23 minor)
  Ootori Shrine (principal deity, major; *Tsukinami, Niiname*)
  Yamai Shrine (mattock, quiver)   Ootori Shrine (mattock, quiver)
  Mitami Shrine                       Oshiwake Shrine
  Ikukuni Shrine (mattock, quiver)
  Inahikari Shrine
  Iwatsuta Shrine                     Tonoki Shrine (mattock, quiver)
  Hachita Shrine (mattock)            Sue-no-arata Shrine—2 [mattocks]
  Kuni Shrine                         Kamo[-ta] Shrine
  Takashi (Takaiwa) Shrine            Ootori-miwahi Shrine
  Tachihayahime-no-mikoto Shrine
  Ootori-ise Shrine
  Ootori-hama Shrine (mattock)        Saka-no-ue Shrine
  Akikuchi Shrine                     Sakurai Shrine
  Ootoshi Shrine (mattock)            Hibe (Kusakabe) Shrine
*Izumi District*—28 (all minor)
  Onouto Shrine—2                     Hakata Shrine
  Yagi Shrine                         Izumi-anashi Shrine—2
  Hyōsu Shrine                        Awa Shrine
  Sone Shrine                         Izumi-inoe Shrine
  Arima (Arimo) Shrine                Yamanao Shrine
  Yashiro(-no-mura) Shrine—2          Hokura Shrine
  Izumi Shrine                        Kusumoto Shrine
  Awaji Shrine                        Okami Shrine

Hata Shrine

Tsugawa (Tsumikawa) Shrine—5 (mattocks)

Marukasa Shrine               Furufu Shrine

Hijiri Shrine

*Hine District*—10 (all minor)

   O (Okami) Shrine—2               Kamusaki Shrine

   Hihashiri Shrine               Hine Shrine (mattock, quiver)

   Kakita Shrine (mattock, quiver)   Hata Shrine

   Kutama (Kunitama) Shrine       Okami Shrine

   Hime Shrine (mattock)

SETTSU Province—75

  26 Major (all *Tsukinami, Niiname*; of these 5 also *Ainame*)

  49 Minor (all *kampei*)

*Sumiyoshi District*—22 (10 major, 12 minor)

   Sumiyoshi Shrine—4 (all principal deities, major; *Tsukinami, Ainame, Niiname*)[501]

   Ooyosami Shrine—4 (all principal deities, major; *Tsukinami, Ainame, Niiname*)

   Kusatsu-Ootoshi Shrine (mattock, quiver)

   Nakatomu-sumuchi Shrine (major; *Tsukinami, Niiname*)

   Kamu-sumuchi Shrine (mattock, quiver)

   Tatehara Shrine

   Sumuchi-sone Shrine           Todorokihime-no-mikoto Shrine

   Akaruhime-no-mikoto Shrine

   Ame-no-mikumari-toyoura-no-mikoto Shrine

   Nunotahime-no-mikoto Shrine

   Oowatatsumi Shrine—2 (formerly Tsumori-no-ujibito-no-kami)[502]

   Tame Shrine                   Funatama Shrine

   Ikune Shrine (major; *Tsukinami, Niiname*)

*Higashinari District*—4 (3 major, 1 minor)

---

[501] In *E-S*, Bk II, the Yasoshima Festival is held to venerate the four Sumiyoshi (earlier name: Suminoe) gods, the four Ooyosami deities, two sea gods, two Tarumi, and two Sumuchi deities. The Sumiyoshi Shrine is the seat of the oldest recorded worship in Settsu Province. In the *Kojiki* and *Nihongi* the Palace of Oojin Tennō is called Oosumi-no-miya: and Nintoku Tennō had his palace at Suminoe on the shore of Naniwa. The *Kojiki* states that the three great gods of Suminoe were: Soko-tsutsu-no-o-no-mikoto, Naka-tsutsu-no-o-no-mikoto and Uwa-tsutsu-no-o-no-mikoto. These three may have been war gods associated with the eastward conquest of the Yamato tribe. In the story of Empress Jingū's conquest of Korea the sea-gods rise to importance, but it is also said these Suminoe deities were taken and transplanted in Silla. Thus the fourth deity at Sumiyoshi is believed to be an enshrinement of the Empress Jingū. See T. Yamane, *The Naniwa Courts and the Sumiyoshi Shrine*, pp. 11 ff.

[502] In the *Kojiki*, Chap. 11, three Watatsumi deities are named: Soko-tsu-watatsumi, Naka-tsu-watatsumi and Uwa-tsu-watatsumi. These deities may also be connected with eastward migration from the Continent in proto-historic times, as we find a Watatsumi Jinja enshrining a *myōjin*, and a Watatsumi-no-mikoto Jinja in Kanzuagata District on Tsushima Island, and a Watatsumi Jinja and Watatsumi *myōjin* shrine both in Shimoagata District in the same province.

Naniwa ni masu Ikukuni(-Sakikuni)-tama Shrine—2 (both principal deities, major; *Tsukinami, Ainame, Niiname*)

Himekoso Shrine (principal deity, major; *Tsukinami, Ainame, Niiname*)

Achihayao Shrine

*Nishinari District*—1 (major)

Igasuri Shrine (major; *Tsukinami, Niiname*)[503]

*Shimanokami District*—3 (all minor)

Akuta (Akuto) Shrine                    Nomi Shrine

Kamuhatori Shrine

*Shimanoshimo District*—17 (5 major, 12 minor)

Niiya ni masu Amateru-mitama Shrine—3 (all principal deities, major; *Tsukinami, Niiname*; of these, for Amateru-mitama only, the *Ainame* is held)

Ama-no-iwatowake Shrine        Sukuku Shrine—2 (mattock, quiver)

Ai Shrine (mattock, quiver)        Inoe Shrine (mattock, quiver)

Hashiriochi Shrine (mattock, quiver)

Sawaragi Shrine

Mitegura Shrine (mattock, quiver)

Mure Shrine

Mishimakamo Shrine

Izanagi Shrine—2 (both major; *Tsukinami, Niiname*)

Mizokui Shrine                    Oota Shrine

*Teshima District*—5 (2 major, 3 minor)

Inatsuhiko Shrine—2            Hosokawa Shrine

Tarumi Shrine (principal deity, major; *Tsukinami, Niiname*)

Aida Shrine (principal deity, major; *Tsukinami, Niiname*)

*Kawanobe District*—7 (all minor)

Isagu Shrine (mattock, quiver)    Takahime-no-fu (Takamefu) Shrine

Kamo Shrine                    Ikota Shrine

Tada Shrine                    Obe Shrine

Himefu Shrine

*Muko District*—4 (2 major, 2 minor)

Hirota Shrine (principal deity, major; *Tsukinami, Ainame, Niiname*)

Natsugi Shrine (mattock, quiver)

Iwashitsu Shrine                Okata Shrine

*Muhara (Uhara) District*—3 (all minor)

Kawachi-no-kunitama Shrine [mattock, quiver][504]

Ookuninushi-no-nishi Shrine (mattock, quiver)

Hokura Shrine (mattock, quiver)

*Yatabe District*—3 (2 major, 1 minor)

Ikuta Shrine (principal deity, major; *Tsukinami, Ainame, Niiname*)

---

[503] Igasuri: see n. 310 above.
[504] Material in brackets has been supplied, | though not appearing in all mss. of *E-S*.

Nagata Shrine (principal deity, major; *Tsukinami, Ainame, Niiname*)
Minume Shrine
*Arima District*—3 (1 major, 2 minor)

Arima Shrine                     Kuchi Shrine (mattock, quiver)
Yu Shrine (major; *Tsukinami, Niiname*)
*Nose District*—3 [all minor]

Kini (Kine) Shrine               Kusasa Shrine
Noma Shrine

731  *kami* in the Tōkaidō
  52  Major (for 19 of these the *Tsukinami* and *Niiname* festivals are held)
  679  Minor
IGA Province—25 (1 major, 24 minor)
  *Ahe District*—9 (1 major, 8 minor)

Yafuta Shrine                    Utsuka Shrine
Hataki Shrine                    Suchiaraki Shrine
Ahekuni Shrine (major)           Sasa Shrine
Anaishi (Anashi) Shrine          Makiyama Shrine
Omiya Shrine
  *Yamada District*—3 (all minor)

Tosaka (Torisaka) Shrine         Awa Shrine
Ashi Shrine
  *Iga District*—11 (all minor)

Kine (Konone) Shrine             Tamori Shrine
Hichi (Hine) Shrine              Oomura Shrine
Hihiki Shrine                    Hishiki Shrine
Enako Shrine                     Ita Shrine
Omine Shrine                     Takase Shrine
Sakato Shrine
  *Nahari District*—2 (both minor)

Nai Shrine                       Unane-no-fushimi Shrine
ISE  Province—253
  18  Major (for 14 of whom *Tsukinami* and *Niiname* festivals are held)
  235  Minor
  *Watarai District*—58 (14 major, 44 minor)[505]

Oomikami-no-miya [Shrine of the Great Deity]—3 (2 *aidono* deities; all
major; *Tsukinami, Niiname*)
Aramatsuri-no-miya (major; *Tsukinami, Niiname*)
Takihara-no-miya (major; *Tsukinami, Niiname*)
Izanagi-no-miya—2 (1 is Izanami-no-mikoto; both major; *Tsukinami,
Niiname*)

---

[505] In this district and other districts of Ise   this list and the ones in *E-S*, Bk IV.
Province, inconsistencies will be found between

Tsukiyomi-no-miya—2 (1 is Aramitama-no-mikoto; both major; *Tsuki-nami, Niiname*)

Watarai-no-miya—4 (3 are *aidono* deities; all major; *Tsukinami, Niiname*)

Taka-no-miya (major; *Tsukinami, Niiname*)

Asakuma Shrine

| | |
|---|---|
| Kano Shrine | Kamo Shrine |
| Satakuninari Shrine | Tanoe Shrine |
| Kusanagi Shrine | Sonō (Sonau) Shrine |
| Iso Shrine | Takihara Shrine |
| Tsukiyomi Shrine | Yuta Shrine |
| Narahara Shrine | Oomizu Shrine |
| Tsunaga-no-ōmizu Shrine | Ookunitamahime Shrine |
| Mike Shrine | Ootsuchi-no-mioya Shrine |
| Tanoe-no-ōmizu Shrine | Kunitsumioya Shrine |
| Sakate-no-kuninari Shrine | Awa-ōji (Awa-no-miko) Shrine |
| Kugutsuhime Shrine | Kawara-no-kuninari Shrine |
| Ooma-no-kuninari Shrine | E (E-no-kami) Shrine |
| Kamusaki Shrine | Kuchira Shrine |
| Emura Shrine | Watarai-no-kuni-no-mikami Shrine |

Watarai-no-ōkunitamahime Shrine

| | |
|---|---|
| Kiyonoiwa Shrine | Shitomi Shrine |
| Kawara Shrine | Yamasue Shrine |
| Ookawachi Shrine | Oihara Shrine |
| Kawara-no-ōyashiro | Usunono Shrine |
| Omata Shrine | Kawara-no-fuchi Shrine |
| Ookaminomifune Shrine | Ikazuchi (Raiten) Shrine |
| (Oihara) (Ogiwara) Shrine | Miyake Shrine |

*Take District*—52 (all minor)

Sumarome (Sumarohime) Shrine  Sana Shrine—2

| | |
|---|---|
| Kushida Shrine | Kasuya Shrine |
| Take Shrine | Naka Shrine |
| Omi Shrine | Hatori-no-itoma Shrine |
| Ookamuyama Shrine—2 | Nanami Shrine |
| Iomi (Ioumi) Shrine—2 | Hayashi Shrine |
| Ooka-no-ue Shrine | Moriyama Shrine |
| Unisakura Shrine | Uni Shrine |
| Hatori-no-matoma Shrine—2 | Ama-no-tamizushiro-ōtoji Shrine |
| Ookakota-no-mikami Shrine | Kishi Shrine |

Urufutsu Shrine

Amekakoyama (Ama-no-kagoyama) Shrine

| | |
|---|---|
| Anashi Shrine | Nagareta Shrine |
| Hataketa Shrine—3 | Nagareta-no-ue Shrine |
| Iwata Shrine | Hichi Shrine |
| Sakikurusu Shrine—2 | Takeōyohi Shrine |
| Take-no-sasafue Shrine | Oikura (Okikura) Shrine |

Izawa Shrine
Uni (Arifuta) Shrine
Ookutama (Ookunitama) Shrine
Kuninomikami Shrine
Isonokami Shrine
Kushita-no-tsukimoto Shrine
Ookushi Shrine

Mure Shrine
Kunari (Kuninari) Shrine
Oowake Shrine
Hitsukura Shrine
Iro-no-ue Shrine
Ushiniwa Shrine

*Iino District*—4 (all minor)

Oita (Iita) Shrine
Iwasaki (Isosaki) Shrine

Kamuyama Shrine
Kamukaki Shrine

*Iitaka District*—9 (all minor)

Tachino Shrine
Mononobe Shrine
Ii (Oi) Shrine
Niu-no-naka Shrine
Kunitsu Shrine

Oowa Shrine
Kasechi Shrine
Niu Shrine
Horisaka Shrine

*Ichishi District*—13 (3 major, 10 minor)

Hata Shrine
Inaba Shrine—2

Mononobe Shrine
Suka Shrine

Asaka Shrine—3 (all principal deities; major)
Hate Shrine
Okawa Shrine
Kawa-ai Shrine

Sayama (Iyama) Shrine
Toshita Shrine

*Ano District*—10 (all minor)

Okisome Shrine
Shifumi Shrine
Minoya Shrine
Okawachi Shrine
Karaino Shrine

Ooichi Shrine
Oni Shrine
Ayuta Shrine
Hisatsuchi Shrine
Funayama Shrine

*Amuki District*—13 (all minor)

Inafu Shrine
Tai Shrine
Kotoimi Shrine
Osaki Shrine
Iwatsumi Shrine
Hatori Shrine
Kuruma Shrine

Kawara Shrine
Oonokoso Shrine
Sakai Shrine
Hisatsuchi Shrine
Minefuri Shrine
Yokomichi-no-shimo Shrine

*Suzuka District*—19 (all minor)

Nakushiri Shrine
Kawamata Shrine
Shihakaki Shrine
Ame-no-hitotsukuwata Shrine
Okishi-no-ōkami Shrine
Miyake Shrine
Fuke Shrine

Shidori (Shizuri) Shrine
Makio Shrine
Agatanushi Shrine
Tsubaki-no-ōkami Shrine
Ooi Shrine—2
E Shrine
Iwa Shrine

Nagase Shrine
Katayama Shrine
*Kawawa District*—20 (all minor)
  Takaichi (Takechi) Shrine
  Kishi (Takashi) Shrine
  Kawa Shrine
  Okata Shrine
  Okawa Shrine
  Iino Shrine
  Takaoka Shrine
  Ashika Shrine
  Suki Shrine
  Hashi Shrine
*Mie District*—6 (all minor)
  Eta (Fukata) Shrine
  Kamusaki Shrine
  Ashimita Shrine
*Asake District*—24 (all minor)
  Ikaruga Shrine
  Kiruta Shrine
  Usagikami Shrine
  Tahika Shrine
  Yasotsumikura Shrine
  Mimitoshi Shrine
  Utsushita Shrine
  Ite Shrine
  Fushi Shrine
  Sakura Shrine
  Nagakura Shrine
  Hase Shrine
*Inabe District*—10 (all minor)
  Kamo 鴨 Shrine
  Heguri Shrine
  Inabe Shrine
  Totori Shrine
  Kamo 賀毛 Shrine
*Kuwana District*—15 (1 major, 14 minor)
  Kuwana Shrine—2
  Otsu Shrine—2
  Noshiri Shrine
  Ono Shrine
  Nukata Shrine
  Nakatomi Shrine
  Tachisaka Shrine

Oshiyama (Imiyama) Shrine
Mimuko Shrine

Mitsukaki Shrine
Onita (Kita) Shrine
Yayori Shrine
Nakato Shrine
Tsubaki Shrine
Kukushimi Shrine
Ooki Shrine
Yafuta Shrine
Fukata Shrine
Ooka-no-miyake Shrine

Kafu Shrine
Okoso Shrine
Tsubakikishi (Tsubakishi) Shrine

Nohara Shrine
Isobe Shrine—2
Oowa (Oo-no-kami) Shrine
Toriichi (Toriide) Shrine
Shite Shrine
Mimitsune Shrine
Kushita Shrine
Uekuri Shrine
Hotsumi Shrine
Ishiri Shrine
Nawashiro Shrine

Ishi (Iwa) Shrine
Tanabe Shrine
Totori-no-yamada Shrine
Ootani Shrine
Hoshikawa Shrine

Sanofu Shrine
Oyama Shrine
Tato Shrine (principal deity, major)
Fukae Shrine
Uka Shrine
Hase Shrine

SHIMA Province—3 (2 major, 1 minor)
  *Tōshi District*—3 (2 major, 1 minor)
    Awashima no Isawa Shrine—2 (both major)
    Awashima no Kamiotanomiko Shrine
OWARI Province—121 (8 major, 113 minor)
  *Amabe District*—8 (all minor)
    Urushibe Shrine            Morokuwa Shrine
    Kunitama Shrine            Fujishima Shrine
    Utashi Shrine              Yunoki Shrine
    Ikuha Shrine               Okamu Shrine
  *Nakashima District*—30 (3 major, 27 minor)
    Sakate Shrine              Minu (Mino) Shrine
    Oomiwa Shrine (principal deity, major)
    Hasoki Shrine
    Harikuma Shrine            Nomi Shrine
    Asai Shrine                Mokuhi Shrine
    Oo(-no-kami) Shrine (principal deity, major)
    Chichihaya Shrine          Oseki Shrine
    Iwato Shrine               Murohara Shrine
    Takata-hasoki Shrine       Ookuchi Shrine
    Himefu Shrine              Masumita Shrine
    Kawawa Shrine              Sakami Shrine
    Asai Shrine                Kuta Shrine
    Tsutsumihari Shrine        Ishitsukuri Shrine
    Chino Shrine               Shioe Shrine
    Fuchi Shrine               Munakata Shrine
    Owari no Ookunitama Shrine Oomitama Shrine
    Tomoe Shrine
  *Hakuri District*—10 (all minor)
    Anaobe Shrine              Ajika Shrine
    Wakakuri Shrine            Kurota Shrine
    Oono Shrine                Ishitsukuri Shrine
    Ubusuna Shrine             Kawashima Shrine
    Ifuribe Shrine             Ooke Shrine
  *Niwa District*—22 (1 major, 21 minor)
    Azura Shrine               Tagata Shrine
    Inaki Shrine               Ishitsukuri Shrine
    Ikakawara Shrine           Yamana Shrine
    Niwa Shrine                Sakito Shrine
    Morokuwa Shrine            Akuma Shrine
    Haritsuna Shrine           Ikuta Shrine
    Takumi Shrine              Narumi-no-tekashi Shrine
    Kezuriguri Shrine          Takumi Shrine
    Mushika Shrine             Tachino (Tateno) Shrine
    Ide Shrine                 Oguchi Shrine

Shiomichi Shrine

*Kasukabe District*—12 (all minor)

Hita Shrine

Toyama Shrine

Kunihara Shrine

Mimari (Misomari) Shrine

Itahato Shrine

Uchiuchi (Uchitsu) Shrine

*Yamada District*—19 (all minor)

Katayama Shrine

Hitsuji Shrine

Kawashima Shrine

Inu Shrine

Wanira Shrine

Wata Shrine

Oonoki Shrine

Wakeoe Shrine

Sakaniwa Shrine

Ishitsukuri Shrine

*Aichi District*—17 (4 major, 13 minor)

Hioki Shrine

Shimotsuchikama Shrine

Mita Shrine

Kawara Shrine

Ifu Shrine

Mononobe Shrine

Hisaki-no-miko Shrine (principal deity, major)

Hikowakamiko Shrine (principal deity, major)

Takakura-no-musubi-miko Shrine (principal deity, major)

Yatsurugi Shrine

Aofusuma Shrine

*Chita District*—3 (all minor)

Irumi (Irimi) Shrine

Hazu Shrine

MIKAWA Province—26 (all minor)

*Kamo District*—7 (all minor)

Nomi Shrine

Hyōsu Shrine

Sanage Shrine

Haiho Shrine

*Nukata District*—2 (both minor)

Inasaki Shrine

*Aomi District*—6 (all minor)

Washitori Shrine

Hinaga Shrine

Ooagata Shrine (principal deity, major)

Oe Shrine

Katayama Shrine

Mutsushi (Mutoshi) Shrine

Mononobe Shrine

Takamu Shrine

Take Shrine

Oome Shrine

Fukawa Shrine

Okuchi Shrine

Kane Shrine

Tanahata Shrine

Shibukawa Shrine

Owari Shrine

Ooi Shrine

Owaribe Shrine

Kamutsuchikama Shrine

Atsuta Shrine (principal deity, major)

Takamu Shrine

Harina Shrine

Narumi Shrine

Ho-no-kami-aneko Shrine

Akuhi Shrine

No Shrine

Iho Shrine

Hirosawa Shrine

Achiha (Yuhata) Shrine

Sakahito (Sakamuto) Shrine

Chiryū Shrine

Hiso Shrine                          Kasume Shrine
*Hazu District*—3 (all minor)
  Kumaku Shrine—2                    Hazu Shrine
*Ho-o District*—6 (all minor)
  Katahara Shrine                    Mitsu Shrine
  Unatari Shrine                     Toka Shrine
  Akahiko Shrine                     Iwakura Shrine
*Yana District*—1 (minor)
  Ishimaki Shrine
*Atsumi District*—1 (minor)
  Ashi Shrine
TŌTOUMI Province—62 (2 major, 60 minor)
  *Hamana District*—5 (1 major, 4 minor)
    Miwayama Shrine                  Eta Shrine
    Ihanako Shrine                   Oomiwa Shrine
    Tsunosakuhiko Shrine (principal deity, major)
  *Fuchi District*—6 (all minor)
    Kisa Shrine                      Kobe Shrine
    Tsumori (Tsukeri) Shrine         Omu (Yasu) Shrine
    Sokonomitachi Shrine             Kakuru Shrine
  *Inasa District*—6 (all minor)
    Ii Shrine                        Otsu Shrine
    Miyake Shrine                    Hachisaki Shrine
    Sube Shrine                      Oosechi (Daisechi) Shrine
  *Aratama District*—4 (all minor)
    Oro Shrine                       Taka Shrine
    Nagatani Shrine                  Wakayamato Shrine
  *Naganoshimo District*—4 (all minor)
    Nagano Shrine                    Oomika Shrine
    Toroku Shrine                    Inoe (Ike) Shrine
  *Naganokami District*—5 (all minor)
    Ootoshi Shrine                   Ifuse (Kose) Shrine
    Hatori Shrine                    Asahihataka Shrine
    Kokura Shrine
  *Iwata District*—14 (all minor)
    Irumi Shrine                     Kasono Shrine
    Aōmi-no-kunitama Shrine          Tanaka Shrine
    Toyoikazuchi-no-mikoto Shrine    Toyoikazuchihime-no-mikoto Shrine
    Ikuikazuchi-no-mikoto Shrine     Ame-no-miko Shrine—2
    Mioya Shrine                     Miko-no-kami Shrine—2
    Yanahime Shrine                  Suwawakamiko Shrine
  *Suchi District*—3 (all minor)
    Hagiwara-no-kawachi Shrine       Okuni Shrine
    Mumanushi Shrine
  *Yamana District*—4 (all minor)

Yamana Shrine                        Kone Shrine
Shimana Shrine                       Kōribe Shrine
*Sano District*—4 (all minor)
Makusa Shrine                        Kotonomachi Shrine
Awawa Shrine                         Toshi Shrine
*Kikō District*—2 (both minor)
Nara Shrine                          Hinatano Shrine
*Haibara District*—5 (1 major, 4 minor)
Ookusu Shrine                        Hatorita Shrine
Kataoka Shrine                       Iitsusawano Shrine
Kyōman Shrine (principal deity, major)
SURUGA Province—22 (1 major, 21 minor)
*Mashitsu District*—4 (all minor)
Miwa Shrine                          Akuwa (Akunami) Shrine
Nahe Shrine                          Yakitsu Shrine
*Udo District*—3 (all minor)
Ikama Shrine                         Iketa Shrine
Kusanagi Shrine
*Abe District*—7 (all minor)
Ashitsuki Shrine                     Kamube (Kambe) Shrine
Takeho Shrine                        Nakatsu Shrine
Oketsuri (Okushi) Shrine             Shirasawa Shrine
Ootoshi-mioya Shrine
*Iohara District*—3 (all minor)
Miho Shrine                          Kusanagi Shrine
Toyotsumi Shrine
*Fuji District*—3 (1 major, 2 minor)
Shidori Shrine
Asama (Sengen) Shrine (principal deity, major)
Fuchi Shrine
*Suruga District*—2 (both minor)
Maroko (Mariko) Shrine               Momosawa Shrine
IZU Province—92 (5 major, 87 minor)
*Kamo District*—46 (4 major, 42 minor)
Izu-no-mishima Shrine (principal deity, major; *Tsukinami, Niiname*)
Hafuhime-no-mikoto Shrine            Igamuhime-no-mikoto Shrine
Ikonahime-no-mikoto Shrine           Sakitamahime-no-mikoto Shrine
Itatewake-no-mikoto Shrine           Atsusawake-no-mikoto Shrine
Takemikaka-no-mikoto Shrine          Monoimina-no-mikoto Shrine
Hayatamawake-no-mikoto Shrine
Iware-no-mikoto Shrine
Itsunahime-no-mikoto Shrine          Ametsuwake-no-mikoto Shrine
Hayashi-no-mikoto Shrine             Uwai-no-mikoto Shrine
Katasuga-no-mikoto Shrine            Kurae-no-mikoto Shrine
Yasu-no-mikoto Shrine                Nakichi-no-mikoto Shrine

Kami-no-mikoto Shrine

Tera-no-mikoto Shrine

Koshiki-no-mikoto Shrine

Takeishizuki-no-mikoto Shrine

Kunitsuhime-no-mikoto Shrine

Iwanohime-no-mikoto Shrine

Sugihokowake-no-mikoto Shrine

Takehokotsukuwake-no-mikoto Shrine

Iwakurawake-no-mikoto Shrine

Iwayo-no-mikoto Shrine

Ametsukatahime-no-mikoto Shrine

Iwahime-no-mikoto Shrine

Awa Shrine (principal deity, major)

Shiritaki Shrine

Achiko Shrine

Minamiko (Minako) Shrine

Hotsusake-no-mikoto Shrine

Iwatewake-no-mikoto Shrine

Hachi Shrine

Ootsu-no-yuki-no-mikoto Shrine

Fusaoki Shrine

Sasawarahime-no-mikoto Shrine

Tsukuma (Takama) Shrine—3

Kamo Shrine—2

*Takata District*—24 (1 major, 23 minor)

Araki Shrine

Fumunashi Shrine

Karono Shrine

Shidori Shrine

Takahashi Shrine

Nagahama Shrine

Kutsumi Shrine

Iwatokunotaka Shrine

Ikamashi Shrine

Hirose Shrine

Ogawa-izumi Shrine

Ooasa Shrine

Tamatsukuri-no-mizu Shrine

Yanagiwara Shrine

Karihayasutakihihayo-no-mikoto Shrine

Tachioyani-no-mikoto Shrine

Ho-no-musubi-no-mikoto Shrine

Shiranaminomina-awa-no-mikoto Shrine

Kanamura-iokimiwake-no-mikoto Shrine

Tachikara(Hikitachikara)-no-mikoto Shrine

Kanamura-iomurahime-no-mikoto Shrine

Ametsuse-no-ketachi-no-mikoto Shrine

Tsurugitachi-iwatokowake-no-mikoto Shrine

Awabitama-shiratamahimewake-no-mikoto Shrine

*Naka District*—22 (all minor)

Minowa Shrine

Ishifu Shrine

Inakami Shrine

Naka Shrine

Ita Shrine

Inashimo Shrine

Naka-no-Ootoshi Shrine

Taniya Shrine

Tako (Oko) Shrine

Ukusu Shrine

Heta Shrine

Sawa Shrine—2

Futonushi-no-wakatama-no-mikoto Shrine

Kuni-no-mihashira-no-mikoto Shrine

Inamiya-no-mikoto Shrine

Iwakura-no-mikoto Shrine

Kunitama-no-mikoto Shrine

Mikatama-no-mikoto Shrine

Kunitama-no-mikoto Shrine

Toyomitama-no-mikoto Shrine

Aotamahime-no-mikoto Shrine
KAI Province—20 (1 major, 19 minor)
  *Yamanashi District*—9 (all minor)
    Kamube (Kambe) Shrine          Mononobe Shrine
    Kaina Shrine                   Kurotona Shrine
    Kanazakura Shrine              Matsu-no-o Shrine
    Tamamoro Shrine                Ooimata Shrine
    Yamanashioka Shrine
  *Koma District*—5 (all minor)
    Kamube (Kambe) Shrine          Homi Shrine
    Uwato Shrine                   Shidori Shrine
    Kasaya Shrine
  *Yatsushiro District*—6 (1 major, 5 minor)
    Saku Shrine                    Yuge Shrine
    Uwato Shrine                   Asama Shrine
    Nakao Shrine                   Hokotsuki Shrine
SAGAMI Province—13 (1 major, 12 minor)
  *Ashinokami District*—1 (minor)
    Samuta Shrine
  *Yoroki District*—1 (minor)
    Kawawa Shrine
  *Oosumi District*—4 (all minor)
    Sakitori Shrine                Takaheya Shrine
    Hihita Shrine                  Afuri Shrine
  *Aikō (Ayukawa) District*—1 (minor)
    Ono Shrine
  *Takakura District*—6 (1 major, 5 minor)
    Oowa Shrine                    Fukami Shrine
    Utsumochi Shrine
    Samukawa Shrine (principal deity; major)
    Arika Shrine                   Iwatateo Shrine
MUSASHI Province—44 (2 major, 42 minor)
  *Ebara District*—2 (both minor)
    Hieta Shrine                   Iwai Shrine
  *Tsutsuki District*—1 (minor)
    Sugiyama Shrine
  *Taba (Tama) District*—8 (all minor)
    Akiru Shrine                   Ono Shrine
    Futate (Futa-no-amatsu) Shrine Oomatonotsunoamatsu Shrine
    Azusami-no-amatsu Shrine       Anasawa Shrine
    Torakashiwa Shrine             Aoi Shrine
  *Adachi District*—4 (1 major, 3 minor)
    Ashitate (Adachi) Shrine
    Hikawa Shrine (principal deity, major; *Tsukinami, Niiname*)
    Tsuki Shrine                   Take-no-hime Shrine

*Yokomi District*—3 ( all minor)
  Yokomi Shrine                Takeuhiko (Takaoi-hiko) Shrine
  Iwahi Shrine
*Iruma District*—5 (all minor)
  Izumo-no-iwahi Shrine       Nakahikawa Shrine
  Hirose Shrine              Mononobe-no-amatsu Shrine
  Kuninuma-no-kunitsukasa Shrine
*Saitama District*—4 (all minor)
  Saitama Shrine—2          Tamashiki Shrine
  Miyame Shrine
*Obusuma District*—3 (all minor)
  Obusuma Shrine           Izumonoiwahi Shrine
  Inanohime Shrine
*Hara District*—4 (all minor)
  Shirakami Shrine         Tanaka Shrine
  Nireyama Shrine         Nara Shrine
*Kami District*—4 (all minor)
  Nagahatabe Shrine       Imaki-aoyasaka-inami Shrine
  Imaki-aosaka-inami-aramitama Shrine
  Imaki-aosaka-inami-no-ikegami Shrine
*Chichibu District*—2 (both minor)
  Chichibu Shrine          Mukura (Muku) Shrine
*Kotama District*—1 (major)
  Kanasana Shrine (principal deity, major)
*Oosato District*—1 (minor)
  Takaki Shrine
*Hiki District*—1 (minor)
  Ikonohayamitamahime Shrine
*Naka District*—1 (minor)
  Mikanoi Shrine
Awa Province 安房—6 (2 major, 4 minor)
  *Awa District*—2 (both major)
    Awa Shrine (principal deity, major; *Tsukinami, Niiname*)
    Mime-no-amehirinohime-no-mikoto Shrine (formerly Susaki-no-kami)
  *Asahina District*—4 (all minor)
    Amatsu Shrine         Nakoshi-no-yama Shrine
    Shimotachi-matsuhara Shrine   Takaie Shrine
Kazusa (Kamitsufusa) Province—5 (1 major, 4 minor)
  *Haniu District*—1 (major)
    Tamasaki Shrine (principal deity, major)
  *Nagara District*—1 (minor)
    Tachibana Shrine
  *Unakami District*—2 (both minor)
    Shima-ana Shrine        Anesaki Shrine
  *Mōda District*—1 (minor)

Akitomi (Ofu) Shrine
SHIMŌSA (SHIMOTSUFUSA) Province—11 (1 major, 10 minor)
  *Katori District*—1 (major)
    Katori Jingū (principal deity, major; *Tsukinami, Niiname*)
  *Chiba District*—2 (both minor)
    Samukawa Shrine          Sokahime Shrine
  *Sōsa District*—1 (minor)
    Oio Shrine
  *Imuba (Imba) District*—1 (minor)
    Magata Shrine
  *Yūki District*—2 (both minor)
    Takahashi Shrine        Taketa Shrine
  *Okada District*—1 (minor)
    Kuwahara Shrine
  *Katsushika District*—2 (both minor)
    Moro Shrine            Ifuhi (Ohohi) Shrine
  *Sōma District*—1 (minor)
    Mitsuchi Shrine
HITACHI Province—28 (7 major, 21 minor)
  *Kashima District*—2 (both major)
    Kashima Jingū (principal deity, major; *Tsukinami, Niiname*)
    Ooaraisozaki no Yakushi Bosatsu Shrine (principal deity, major)
  *Makabe District*—1 (minor)
    Ookunitama Shrine
  *Shida District*—2 (both minor)
    Tatenui Shrine         Ami Shrine
  *Kuji District*—7 (1 major, 6 minor)
    Nagahatabe Shrine      Satsu (Sachitsu) Shrine
    Amanoshiraha Shrine
    Ame-no-hayatamahime-no-mikoto Shrine
    Shizu Shrine (principal deity, major)
    Inamura Shrine        Tachino Shrine
  *Tsukuba District*—2 (1 major, 1 minor)
    Tsukuba-no-yama Shrine (1 principal deity, major; 1 minor)
  *Naka District*—7 (2 major, 5 minor)
    Ooi Shrine           Aoyama Shrine
    Yoshida Shrine (principal deity, major)
    Awa-no-yama-no-ue Shrine
    Sakatsura-isozaki Yakushi Bosatsu Shrine (principal deity, major)
    Fujiuchi Shrine       Iwafune Shrine
  *Niihari District*—3 (1 major, 2 minor)
    Inada Shrine (principal deity, major)
    Sashino Shrine
    Kamo-no-ōkami-no-miko-kamutama Shrine
  *Mubaraki District*—3 (all minor)

Ihari Shrine                    Hanashiyama Shrine
Nushiishi (Nushishi) Shrine
*Taka District*—1 (minor)
Sawawa-no-kunitsukami Shrine

    *  *  *  *  *

End of Book Nine of the *Engi-shiki*
 Enchō 5th Year, 12th Month, 26th Day
  [same signatures as at end of Book Six]

# BOOK TEN

## REGISTER OF DEITIES (B)

### TŌSAN, HOKURIKU, SAN'IN, SAN'YŌ, NANKAI,

### AND SAIKAI CIRCUITS

382 *kami* of the Tōsandō

  42 Major (for 5 of whom the *Tsukinami* and *Niiname* are celebrated with offerings on top of the tables)

340 Minor

Oomi (Chikatsu-ōmi) Province—155 (13 major, 142 minor)

  *Shiga District*—8 (3 major, 5 minor)

| | |
|---|---|
| Nawaka Shrine | Shidori (Shizuri) Shrine |
| Iwai (Iwakura) Shrine | Kamuta (Kanda) Shrine |
| Ono Shrine—2 (principal deities, major) | |
| Hiyoshi Shrine (principal deity, major) | |
| Ogura Shrine | |

  *Kurimoto District*—8 (2 major, 6 minor)

| | |
|---|---|
| Io-no-i Shrine | Ibuki Shrine |
| Otsuki-no-ōyashiro | Otsuki Shrine |
| Takano Shrine | Ikishiro Shrine |
| Sakunado Shrine | Takebe Shrine (principal deity, major) |

  *Kōka District*—8 (2 major, 6 minor)

| | |
|---|---|
| Yakawa Shrine | Minakuchi Shrine |
| Iwabe-no-kashio-no-kami Shrine | |
| Kawata Shrine—2 (both principal deities, major; *Tsukinami, Niiname*) | |
| Iimichi (Iichi) Shrine | Kawakare Shrine—2 |

  *Yasu District*—9 (2 major, 7 minor)

| | |
|---|---|
| Mikamu (Mikami) Shrine (principal deity, major; *Tsukinami, Niiname*) | |
| Otsu Shrine | Shimo-no-niikawa Shrine |
| Hyōsu Shrine (principal deity; major) | |
| Hirita Shrine | Kami-no-niikawa Shrine |
| Mumamichi-no-isobe Shrine | Konino Shrine—2 |

  *Gamō District*—11 (1 major, 10 minor)

| | |
|---|---|
| Ooshima Shrine | Oiso Shrine |
| Isobe Shrine | Ooya Shrine |
| Hitosa (Hitsusa) Shrine | Nagasu (Nagani) Shrine |

Sasaki Shrine                        Sugata Shrine
Mumamioka Shrine—2
Oitsushima Shrine (principal deity, major)
*Kamusaki (Kanzaki) District*—2 (both minor)
Oka Shrine                           Kawaketa Shrine
*Echi District*—3 (all minor)
Karuno Shrine                        Isobe Shrine—2
*Inukami District*—7 (all minor)
Ajiki Shrine—2                       Taka Shrine—2
Himukai Shrine                       Tsue Shrine
Yamada Shrine
*Sakata District*—5 (all minor)
Yamada Shrine                        Hinade Shrine
Ifuki Shrine                         Oka Shrine
Yamatsu-terasu Shrine
*Asai District*—14 (all minor)
Shiotsu Shrine                       Yutsuki Shrine
Hakunu Shrine                        Oe Shrine
Shimo-no-shiotsu Shrine              Ya-ai Shrine
Okamoto Shrine                       Katayama Shrine—2
Hikitari Shrine                      Masota Shrine
Kamikoso Shrine                      Oowa Shrine
Tsukufushima (Tsukubusuma) Shrine
*Ikago District*—46 (1 major, 45 minor)
Ikago Shrine (principal deity, major)
Nomi Shrine
Kamusaki (Kansaki) Shrine            Oosawa Shrine
Ame-no-yaotsura Shrine               Omi Shrine
Hashiriochi Shrine                   Ashisaki Shrine
Kurumita Shrine                      Himeta Shrine
Iwahe (Owahe) Shrine                 Akaho Shrine
Sakura-ichi Shrine                   Toha Shrine
Yokoyama Shrine                      Oota Shrine
Hyōsu Shrine                         Akami Shrine
Hami Shrine                          Sakurahashi Shrine
Ichiisaki Shrine                     Sami Shrine
Tsubaki Shrine                       Sawakato Shrine
Ikagokusaka Shrine                   Yoshiro Shrine
Fuse-no-tateishi Shrine              Nokita Shrine
Ishitsukuri Shrine                   Tamatsukuri Shrine
Ifufura (Oofura) Shrine              Iwataki Shrine
Takano Shrine                        Erehiko Shrine
Ookura Shrine                        Kuroda Shrine
Niu Shrine—2                         Kamutakatsuki Shrine
Ame-no-iwatowake-no-mikoto Shrine

Ame-no-hihiki-no-mikoto Shrine

Kusaoka Shrine                    Ita Shrine
Ooami Shrine                      Oomizuwake Shrine

Amatsukawa-no-mikoto Shrine

*Takashima District*—34 (2 major, 32 minor)
  Mio Shrine—2 (both major, *Tsukinami, Niiname*)
  Ashitomi (Ashitsumi) Shrine     Yoroki Shrine
  Tabe Shrine                     Kumano Shrine
  Mishima Shrine                  Ookawa Shrine
  Ono Shrine                      Machi Shrine
  Ichiihara Shrine                Oota Shrine
  Tomoyui Shrine                  Hioki Shrine
  Tsuno Shrine                    Ooarahiko Shrine—2
  Oosaki Shrine                   Sakamoto Shrine
  Ootokoro Shrine                 Make Shrine
  Yuge Shrine                     Shiroshi Shrine
  Hanifu Shrine                   Oomizuwake Shrine
  Oono Shrine                     Oumi Shrine
  Oone (Ooni) Shrine              Arakura Shrine
  Mieu Shrine—2                   Tsuki Shrine
  Nagata Shrine                   Ukita Shrine

MINO Province—39 (1 major, 38 minor)
  *Taki District*—4 (all minor)
    Taki Shrine                   Oomuwa (Oomiwa) Shrine
    Mii Shrine                    Kukumiohiko Shrine
  *Fuwa District*—3 (1 major, 2 minor)
    Nakayama-kanayamahiko Shrine (principal deity, major)
    Tairyō Shrine                 Ibuki Shrine
  *Ikeda District*—1 (minor)
    Yaki Shrine
  *Ahachi District*—4 (all minor)
    Uwato Shrine                  Kamo Shrine
    Sumumata Shrine               Arakata Shrine
  *Oono District*—3 (all minor)
    Hananaga Shrine               Hananaga-no-shimo Shrine
    Koburi Shrine
  *Katagata District*—2 (both minor)
    Katagatatsu Shrine            Wakae Shrine
  *Atsumi District*—3 (all minor)
    Hinamori Shrine               Akanebe Shrine
    Mononobe Shrine
  *Kakami District*—7 (all minor)
    Iwanonishi Shrine             Murakuni Shrine—2
    Asukada Shrine                Murakuni-masumida Shrine
    Kasami Shrine                 Mii Shrine

*Kamo District*—9 (all minor)

Agatanushi Shrine              Sakahafuri Shrine
Ooyama Shrine                  Tabe Shrine
Afushina Shrine                Kamuta Shrine
Sakuta Shrine                  Tai Shrine
Nakayama Shrine

*Ena District*—3 (all minor)

Sakamoto Shrine                Nakagawa Shrine
Ena Shrine

HIDA Province—8 (all minor)

*Oono District*—3 (all minor)

Mizunashi Shrine               Tsukimoto Shrine
Ena Shrine

*Araki District*—5 (all minor)

Ootsu Shrine                   Araki Shrine
Takata Shrine                  Atayuta Shrine
Kurihara Shrine

SHINANO Province—48 (7 major, 41 minor)

*Ina District*—2 (both minor)

Ooyamada Shrine                Achi Shrine

*Suwa District*—2 (both major)

Minakatatomi Shrine—2 (principal deities, major)

*Tsukama District*—3 (all minor)

Okata Shrine                   Isakota (Sata) Shrine
Are Shrine

*Azumi District*—2 (1 major, 1 minor)

Hodaka Shrine (principal deity, major)
Kawa-ai Shrine

*Sarashina District*—11 (1 major, 10 minor)

Fuse Shrine                    Haheshina Shrine
Sarashina Shine                Tagishina Shrine
Nagatani Shrine                Hioki Shrine
Shimizu Shrine                 Hikanatome Shrine
Ike Shrine                     Hata (Haruta) Shrine
Takemizuwake Shrine (principal deity, major)

*Minochi District*—9 (1 major, 8 minor)

Miwa Shrine                    Izumo Shrine
Tsumashina Shrine              Ogawa Shrine
Morita Shrine                  Awano Shrine
Kazema (Kazama) Shrine         Shiratamatariho-no-mikoto Shrine
Takeminakatatomi-no-mikoto-hiko-kamiwake Shrine
    (principal deity, major)

*Takai District*—6 (all minor)

Sumisaka Shrine                Ochi Shrine
Ouchi Shrine                   Kasahara Shrine

Osaka Shrine                    Takamori Shrine
*Hanishina District*—5 (all minor)
  Awasa Shrine                  Sakaki Shrine
  Nakamura Shrine               Tamayorihime-no-mikoto Shrine
  Hafuri Shrine
*Chiisagata District*—5 (2 major, 3 minor)
  Ikushima-tarushima Shrine—2 (principal deities, major)
  Yamaie (Yamaga) Shrine        Shiono Shrine
  Komayumi-no-mine Shrine
*Saku District*—3 (all minor)
  Eta Shrine                    Nagakura Shrine
  Ootomo Shrine

KŌZUKE (KAMITSUKE) Province—12 (3 major, 9 minor)
  *Kataoka District*—1
    Ohafuri Shrine
  *Kanra District*—2 (1 major, 1 minor)
    Nuki-no-saki Shrine (principal deity, major)
    Uke (Uki) Shrine
  *Kuruma District*—3 (1 major, 2 minor)
    Ikaho Shrine (principal deity, major)
    Haruna Shrine               Kawasukune Shrine
  *Seta District*—1 (major)
    Akagi Shrine (principal deity, major)
  *Yamada District*—2 (both minor)
    Kamo Shrine                 Miwa Shrine
  *Nawa District*—2 (both minor)
    Hono-ikazuchi Shrine        Shidori (Shizuri) Shrine
  *Sai District*—1 (minor)
    Ookuni Shrine

SHIMOTSUKE Province—11 (1 major, 10 minor)
  *Tsuga District*—3 (all minor)
    Oomiwa-no-yashiro           Oosaki Shrine
    Murahi Shrine
  *Kawachi (Kafuchi) District*—1 (major)
    Futaarayama Shrine (principal deity, major)
  *Haga District*—2 (both minor)
    Oosaki Shrine               Arakashi Shrine
  *Nasu District*—3 (minor)
    Takemuyama Shrine           Yu Shrine
    Miwa Shrine
  *Samukawa District*—2 (minor)
    Awa Shrine                  Munakata Shrine

MUTSU (MICHINOKU) Province—100 (15 major, 85 minor)
  *Shirakawa District*—7 (1 major, 6 minor)
    Tsutsukowake Shrine (principal deity, major)

Iwatowake Shrine
Yamizo-no-mine Shrino
Nagakura Shrine

Shirakawa Shrine
Iitoyohime Shrine
Iwatsutsukowake Shrine

*Kamata District*—1 (major)
Kamutamine Shrine (principal deity, major)
*Natori District*—2 (both minor)
Taka Shrine                              Sakue Shrine
*Miyagi District*—4 (2 major, 2 minor)
Izusahime (Izusanome) Shrine
Shiwahiko Shrine (principal deity, major)
Hanafushi Shrine (principal deity, major)
Taga Shrine
*Kurokawa District*—4 (all minor)
Suki Shrine                              Iwakamiyamasumi Shrine
Kashima-no-amatariwake Shrine
Yuku Shrine
*Kami District*—2 (both minor)
Iitoyo Shrine                            Kamiishi Shrine
*Shikama District*—1 (major)
Itate Shrine (principal deity, major)
*Tamatsukuri District*—3 (all minor)
Yu Shrine                                Araokawa Shrine
Yu-no-ishi Shrine
*Watari District*—4 (all minor)
Kashima-no-itsunohike Shrine   Kashima-no-onata Shrine
Afukawa Shrine                 Kashima-no-amatariwake Shrine
*Shinobu District*—5 (1 major, 4 minor)
Kashima Shrine                 Kuronuma Shrine
Azumaya-no-numa Shrine (principal deity, major)
Shirawase Shrine               Azumaya-no-kuni Shrine
*Shida District*—1 (minor)
Shikitama-hayamitama Shrine
*Iwaki District*—7 (all minor)
Ookunitama Shrine              Futamata Shrine
Yu Shrine                      Samaku-no-mine Shrine
Sumiyoshi Shrine               Kashima Shrine
Kokuwakura Shrine
*Shineha (Shimeha) District*—1 (minor)
Kusano Shrine
*Ojika District*—10 (2 major, 8 minor)
Hitsujisaki Shrine (principal deity, major)
Katori-no-izunomiko Shrine
Ikohayawake-no-mikoto Shrine   Sowa Shrine
Ogaminoshi Shrine (principal deity, major)
Toriya Shrine

Ooshima Shrine                    Kashima-no-miko Shrine
Kusuhina Shrine                   Kesema Shrine
*Momonou District*—6 (1 major, 5 minor)
Iinoyama Shrine                   Hitakami Shrine
Futamata Shrine                   Ishigami Shrine
Kesema-no-ōshima Shrine (principal deity, major)
Oto Shrine
*Namekata District*—8 (1 major, 7 minor)
Takakura Shrine                   Himatsuri Shrine
Sakamine Shrine                   Mito Shrine
Kashima-no-miko Shrine            Masuta-no-mine Shrine
Taka Shrine (principal deity, major)
Oshio Shrine
*Kurihara District*—7 (1 major, 6 minor)
Uwato Shrine
Shiwahime Shrine (principal deity, major)
Oto Shrine                        Komagatane Shrine
Waga Shrine                       Katori-no-miko Shrine
Orushiwake-no-ishi Shrine
*Isawa District*—7 (all minor)
Iwa Shrine                        Komagata Shrine
Wagaetono Shrine                  Iwade-no-i Shrine
Isawagawa Shrine                  Todoi Shrine
Oroheshi Shrine
*Niita District*—1 (minor)
Komatsu Shrine
*Iwase District*—1 (minor)
Hokotsuki Shrine
*Aizu District*—2 (1 major, 1 minor)
Isasumi Shrine (principal deity, major)
Kokai-no-kuni Shrine
*Oda District*—1 (minor)
Koganeyama Shrine
*Yama District*—1 (minor)
Iwaki (Iwasaki) Shrine
*Shiba District*—1 (minor)
Shigariwake Shrine
*Kese District*—3 (all minor)
Rikukotan Shrine                  Tonakoshi Shrine
Edate (Kinudate) Shrine
*Asaka District*—3 (1 major, 2 minor)
Unakorowake Shrine (principal deity, major)
Iitoyowake Shrine
Oitsushima (Kakushitsushima) Shrine
*Shibata District*—1 (major)

Ootakayama Shrine (principal deity, major)
*Uta District*—1 (major)
    Koimine Shrine (principal deity, major)
*Igu District*—2 (both minor)
    Atsuhitakahiko Shrine        Toriyamine Shrine
*Iwai District*—2 (both minor)
    Haishiwa Shrine              Maikusa Shrine
*Esashi District*—1 (minor)
    Shizuoka Shrine
DEWA (IDEWA) Province—9 (2 major, 7 minor)
    *Akumi District*—3 (2 major, 1 minor)
        Oomonoimi Shrine (principal deity, major)
        Omonoimi Shrine
        Tsukiyama Shrine (principal deity, major)
    *Tagawa District*—3 (all minor)
        Oga Shrine               Yuzusa-hime Shrine
        Idewa Shrine
    *Hiraka District*—2 (both minor)
        Shioyu-hiko Shrine       Haushiwake Shrine
    *Yamamoto District*—1 (minor)
        Soikawa Shrine

352  *kami* in the Hokurikudō
  14  Major (of these one has *Tsukinami* and *Niiname*)
338  Minor
WAKASA Province—42 (3 major, 39 minor)
    *Oniu District*—16 (2 major, 14 minor)
        Tada Shrine
        Wakasahiko Shrine—2 (principal deities, major)
        Oami Shrine              Iwakurahiko Shrine
        Iwakurahime Shrine       Shiimura Shrine
        Hako Shrine              Kusuya Shrine
        Iwa (Miwa) Shrine        Niu Shrine
        Anashi Shrine            Sobi Shrine
        Kowaki Shrine            Kamutahiko Shrine
        Kamutahime Shrine
    *Ooii District*—7 (all minor)
        Aoumi Shrine             Izanagi Shrine
        Kagoyama Shrine          Shizushi Shrine
        Hioki Shrine             Ooii Shrine
        Sakichi Shrine
    *Mikata District*—19 (1 major, 18 minor)
        Sukama Shrine            Mikata Shrine
        Imui Shrine              Tayuhi Shrine
        Niu Shrine               Orita Shrine

Wanibe Shrine                           Saki Shrine
Uwanishi Shrine (principal deity, major; *Tsukinami, Niiname*)
Takanami Shrine
Nifu Shrine                             Suhe Shrine
Kono Shrine                             Imi (Mimi) Shrine
Ose Shrine                              Tsune Shrine
Noto Shrine                             Kurami Shrine
Yamatsuta Shrine
ECHIZEN Province—126 (8 major, 118 minor)
  *Tsuruga District*—43 (7 major, 36 minor)
    Kehi Shrine—7 (all principal deities, major)
Kahiru Shrine                           Tsurugi Shrine
Niu Shrine                              Tayui Shrine
Kuzumi Shrine                           Nosaka Shrine
Shihisaki Shrine                        Tsuruga (Tsunuga) Shrine
Ookura Shrine                           Washisaki Shrine
Ichiburi Shrine                         Kanasaki Shrine
Itsuhata Shrine                         Asomura-no-tokura Shrine
Shiraki Shrine                          Yokokura Shrine
Yokoyama Shrine                         Itakiya Shrine
Chiwamuramine Shrine                    Ibeiwakura Shrine
Takaoka Shrine                          Kahiru Shrine
Kahiru-tanokuchi Shrine                 Oomiwa-no-shimosaki Shrine
Orita Shrine                            Misaki Shrine
Ameyaoyorozuhime Shrine                 Iwata Shrine
Amahime-no-wakamiko Shrine              Ametotsurugi Shrine
Amekunitsuhiko Shrine                   Isanahiko Shrine
Amesuzu Shrine                          Amekunitsuhime Shrine
Shirakihiko Shrine                      Tamasasarahiko Shrine
  *Niu District*—14 (1 major, 13 minor)
Aniko Shrine                            Amayo Shrine
Oomushi Shrine (principal deity, major)
Nagaoka Shrine                          Tofu Shrine
Hiraite Shrine                          Make Shrine
Sasamushi Shrine—4                      Ooyamamita Shrine
Ikazuchi Shrine                         Omushi Shrine
  *Imatachi District*—14 (all minor)
Hoyama Shrine                           Kunaka (Kuninaka) Shrine—2
Ishibe Shrine                           Okamoto Shrine
Suwa-asuki Shrine—3                     Nitsu Shrine
Tona Shrine                             Oyamada Shrine
Ukamu Shrine                            Katashiwa Shrine
Shikiyama Shrine
  *Asuha District*—13 (all minor)
Sugimori-no-kōri Shrine                 Haniwa (Tsuchi-no-wa) Shrine

Naono Shrine
Tochii Shrine
Yosuna Shrine
Mikado Shrine
Kamusoi Shrine
Asuha Shrine

Make Shrine
Shiisaki Shrine
Yamakata Shrine
Wake Shrine
Ue Shrine

*Oono District*—9 (all minor)

Iwakura Shrine
Kamuba (Kaniha) Shrine
Sakato-hitokoto Shrine
Kuninari-ōno Shrine
Arashima Shrine

Shinokura Shrine
Ootsuki-iwakura Shrine
Kazahaya Shrine
Takao-iwakura Shrine

*Sakanoi District*—33 (all minor)

Fukuro Shrine
Misaki Shrine
Tane Shrine
Okami Shrine
Kunitsukami Shrine
Yanagise Shrine
Katakishi Shrine
Hikona Shrine
Kibe Shrine
Ketani Shrine
Eta Shrine
Iki Shrine
Yokoyama Shrine
Iwata Shrine
Takamuku Shrine
Ietsu Shrine
Itosaki Shrine

Sakanai Shrine
Tsunakoshi Shrine
Kumeta Shrine
Achiwase Shrine
Ikuchi Shrine
Konosumi Shrine
Oomizo Shrine
Heita Shrine
Hiraoka Shrine
Shiba Shrine
Ukuso Shrine
Hosoroki Shrine
Mikuni Shrine
Misaka (Umasaka) Shrine
Kasama Shrine
Oominato Shrine

KAGA Province—42 (all minor)

*Enu (Enuma) District*—11 (all minor)

Shinohara Shrine
Miki Shrine
Hatori Shrine
Imunami (Inami) Shrine
Izumi Shrine
Shiotsu (Ushiotsu) Shrine

Tokari Shrine
Miyamura-isobe Shrine
Sugau-no-isobe Shrine
Hioki Shrine
Keta-no-miko Shrine

*Nomi District*—8 (all minor)

Sano Shrine
Isobe Shrine
Hatasaka (Hatanari) Shrine
Takinami Shrine

Tata Shrine
Kasugami Shrine
Usagihashi (Uhashi) Shrine
Kumata Shrine

*Ishikawa District*—10 (all minor)

Shirayamahime Shrine

Motomurai Shrine

Nukahimukashi (Nukanohigashi) Shrine
Nukanishi Shrine
Mima (Mimuma) Shrine          Saki Shrine
Naramoto Shrine                Kasama Shrine
Misochi Shrine                 Kamuta Shrine
   *Kaga District—13 (all minor)*
Obama Shrine                   Noma Shrine
Miwa Shrine                    Kamo Shrine
Kamuta Shrine                  Shimo-no-ma Shrine
Kumuke Shrine                  Suki Shrine
Notsuchi Shrine                Hajikami Shrine
Oonominato Shrine              Noka Shrine
Kasano Shrine
NOTO Province—43 (1 major, 42 minor)
   *Hakui District—14 (1 major, 13 minor)*
Aimi Shrine                    Shio Shrine
Keta Shrine (principal deity, major)
Kamushiro Shrine
Hakui Shrine                   Setohiko Shrine
Tehayahime Shrine              Shiiha-no-tsuburahime Shrine
Natsumihime Shrine             Moro-okahiko Shrine
Momonu-no-hiko Shrine          Kumakafutsu-arakashihiko Shrine
Fujitsuhiko Shrine             Ooanamochi-no-mikata-ishi Shrine
   *Noto District—17 (all minor)*
Notohime Shrine                Fujiwarahiko Shrine
Sugaoshihime Shrine            Kafutohiko Shrine
Amenohikagehime Shrine         Toriyahiko Shrine
Araishihiko Shrine             Kutehiko Shrine
Noto-no-ikukunitamahiko Shrine Shirahiko Shrine
Isurukihiko Shrine             Yokihiko Shrine
Arakashihiko Shrine            Kushi-inadakihime Shrine
Iyahime Shrine                 Mikadonushihiko Shrine
Sukunahiko-no-kami-no-kataishi Shrine
   *Fugeshi District—9 (all minor)*
Fugeshihiko Shrine             Iwasehiko Shrine
Kamusugi-no-izumuhime Shrine Iwakurahiko Shrine
Mimanahiko Shrine              Mimanahime Shrine
Kamume-itsukihiko Shrine       Okitsuhime Shrine
Hetsuhime Shrine
   *Suzu District—3 (all minor)*
Suzu Shrine                    Komashihiko Shrine
Kashiwarahiko Shrine
ETCHŪ Province—34 (1 major, 33 minor)
   *Tonami District—7 (all minor)*
Takase Shrine                  Nagaoka Shrine

Hayashi Shrine

Hime Shrine

Asai Shrine

Ubara Shrine

Ogami Shrine

*Imizu District*—13 (1 major, 12 minor)

Imizu Shrine

Mononobe Shrine

Kume Shrine

Hayakawa Shrine

Isobe Shrine

Kusaoka Shrine

Michi Shrine

Kakumi Shrine—2

Fuse Shrine

Fushita Shrine

Yashiro Shrine

Keta Shrine [principal deity, major]

*Nehi District*—7 (all minor)

Anekurahime Shrine

Shiratori Shrine

Kumano Shrine

Usaka Shrine

Hayahoshi Shrine

Takuhireshi Shrine

Sugiwara Shrine

*Niikawa District*—7 (all minor)

Kamuto Shrine

Ichiiwara Shrine

Hioki Shrine

Oyama Shrine

Takeiwakatsu Shrine

Yagokoro-ōichihiko Shrine

Fuse Shrine

ECHIGO Province—56 (1 major, 55 minor)

*Kubiki District*—13 (all minor)

Nunakawa Shrine

Ahita Shrine

Sata Shrine

Mizushima-no-isobe Shrine

Iogimi Shrine

Aomi Shrine

Hida Shrine

Oo Shrine

Keta (Ita) Shrine

Mononobe Shrine

Sugawara Shrine

Eno Shrine

Matota (Marita) Shrine

*Koshi District*—6 (all minor)

Miyake Shrine—2

Tsuno Shrine

Unagushi Shrine

Kirihara-no-isobe Shrine

Oniu Shrine

*Mishima District*—6 (all minor)

Mishima-no-isobe Shrine

Ukawa Shrine

Mishima Shrine

Mononobe Shrine

Taki Shrine

Iwai Shrine

*Ionu District*—5 (all minor)

Ionu Shrine

Sakamoto Shrine

Kawa-ai Shrine

Oosaki Shrine

Ime Shrine

*Kambara (Kamuhara) District*—13 (1 major, 12 minor)

Aomi Shrine—2

Ikure Shrine

Ofuse Shrine

Utsurawashi Shrine

Tsukita Shrine

Ikarashi Shrine

Iyahiko Shrine (principal deity, major)
Nagase Shrine
Nakayama Shrine                  Asaiino Shrine
Funae Shrine                     Tsuchifuta (Hanifuta) Shrine
*Nutari District*—5 (all minor)
Oogata Shrine                    Ichikawa Shrine
Ishii Shrine                     Mikuri Shrine
Kawa-ai Shrine
*Iwafune District*—8 (all minor)
Iwafune Shrine                   Kambara Shrine
Nishinami Shrine                 Arakawa Shrine
Taki Shrine                      Urushiyama Shrine
Momokawa Shrine                  Minato Shrine
Sado Province—9 (all minor)
*Umo District*—2 (both minor)
Watatsu Shrine                   Oome Shrine
*Sawada District*—5 (all minor)
Hikitabe Shrine                  Mononobe Shrine
Mike Shrine                      Iimochi Shrine
Oshiki Shrine
*Kamo District*—2 (both minor)
Oohata Shrine                    Atsukushihiko Shrine


560  *kami* of the San'indō
37 Major (of whom one has *Tsukinami* and *Niiname*)
523 Minor
Tamba Province—71 (5 major, 66 minor)
*Kuwada District*—19 (2 major, 17 minor)
Izumo Shrine (principal deity, major)
Kuwada Shrine                    Miyake Shrine
Ogawatsuki Shrine (principal deity, major)
Miagata Shrine                   Kamuno Shrine
Yamakuni Shrine                  Atago Shrine
Ohata Shrine                     Hashirida Shrine
Matsuno-o Shrine                 Idate Shrine
Ooi Shrine                       Iwaho Shrine
Yono Shrine                      Taki Shrine
Murayama Shrine                  Kuwayama Shrine
Hietano Shrine
*Funai District*—10 (1 major, 9 minor)
Funai Shrine                     Shitahi Shrine
Izushi-no-ka-no-isobe Shrine     Shima-no-mononobe Shrine
Hatahisa Shrine                  Shiwaka Shrine
Benaki Shrine                    Make Shrine (principal deity, major)
Sakachishi Shrine                Tachii (Tanuma) Shrine

*Taki District*—9 (2 major, 7 minor)
    Kushi-iwamado Shrine—2 (principal deities, major)

| | |
|---|---|
| Kamuta Shrine | Kawachi-no-tatanuhi Shrine—2 |
| Oohime Shrine | Sasaba Shrine |
| Futamura Shrine | Kumakura Shrine |

*Hikami District*—17 (all minor)

| | |
|---|---|
| Takakura Shrine | Samiya Shrine |
| Karino Shrine | Isobe Shrine |
| Chino Shrine | Ine (Ichino) Shrine |
| Sachi Shrine | Adaoka Shrine |
| Tatenui Shrine | Serida Shrine |
| Hyōsu Shrine | Nii Shrine |
| Nunuki Shrine | Ionoi Shrine |
| Kawara Shrine | Itsuki Shrine |
| Kamuno Shrine | |

*Amata District*—4 (all minor)

| | |
|---|---|
| Ikuno Shrine | Amuka Shrine |
| Amaterutama-no-mikoto Shrine | Araki Shrine |

*Ikaruga District*—12 (all minor)

| | |
|---|---|
| Suwakibe Shrine | Aichi Shrine |
| Asusuki Shrine | Mitetsuki Shrine |
| Sada Shrine | Kamunabi Shrine |
| Iya Shrine | Akakuni Shrine |
| Takakura Shrine | Sasuga Shrine |
| Shimama Shrine | Fukuda Shrine |

TANGO Province—65 (7 major, 58 minor)
    *Kasa District*—11 (1 major, 10 minor)

| | |
|---|---|
| Nagu Shrine | Ichifuse Shrine |
| Iyakaki Shrine | Shidori Shrine |
| Takata Shrine | Ookawa Shrine (principal deity, major) |
| Arasu Shrine | Yahara Shrine |
| Marata Shrine | Miyake Shrine |
| Hihara Shrine | |

*Yosa District*—20 (3 major, 17 minor)
    Komori Shrine (principal deity, major; *Tsukinami, Niiname*)

| | |
|---|---|
| Mononobe Shrine | Iyato (Mito) Shrine |
| Sushiro Shrine | Fukō Shrine |
| Uzuki Shrine | Achie Shrine |
| Kurida Shrine | Tayu Shrine |
| Ura Shrine | Yatabe Shrine |
| Achie-no-isobe Shrine | Shidori Shrine |
| Mie Shrine | Kotsumi Shrine |
| Itatsura Shrine | Sugisue Shrine |
| Wagano Shrine | Oomushi Shrine (principal deity, major) |

    Omushi (Komushi) Shrine (principal deity, major)

*Tawa District*—9 (2 major, 7 minor)
 Oomiya-no-me Shrine—2 (principal deities, major)

| | |
|---|---|
| Kuioka Shrine | Hami Shrine |
| Taku Shrine | Inashiro Shrine |
| Naki Shrine | Yata Shrine |
| Hichimanai Shrine | |

*Takano District*—14 (1 major, 13 minor)

| | |
|---|---|
| Oouka Shrine | Nagu Shrine |
| Mizotani Shrine | Kunihara Shrine |
| Amino Shrine | Echi Shrine |
| Oono Shrine | Takano Shrine (major) |
| Ikuōbe Shrine | Shifuhi Shrine |
| Fukatabe Shrine | Yukao Shrine |
| Karatachi Shrine | Himefu (Mefu) Shrine |

*Kumano District*—11 (all minor)

| | |
|---|---|
| Kumano Shrine | Ibuki Shrine |
| Izushimi Shrine | Yata Shrine |
| Marota Shrine | Himefu (Mefu) Shrine |
| Moroyoshi Shrine | Mishimata Shrine |
| Kamutani Shrine | Muraoka Shrine |
| Kikibe Shrine | |

TAJIMA Province—131 (18 major, 113 minor)
 *Asako District*—9 (1 major, 8 minor)

| | |
|---|---|
| Awaka Shrine | Asako-no-isobe Shrine |
| Toka-no-isobe Shrine | Hyōsu Shrine |
| Akafuchi Shrine | Iyu Shrine |
| Shidori Shrine | Ashika Shrine |
| Sana Shrine | |

*Yabu District*—30 (3 major, 27 minor)
 Yabu Shrine—5 (2 principal deities, major; 3 minor)

| | |
|---|---|
| Uruwa Shrine | Mizutani Shrine (principal deity, major) |
| Asama Shrine | Yaoka Shrine |
| Ikuto Shrine | Tatenui Shrine |
| Hyōsu Shrine | Osaka Shrine |

 Sakitsuhiko-aruchi-no-mikoto Shrine—2

| | |
|---|---|
| I-no-e Shrine—2 | Tetani Shrine |
| Itafuki Shrine | Honama Shrine |
| Kuzu (Katsura) Shrine | Ooyohi Shrine |
| Kirihara Shrine | Mitsuoka Shrine |
| Sarakimura-no-ōhyōsu Shrine | Mii Shrine |
| Nakusa Shrine | Moriuchi Shrine |
| Wanami Shrine | Yakimura-ni-masu-yama Shrine |

*Izushi District*—23 (9 major, 14 minor)
 Izushi Shrine—8 (all principal deities; major)
 Miizushi Shrine (principal deity, major)

Kirino Shrine

Morosugi Shrine

Suru Shrine

Sasaki Shrine

Hide Shrine

Sugi Shrine

Ono Shrine

Tetani Shrine

Nakashima Shrine

Ooyube-no-hyōsu Shrine

Amuka Shrine

Hiji Shrine

Isobe Shrine

Osaka Shrine

*Keta District*—21 (4 major, 17 minor)

Tamaraki Shrine

Keta Shrine

Ashita Shrine

Mino Shrine

Himefu Shrine

Takanuki Shrine

Kutone-hyōsu Shrine

Hioki Shrine

Tatenui Shrine

Ita Shrine

Omoiyari Shrine

Mii Shrine

Takafu Shrine

Saku Shrine

Kanto Shrine

Ichi Shrine

Sutani Shrine

Yama Shrine (principal deity, major)

He (To) Shrine (principal deity, major)

Ikazuchi Shrine (principal deity, major)

Hosoki Shrine (principal deity, major)

*Kinosaki District*—21 (1 major, 20 minor)

Mononobe Shrine

Kuma Shrine

Anameki Shrine

Meshiro Shrine

Yosaki Shrine

Fukuhi Shrine

Oe Shrine

Kukuhi Shrine

Mimii Shrine

Momoshima Shrine

Hyōsu Shrine

Fukasaka Shrine

Hyōsu Shrine—2

Kehi Shrine

Kuruhi Shrine

Shikinami Shrine

Agata Shrine

Sakatare Shrine

Nishito (Seto) Shrine

Ama Shrine (principal deity, major)

*Mikumi District*—12 (all minor)

Sauke Shrine

Takano Shrine

Ikisa Shrine—3

Noriwa Shrine

Mii Shrine

Kurahashi Shrine

Akotani Shrine

Kuwahara Shrine

Iroki Shrine

Niu Shrine

*Futakata District*—5 (all minor)

Futakata Shrine

Ooie Shrine

Ootoshi Shrine

Menu Shrine

Suka Shrine

*Shitsumi District*—10 (all minor)

Tata Shrine

Oshiro Shrine—2

Shitsumi Shrine—2

Isofu Shrine

Toyo Shrine

Takasaka Shrine

Kurono Shrine                    Haruki Shrine

INABA Province—50 (1 major, 49 minor)

   *Kono District*—9 (all minor)

    Oshiro Shrine                    Oo Shrine

    Saminohyōsu Shrine               Takano Shrine

    Koyanohyōsu Shrine               Futakami Shrine

    Miyu Shrine                      Hino Shrine

    Kamuro Shrine

   *Hōmi District*—9 (1 major, 8 minor)

    Takonoue Shrine—2               Ikamu Shrine

    Tsukiori Shrine                 Arasaka Shrine

    Temi Shrine                     Hatori Shrine

    Mitani Shrine                   Ube Shrine (principal deity, major)

   *Yakami District*—19 (all minor)

    Ooe Shrine—3                    Tsubakichi-no-kami Shrine—2

    Shionokami Shrine—2             Tsubanami Shrine—2

    Isonosashi Shrine—2             Takamuku Shrine—2

    Ihi (Ohi) Shrine                Himenu Shrine

    Watari Shrine                   Kutami Shrine

    Furutachi Shrine                Miteguranu Shrine

   *Oumi District*—1

    Nakatomi-takatake Shrine

   *Takakusa District*—7 (all minor)

    Iwa Shrine                      Shidori Shrine

    Ame-no-hohi-no-mikoto Shrine  Ame-no-hinatori-no-mikoto Shrine

    Atakatsutake-mikuma-no-mikoto Shrine

    Oonomi-no-sukune-no-mikoto Shrine

    Oowasami-no-mikoto Shrine

   *Keta District*—5 (all minor)

    Hayakawa Shrine                 Hatai Shrine

    Kachimi Shrine                  Itai Shrine

    Shikanu Shrine

HŌKI (HAHAKI) Province—6 (all minor)

   *Kawamura District*—2 (minor)

    Shidori Shrine                  Hahaki Shrine

   *Kume District*—2 (minor)

    Shidori Shrine                  Kusaka Shrine

   *Oomi District*—2 (minor)

    Munakata Shrine                 Oomiwa-no-yama Shrine

IZUMO Province—187 (2 major, 185 minor)[506]

   *Ou District*—48 (1 major, 47 minor)

    Kumano Shrine (principal, major)

---

[506] In Izumo Province the names of shrines in this list will show discrepancies when compared with the (older) text of *Izumo fudoki*.

Saki Shrine
Norito Shrine     Tanaka Shrine
Tatei Shrine     Hayatama Shrine
Fugomi Shrine     Iwasaka Shrine
Sakusa Shrine     Manai Shrine
Takahi Shrine     Yamashiro Shrine
Himezuki Shrine     Noshiro Shrine
Fujina-Oonamochi Shrine     Fujina Shrine
Kutami Shrine     Tamatsukuriyu Shrine
Karakuni-itate in same Shrine     Himefu Shrine
Kumachi (Kimachi) Shrine     Sai Shrine
Sai-no-takamori Shrine     Shishimichi Shrine
Urufu Shrine     Suta Shrine
Yuya Shrine     Karakuni-itate in same Shrine
Chikuya (Tsukiya) Shrine     Hayatsumushiwake in same Shrine
Yamasa Shrine     Kushimikeno in same Shrine
Fube Shrine     Tsubeshiro Shrine
Noki Shrine     Ooanamochi in same Shrine
Oonamochi-no-miko in same Shrine
Sakuta Shrine
Karakuni-itate in same Shrine     Shiomi Shrine
Otaki Shrine     Miosa in same Shrine
Ichihara Shrine     Yuki Shrine
Kachihi Shrine     Kachihi-no-takamori Shrine
Taomote Shrine     Kume Shrine

*Shimane District*—14 (all minor)
Fujikimi Shrine     Take Shrine
Kurami Shrine     Hayatsutakeshi in same Shrine
Kawakami Shrine     Nagami Shrine
Kadoe Shrine     Yokota Shrine
Kaga Shrine     Nisa Shrine
Nisa-no-kashinoi Shrine     Noriyoshi (Hōki) Shrine
Ikuma Shrine     Miho Shrine

*Aika (Akika) District*—10 (all minor)
Sada Shrine     Utaki Shrine
Ooi Shrine     Hita Shrine
Mii Shrine     Uchi Shrine
Tarumi Shrine     Etomo Shrine
Kososhi Shrine     Oonotsu Shrine

*Tatenui District*—9 (all minor)
Kutami Shrine     Saka Shrine
Umi Shrine     Taku Shrine
Mitsu Shrine     Noroshi Shrine
Kozu Shrine     Kozu Shrine
Mi (Mizu) Shrine

*Izumo District*—58 (1 major, 57 minor)

Ooanamochi Shrine
Kizuki-no-ōyashiro (principal deity, major)
Ookami no Ookisaki in same Shrine
Inochihime in same Shrine
Kamutama-no-miko in same Shrine
Kamutama-inochinushi in same Shrine
Ooanamochi-miko in same Shrine
Ooanamochi-no-inasewagi in same Shrine
Ooanamochi-miko-no-tamae in same Shrine
Asuki Shrine
Kamukarakuni-itate in same Shrine
Amewakahiko in same Shrine

Susano-o in same Shrine        Kami-musubi-ohotoji in same Shrine
Kan'asuki in same Shrine       Kan'isanaki in same Shrine
Kami-ama-no-hinatori in same Shrine
Kan'isaka in same Shrine
Ajisuki in same Shrine         Amewakahiko in same Shrine
Misaki Shrine                  Inasa Shrine
Kusaka Shrine                  Inu Shrine
Ooanamochi-amashirohiko in same Shrine
Ooanamochi-amashirohime in same Shrine
Kantama-izunome in same Shrine
Kantama in same Shrine
Hikosawake in same Shrine      Ibuki Shrine
Tsugari Shrine                 Izawa Shrine
Mitami Shrine                  Himeji in same Shrine
Agata Shrine                   Wakafutsunushi in same Shrine
Iwa Shrine                     Tsumuji Shrine
Uka Shrine                     Minuma Shrine
Fuse Shrine                    Ihomi (Oomi) Shrine
Izumo Shrine                   Karakuni-itate in same Shrine
Hishiro Shrine                 Karakama Shrine
Toriya Shrine                  Kanshiro Shrine
Sokinoya Shrine                Karakuni-itateho in same Shrine
Isaga Shrine                   Kumu Shrine
Kamori Shrine                  Mii Shrine
Ishi Shrine                    Hachi Shrine
Tachimushi Shrine              Ago Shrine

*Kamuto District*—27 (all minor)

Mikuga Shrine                  Ane Shrine
Sashimu Shrine                 Takigi Shrine
Taki Shrine                    Ooanamochi in same Shrine
Kumura (Kunimura) Shrine       Namesa Shrine
Wakasuserihime in same Shrine  Saheki Shrine

Chii Shrine                          Hifuchi Shrine
Kantama-mikotsunotama in same Shrine
Asayama Shrine
Ari Shrine                           Karihime in same Shrine
Yano Shrine                          Ooyama Shrine
Kunai Shrine                         Yamuya Shrine
Honoka Shrine                        Yamuyahiko Shrine
Yamuyahiko-mayumi Shrine             Hina Shrine
Asuri Shrine                         Kamimusubi-no-mikoto Shrine
Yamuyahiko-no-mikoto-no-miko Yakitachi-ame-no-hohiko-no-mikoto
   Shrine

*Iishi District*—5 (all minor)
   Mitoya Shrine                     Tabe Shrine
   Iishi Shrine                      Susa Shrine
   Kawabe Shrine
*Nita District*—2 (both minor)
   Ikatake Shrine                    Misawa Shrine
*Oohara District*—13 (all minor)
   Unoji Shrine                      Sumine in same Shrine
   Kambara Shrine                    Yakuchi Shrine
   Mishiro Shrine                    Fusu Shrine
   Hii 斐伊 Shrine                    Hii-no-hayahiko in same Shrine
   Kosuki (Kisuki) Shrine            Kata Shrine
   Sase Shrine                       Serita Shrine
   Ushio Shrine
*Nogi District*—1 (minor)
   Ame-no-hohi-no-mikoto Shrine
IWAMI Province—34 (all minor)
   *Ano District*—10 (all minor)
      Mononobe Shrine                Kamuta Shrine
      Sasuka Shrine                  Asakurahiko-no-mikoto Shrine
      Niigusohime-no-mikoto Shrine   Nihehime Shrine
      Sahimeyama Shrine              Noi (No-no-i) Shrine
      Shizuma Shrine                 Kamube (Kambe) Shrine
   *Nima District*—5 (all minor)
      Ki-no-ue Shrine
      Yama-no-be-no-yashirohime-no-mikoto Shrine
      Hyakuraku Shrine               Mizukami Shrine
      Kokubunji no Hyakuraku Shrine
   *Naka District*—11 (all minor)
      Tahato Shrine                  Tsudo Shrine
      Ikamu Shrine                   Oomayama Shrine
      Iwami-no-ametoyotarikarahime-no-mikoto Shrine
      Oomatsuri-no-ame-no-iwatohiko Shrine
      Ooiihiko-no-mikoto Shrine

Kushiro-no-ame-no-kokekahiko-no-mikoto Shrine

Ootoshi Shrine                      Yama-no-be Shrine

Yasu Shrine

*Oochi District*—3 (all minor)

Amatsu Shrine                       Tatachitakehorine-no-mikoto Shrine

Oohara Shrine

*Mino District*—5 (all minor)

Sugano-no-ameiruwakako-no-mikoto Shrine

Sahime-no-yama Shrine

Shimiwa-no-amaiwakatsu-no-mikoto Shrine

Kushirogahime-no-mikoto Shrine

Ono-no-ame-no-ōkamishitasoazuwake-no-mikoto Shrine

Oki Province—16 (4 major, 12 minor)

*Chifuri District*—7 (1 major, 6 minor)

Yurahime Shrine (principal deity, major; former name, Watasu-no-kami)

Ooyama Shrine

Ama Shrine                          Hinamajihime-no-mikoto Shrine

Make-no-mikoto Shrine               Amasashihiko-no-mikoto Shrine

*Ama District*—2 (1 major, 1 minor)

Nakirahime-no-mikoto Shrine

Ukeka-no-mikoto Shrine (principal deity; major)

*Suki District*—4 (all minor)

Kamonabi Shrine                     Mioya Shrine

Tamawakasu-no-mikoto Shrine   Wakenosu-no-mikoto Shrine

*Ochi District*—3 (2 major, 1 minor)

Amatakekanakusa Shrine

Mizuwakasu-no-mikoto Shrine (principal deity, major)

Ise-no-mikoto Shrine (principal deity, major)

140    *kami* of the San'yōdō

16 Major (of whom four have *Tsukinami* and *Niiname*)

124 Minor

Harima Province—50 (7 major, 43 minor)

*Akashi District*—9 (3 major, 6 minor)

Uru Shrine                          Mononobe Shrine

Tarumi Shrine—3 (principal deities, major; *Tsukinami, Niiname*)

Mikatata Shrine

Hayashi Shrine                      Akawa Shrine

Iwatsuhime Shrine

*Kako District*—1 (minor)

Hioka ni masu Ame-no-isasahiko Shrine

*Shikama District*—4 (all minor)

Itate-hyōsu Shrine—2             Shirakuni Shrine

Takaoka Shrine

*Iio (Iibo) District*—7 (3 major, 4 minor)

Ibo ni masu Amaterasu Shrine (principal deity, major)
Aso Shrine
Hafurita Shrine                    Awaji Shrine
Nakatomi-no-itate Shrine (principal deity, major)
Yahira Shrine
Ieshima Shrine (principal deity, major)
*Akaho District*—3 (all minor)
Iwatsuhime Shrine                  Yaho Shrine
Kuraoki Shrine
*Shisawa District*—7 (1 major, 6 minor)
Iwa no Oonamochi-no-mitama Shrine (principal deity, major)
Mikata Shrine                      Amagoi Shrine
Niwata Shrine                      Ooyamato no Kotoshironushi Shrine
Yohi Shrine                        Nishi Shrine
*Sayo District*—2 (both minor)
Sayotsuhime Shrine                 Amehitotsu-kamutama Shrine
*Minagi District*—1 (minor)
Misaka Shrine
*Kamusaki District*—2 (both minor)
Niisuki Shrine                     Tagawa Shrine
*Taka District*—6 (all minor)
Arata Shrine                       Hyōsu Shrine
Konai Shrine                       Katsuranomikoto Shrine
Ootsunomikoto Shrine               Ame-no-mahitotsu Shrine
*Kamo District*—8 (all minor)
Takatake Shrine                    Isobe Shrine
Saka-ai Shrine                     Sumiyoshi Shrine
Sugata Shrine                      Konashi Shrine
Kakita Shrine                      Ogihara Shrine
MIMASAKA Province—11 (1 major, 10 minor)
*Oonba District*—8 (all minor)
Sawara Shrine                      Katabe Shrine
Ichiawa Shrine—2                   Yokomi Shrine
Kuto Shrine                        Ukami Shrine
Nagata Shrine
*Tomahiukashi District*—2 (1 major, 1 minor)
Kōya (Takano) Shrine
Chūsan (Nakayama) Shrine (principal deity; major)
*Aita District*—1 (minor)
Ame-no-iwatowake Shrine
BIZEN Province—26 (1 major, 25 minor)
*Ooku District*—3 (1 major, 2 minor)
Miwa Shrine                        Katayamahiko Shrine
Ani Shrine (principal deity, major)
*Akasaka District*—6 (all minor)

Kamo Shrine—3                     Munakata Shrine
Iso-no-kami-no-futsunomitama Shrine
Fuse Shrine
*Wake District*—1 (minor)
Kamine Shrine
*Kōtsumichi District*—4 (all minor)
Oomuwa (Oomiwa) Shrine—4
*Mino District*—8 (all minor)
Iwatowake Shrine               Ohari Shrine
Ama-no-kami (Amatsukami) Shrine
Ise Shrine
Amahakari Shrine               Kuni Shrine
Iwatowake Shrine               Ochihari-no-namawakahime Shrine
*Tsutaka District*—2 (both minor)
Kamo Shrine                    Munakata Shrine
*Kojima District*—2 (both minor)
Kamo Shrine                    Tatsuchiura Shrine
BITCHŪ Province—18 (1 major, 17 minor)
*Kuboya District*—3 (all minor)
Momoiyama Shrine               Ashitaka Shrine
Sugau Shrine
*Kaya District*—4 (1 major, 3 minor)
Furukōri Shrine                Nomata Shrine
Tsuzumi Shrine
Kibitsuhiko Shrine (principal deity, major)
*Shimotsumichi District*—5 (all minor)
Ishitatami Shrine              Miwa Shrine
Masaki Shrine                  Yokota Shrine
Anatoyama Shrine
*Oda District*—3 (all minor)
Arita Shrine                   Kanshima Shrine
Ue Shrine
*Shitsuki District*—1 (minor)
Ashitsukiyama (Asukinoyama) Shrine
*Aka District*—2 (both minor)
Himesaka-no-ishi-no-chi-no-ana Shrine
Ido-no-ishi-no-chi-no-ana Shrine
BINGO Province—17 (all minor)
*Ana (Yasuna) District*—2 (both minor)
Takeinatakisayafutsu Shrine    Amawaketoyohime Shrine
*Fukatsu District*—1 (minor)
Susanoono Shrine
*Nuka District*—1 (minor)
Niitsuhime Shrine
*Nunokuma District*—3 (all minor)

Takamoro Shrine    Nunasaki Shrine
Hikosasuki Shrine
*Homuji District*—1 (minor)
Tarihiri Shrine
*Ashida District*—2 (both minor)
Kamunabi Shrine    Kunitakayorihiko Shrine
*Kafunu (Kōnu) District*—1 (minor)
Okami Shrine
*Mikami District*—1 (minor)
Sorahiko Shrine
*Eso District*—1 (minor)
Takaokami Shrine
*Mitsuki District*—1 (minor)
Karakawa Shrine
*Sera District*—1 (minor)
Warihime Shrine
*Mitani District*—1 (minor)
Chihayahiko Shrine
*Miyoshi District*—1 (minor)
Chihayahime Shrine
AKI Province—3 (all major)
*Saeki District*—2 (both major)
Hayatani Shrine (principal deity, major; *Tsukinami, Niiname*)
Itsukishima Shrine (principal deity, major)
*Aki District*—1 (major)
Take Shrine (principal deity, major)
SUŌ Province—10 (all minor)
*Kumake District*—2 (both minor)
Kumake Shrine    Iwaki Shrine
*Sawa District*—6 (all minor)
Tama-no-oya Shrine—2    Izumo Shrine—2
Misaka Shrine    Tsurugi Shrine
*Yoshiki District*—1 (minor)
Nikabe Shrine
*Tsuno District*—1 (minor)
Futamata Shrine
NAGATO Province—5 (3 major, 2 minor)
*Toyora District*—5 ( 3 major, 2 minor)
Sumiyoshi no Aramitama Shrine—3 (all principal deities, major)
Imumiya Shrine    Muraya Shrine

163  *kami* of the Nankaidō
29 Major (of whom 10 have *Tsukinami* and *Niiname*; of those 4 also have
*Ainame*)
134 Minor

Kɪɪ Province—31 (13 major, 18 minor)
  *Ito District*—2 (1 major, 1 minor)
    Ota Shrine
    Niutsuhime Shrine (principal deity, major; *Tsukinami, Niiname*)
  *Naka District*—3 (all minor)
    Arata Shrine—2                    Ama Shrine
  *Nakusa District*—19 (9 major, 10 minor)
    Hi-no-kuma Shrine (principal deity, major; *Tsukinami, Ainame, Niiname*)
    Kunikakasu Shrine (principal deity, major; *Tsukinami, Ainame, Niiname*)
    Itakiso Shrine (principal deity, major; *Tsukinami, Ainame, Niiname*)
    Ooyatsuhime Shrine (principal deity, major; *Tsukinami, Niiname*)
    Tsumatsuhime Shrine (principal deity, major; *Tsukinami, Niiname*)
    Narukami Shrine (principal deity, major; *Tsukinami, Ainame, Niiname*)
    Katsuchi (Kagutsuchi) Shrine    Kata Shrine
    Ikuhime Shrine                   Asakura Shrine
    Sashitahiko Shrine               Maihime Shrine
    Kamayama Shrine                  Takatsumihiko Shrine
    Takatsumihime Shrine             Itachi Shrine (principal deity, major)
    Shima Shrine (principal deity, major)
    Shizuhi Shrine (principal deity, major)
    Katama(-no-oto) Shrine
  *Arita District*—1 (major)
    Susa Shrine (principal deity, major; *Tsukinami, Niiname*)
  *Muro District*—6 (2 major, 4 minor)
    Kumanohayatama Shrine (major)
    Kumano Shrine (principal deity, major)
    Ama Shrine—3                     Ame-no-tajikara-o Shrine
Awaji Province—13 (2 major, 11 minor)
  *Tsuna District*—9 (1 major, 8 minor)
    Awaji-Izanagi Shrine (principal deity, major)
    Ise-kuruma Shrine                Iwaya Shrine
    Tsukisa Shrine                   Kamo Shrine
    Yura-no-minato Shrine            Shichiku Shrine
    Kishikawa Shrine                 Kawakami Shrine
  *Mihara District*—4 (1 major, 3 minor)
    Yahara Shrine                    Minatokuchi Shrine
    Yamato no Ookunitama Shrine (principal deity, major)
    Kudo Shrine
Awa 阿波 Province—50 (3 major, 47 minor)
  *Itano District*—4 (1 major, 3 minor)
    Ooasahiko Shrine (principal deity, major)
    Kaehime Shrine                   Ushihiko Shrine
    Oka-no-ue Shrine
  *Awa District*—2 (both minor)
    Takefutsu Shrine                 Kotoshironushi Shrine

*Mima District*—12 (all minor)

| | |
|---|---|
| Kamo Shrine | Tawa (Tane) Shrine |
| Yokota Shrine | Izanami Shrine |
| Take Shrine | Ameyoritachi Shrine |
| Amatsukasahiko Shrine | Yasoko Shrine |
| Haniyamahime Shrine | Mitsuwanome Shrine |

Yamato Ookunitama-no-kami Ookunishiki Shrine—2

*Oe District*—8 (1 major, 7 minor)

Imube Shrine (principal deity, major; *Tsukinami, Niiname*)

Ame-no-murakumo-no-kami Ishiwayahime Shrine—2

Ikakashi Shrine

Ame-no-minumahiko Ame-no-mizusekihime Shrine—2

Hiwame-no-kami Awamadohime Shrine—2

*Nakata District*—9 (1 major, 8 minor)

Ame-no-iwatowake Yakurahime Shrine (principal deity, major; *Tsuki-nami, Niiname*)

Ame-no-iwatowake Toyotamahime Shrine

Manotohiko Shrine

Watatsumi Toyotamahime Shrine

Oomiwa Shrine

| | |
|---|---|
| Amasashinowake Shrine | Mimatsuhiko Shrine |
| Ofutomahime Shrine | Takeminatomi Shrine |

*Katsura District*—8 (all minor)

| | |
|---|---|
| Katsura Shrine | Kotoshironushi Shrine |
| Yamagatahiko Shrine | Umorihiko Shrine |
| Asatachihiko Shrine | Hayasame Shrine |
| Mikata (Miagata) Shrine | Takeshima-meoya-no-mikoto Shrine |

*Naka District*—7 (all minor)

| | |
|---|---|
| Waya Shrine | Unai Shrine |
| Wanasaifuso Shrine | Murohime Shrine |
| Takehime Shrine | Yahoko Shrine |
| Kashiwahime Shrine | |

SANUKI Province—24 (3 major, 21 minor)

*Samukawa District*—5 (all minor)

| | |
|---|---|
| Shitahari Shrine | Fuse Shrine |
| Kansaki Shrine | Tawa Shrine |
| Oominohiko Shrine | |

*Miki District*—1 (minor)

Wanikawa Shrine

*Kagawa District*—1 (major)

Tamura Shrine (principal deity, major)

*Aya District*—3 (1 major, 2 minor)

| | |
|---|---|
| Kamo Shrine | Kamutani Shrine |

Kiyama Shrine (principal deity, major)

*Utari District*—2 (both minor)

Ii Shrine                              Ube Shrine
*Naka District*—2 (both minor)
Kushinashi Shrine                      Kamuno (Kaminu) Shrine
*Tado District*—2 (both minor)
Ooasa Shrine                           Kumoke Shrine
*Katsuta (Karita) District*—6 (1 major, 5 minor)
Takaya Shrine                          Yamada Shrine
Kamara Shrine                          Uhe Shrine
Awai Shrine (principal deity; major)
Kuroshima Shrine
*Oouchi District*—1 (minor)
Minushi Shrine
*Mino District*—1 (minor)
Oomizukami Shrine
Iyo Province—24 (7 major, 17 minor)
*Ume District*—1 (major)
Murayama Shrine (principal deity, major)
*Niï* 新居 *District*—2 (1 major, 1 minor)
Isono Shrine (principal deity; major)
Kuroshima Shrine
*Kuwamura District*—3 (all minor)
Sasaku Shrine                          Futo Shrine
Sufu Shrine
*Ochi District*—7 (2 major, 5 minor [sic])
Oosuki Shrine                          Ikanashi Shrine
Ooyamatsumi Shrine (principal deity; major)
Oono Shrine
Himesaka Shrine (principal deity; major [but 'minor' in *Shinten* ed.])
Taki Shrine (principal deity; major)
Kusumoto (Makimoto) Shrine
*Noma District*—1 (major)
Noma Shrine (principal deity; major)
*Kasahaya District*—2 (both minor)
Kunitsuhiko-no-mikoto Shrine    Kushitamahime-no-mikoto Shrine
*Yu District*—4 (1 major, 3 minor)
Ajimi Shrine (principal deity, major)
Izumo-oka Shrine                       Yu Shrine
Isaniwa Shrine
*Iyo District*—4 (1 major, 3 minor)
Iyo Shrine (principal deity; major)
Isono Shrine
Takaoshihime Shrine             Iyotsuhiko-no-mikoto Shrine
Tosa Province—21 (1 major, 20 minor)
*Aki District*—3 (all minor)
Murotsu Shrine                         Take Shrine

Sakamoto Shrine
*Kagami District*—4 (all minor)
    Ame-no-oshihowake Shrine        Komatsu Shrine
    Fukafuchi Shrine                Ookawakami-no-mirafu Shrine
*Nagaoka District*—5 (all minor)
    Toyo-okanokaminoamatsukami Shrine
    Asamine Shrine
    Ueta Shrine                     Ono Shrine
    Iwatsuchi Shrine
*Tosa District*—5 (1 major, 4 minor)
    Tosa Shrine (major)             Katsurakio Shrine
    Katsurakime Shrine              Kōritsu Shrine
    Asakura Shrine
*Agawa District*—1 (minor)
    Ame-no-iwatowake-no-yasukunitama Shrine
*Hata District*—3 (all minor)
    Izuta Shrine                    Takashiri Shrine
    Kamo Shrine

107   *kami* of the Saikaidō
  38 Major
  69 Minor
  CHIKUZEN Province—19 (16 major, 3 minor)
    *Munakata District*—4 (all major)
      Munakata Shrine—3 (all principal deities, major)
      Orihata Shrine (principal deity, major)
    *Naka District*—4 (all major)
      Hachiman Daibosatsu Hakosaki-no-miya (principal deity, major)
      Sumiyoshi Shrine—3 (all principal deities, major)
    *Kasuya District*—3 (all major)
      Shikaumi Shrine—3 (all principal deities, major)
    *Ito District*—1 (major)
      Shito Shrine
    *Mikasa District*—2 (both major)
      Chikushi Shrine (principal deity, major)
      Kamado Shrine (principal deity, major)
    *Kamitsuasakura District*—1 (minor)
      Materafu Shrine
    *Shimotsuasakura District*—3 (all major)
      Minagi Shrine—3 (principal deities, major)
    *Yasu District*—1 (minor)
      Oonamochi (Oonamuchi) Shrine
  CHIKUGO Province—4 (2 major, 2 minor)
    *Mii District*—3 (2 major, 1 minor)
      Takara-no-tamatare-no-mikoto Shrine (principal deity, major)

Ise no Amaterasu-mioya Shrine
Toyohime Shrine (principal deity, major)
*Mihara District*—1 (minor)
Mise-no-ōmitama-ishi Shrine
BUZEN Province—6 (3 major, 3 minor)
  *Usa District*—3 (all major)
    Hachiman Daibosatsu Usa-no-miya (principal deity, major)
    Hime Shrine (principal deity, major)
    Ootarashihime-no-byō Shrine (principal deity, major)
  *Tagawa District*—3 (all minor)
    Karakuni-okinaga-ōhime-ōma-no-mikoto Shrine
    Oshihone-no-mikoto Shrine
    Toyohime-no-mikoto Shrine
BUNGO Province—6 (1 major, 5 minor)
  *Naori District*—1 (minor)
    Takeo-no-shimokorihiko Shrine
  *Ooita District*—1 (major)
    Samuta (Sasamuta) Shrine (major)
  *Hayami District*—3 (minor)
    Unakihime Shrine                Hiohime Shrine—2
  *Ama District*—1 (minor)
    Hayasuihime Shrine
HIZEN Province—4 (1 major, 3 minor)
  *Matsura District*—2 (1 major, 1 minor)
    Tajima Shrine (principal deity, major)
    Shishiki Shrine
  *Kii District*—1 (minor)
    Araho Shrine
  *Saka District*—1 (minor)
    Yotohime Shrine
HIGO Province—4 (1 major, 3 minor)
  *Aso District*—3 (1 major, 2 minor)
    Takeiwatatsu-no-mikoto Shrine (principal deity, major)
    Kunitsukuri Shrine              Asohime Shrine
  *Tamana (Tamaina) District*—1 (minor)
    Hikino Shrine
HIMUKA (HYŪGA) Province—4 (all minor)
  *Koyu District*—2 (both minor)
    Tsuno Shrine                    Tsuma Shrine
  *Miyazaki District*—1 (minor)
    Eta Shrine
  *Murakata (Murokata) District*—1 (minor)
    Kirishima Shrine
OOSUMI Province—5 (1 major, 4 minor)
  *Kuwahara District*—1 (major)

Kagoshima Shrine (major)
*So-o District*—3 (all minor)
  Oonamochi Shrine             Miya-no-ura Shrine
  Karakuni-no-uzumine Shrine
*Komu District*—1 (minor)
  Sukuhi (Yaku) Shrine
SATSUMA Province—2 (both minor)
*Eno (E) District*—1 (minor)
  Hirakiki Shrine
*Izumi District*—1 (minor)
  Kashikuri Shrine
IKI ISLAND (IKI NO SHIMA)—24 (7 major, 17 minor)
*Iki District*—12 (4 major, 8 minor)
  Mizu Shrine               Atami Shrine
  Sumiyoshi Shrine (principal deity, major)
  Hyōsu Shrine (principal deity, major)
  Tsukiyomi Shrine (principal deity, major)
  Kunikatanushi Shrine
  Takamioya Shrine         Tanagahime Shrine
  Sashifutsu Shrine        (same Shrine) Sashifutsu
  Nakatsu Shrine (principal deity, major)
  Tsunoe (Tsunokamu) Shrine
*Ishida District*—12 (3 major, 9 minor)
  Ametanagao Shrine (principal deity, major)
  Ametanagahime Shrine (principal deity, major)
  Misakito Shrine          Kunitsu Shrine
  Ama Shrine (major)       Tsu Shrine
  Yo Shrine               Ookunitama Shrine
  Niji Shrine              Minoe Shrine
  Kunitsu-okami Shrine    Mononobe-no-futsu Shrine
TSUSHIMA ISLAND (TSUSHIMA NO SHIMA)—29 (6 major, 23 minor)
*Kanzuagata District*—16 (2 major, 14 minor)
  Watatsumi Shrine (principal deity, major)
  Shima-no-ōkunitama Shrine   Norito Shrine
  Ama-no-moroha-no-mikoto Shrine
  Unuto (Utoto) Shrine
  Ama-no-takutsutama-no-mikoto Shrine
  Ohira-no-sukune-no-mikoto Shrine
  Nasukami-no-kane-no-miko Shrine
  Inakuhi Shrine           Yukiai Shrine
  Watatsumi-no-miko Shrine (principal deity, major)
  Koroku Shrine            Koroku-no-miko Shrine
  Shimano-ōkunitama-no-kami-no-miko Shrine
  Ooshima Shrine         Warawa (Harawa) Shrine
*Shimo(tsu)agata District*—13 (4 major, 9 minor)

Takamitama (Takami-musubi) Shrine (principal deity, major)
Shirokane-no-kami (Kanayamanoue) Shrine
Ikazuchi-no-mikoto Shrine
Watatsumi Shrine (principal deity, major)
Takutsu Shrine                    Futonoto Shrine (principal deity, major)
Amateru Shrine
Sumiyoshi Shrine (principal deity, major)
Watatsumi Shrine               Taira Shrine
Shikishima Shrine               Tsutsuchi Shrine
Kanayama Shrine

*        *        *        *        *

End of Book Ten of the *Engi-shiki*
  Enchō 5th Year, 12th Month, 26th Day
    [same signatures as at end of Book Six]

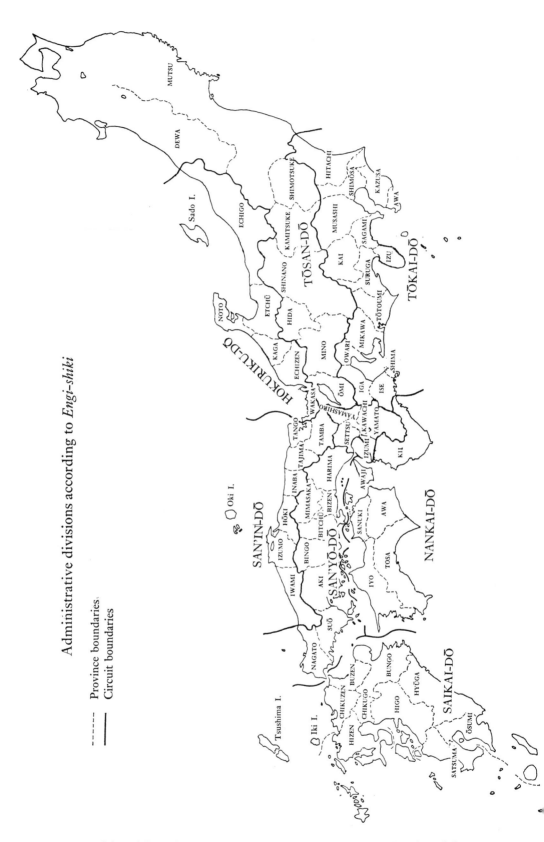

Administrative divisions according to *Engi-shiki*

----- Province boundaries.
—— Circuit boundaries

Adopted from Torao Toshiya's *Engi-shiki* (vol. 8, *Nihon rekishi sōsho* series)

# TABLE OF MEASUREMENTS

I MEASURE OF LENGTH (for cloth, etc.):

    1 *bu* 分   = 0.15 inch

    10 *bu* 分   = 1 *sun*   = 1.5 in.

    10 *sun* 寸   = 1 *shaku* = 1.243 ft.

    10 *shaku* 尺 = 1 *jō* 丈 = 4.14 yds.

    1 *tan* 反 or 段 = varies from 2 *jō* 8 *shaku* up to 4 *jō*, according to textile type

    1 *hiki* 疋 or 匹 = 2 *tan* (50 to 80 *shaku*)

    1 *ryō* 兩 = 1 *hiki* or 2 *tan* ('a double')

    1 *ryō* 了 = 7 *shaku* (?)

II CAPACITY:

    1 *tsubu* (or *ka*) 顆   = a grain (of rice, cereal, etc.)

    1 *satsu* 撮   = a pinch (0.0048 oz.)

    10 *satsu*   = 1 *sai* (0.048 oz.)

    10 *sai* 才   = 1 *shaku*   = 0.03 pint

    10 *shaku* 勺   = 1 *gō*   = 0.31 pint

    10 *gō* 合   = 1 *shō*   = 3.18 pints

    10 *shō* 升   = 1 *to*   = *c.* 4 gals.

    10 *to* 斗   = 1 *koku* 石 or 斛 = *c.* 4.9 bushels

    1 *wa* (or *taba*) 把   = 'a bundle'

    1 *soku* (or *tsuka*) 束 = 10 *wa* (except in 'small tax', when it equals one *wa*)

    1 *hyō* 俵, a bale   = 4 *to*

  Variables:

    1 *tan* 擔 'a burden'

    1 *i* 圍 'an armload'

    1 *kago* 籠 'basketful'

III WEIGHT:

    12 *bu* 分   = 1 *shu*

    24 *shu* 銖   = 1 *ryō*

    16 *ryō* 兩   = 1 *kin* 斤 = 1.32 lbs.

    1 *mochi* (or *ton*) 屯   = 10 *ryō* (*c.* 13 oz.)

             *Wamyōshō* says: 6 *ryō* (*c.* 7.8 oz.) = 1 *mochi*

    1 *ko* 絢   = 1 skein of thread:

         fine thread, 1 *ko* = 4 *ryō*

         medium thread, 1 *ko* = 5 *ryō*

         coarse thread, 1 *ko* = 7 *ryō*

    *tei* 廷 ingot, or bar (of metals)

IV LINEAR MEASURE:

    1 *chō* 町   = 60 *ken* 間   (*c.* 119 yds.)

    1 *ri* 里   = 36 *chō* 町   (*c.* 2.44 miles)

V AREA:

    1 *tan* 段 or 端 = 9.9 ares; 0.24 acre

    1 *chō* 町 = 10 *tan* or 3,000 *tsubo* (*c.* 2.45 acres)

VI COINAGE:

    1 *mon* 文   = a copper coin

    1 *kan* 貫   = 1,000 *mon* = 'a string of cash'

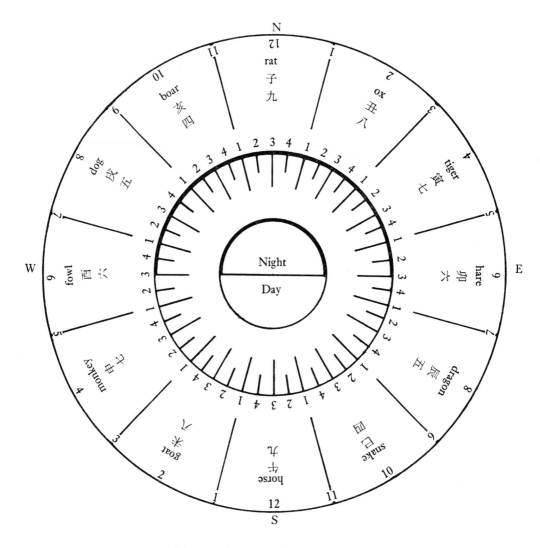

Diagram of Intervals of Day and Night

# APPENDIX I

## LIST OF PRINCESSES WHO SERVED
## AT KAMO SHRINES

### (*Kamo Saiin-ki*)[1]

| | | APPOINTED BY | YEAR | A.D. |
|---|---|---|---|---|
| 1 | *Uchiko Naishinnō* 有智子内親王, 2nd or 8th daughter of Saga Tennō. | Saga Tennō | Kōnin 14 or Kōnin 1 | 823 810 |
| 2 | *Tokiko Naishinnō* 時子, 9th daughter of Nimmyō Tennō. | Junna T. | Tenchō 8 | 831 |
| 3 | *Takako Naishinnō* 高子, 12th daughter of Nimmyō T. | Junna T. | Tenchō 10 | 833 |
| 4 | *Keishi Naishinnō* 惠子, 8th daughter of Montoku T. | Nimmyō T. | Kashō 3 | 850 |
| 5 | *Nobuko Naishinnō* 述子, 5th daughter of Montoku T. | Montoku T. | Ten'an 1 | 857 |
| 6 | *Noriko Naishinnō* 儀子, 3rd daughter of Montoku T. | Seiwa T. | Jōgan 1 | 859 |
| 7 | *Atsuko Naishinnō* 敦子, 10th daughter of Seiwa T. | Yōzei T. | Genkei 1 | 877 |
| 8 | *Bokushi Naishinnō* 穆子, 7th daughter of Kōkō T. | Yōzei T. | Genkei 8 | 884 |
| 9 | *Chokushi Nyoō* 直子女王, daughter of Prince Korehiko (chief of the Ministry of Central Affairs). | Kōkō T. | Ninna 5 | 889 |
| 10 | *Kimiko Naishinnō* 君子, 10th daughter of Uda Tennō. | Uda T. | Kampyō 5 | 893 |
| 11 | *Kyōshi Naishinnō* 恭子, 19th (?) daughter of Daigo T. | Daigo T. | Engi 3 | 903 |
| 12 | *Nobuko Naishinnō* 宣子, 2nd daughter of Daigo T. | Daigo T. | Engi 15 | 915 |
| 13 | *Akiko Naishinnō* 韶子, 13th (?) daughter of Daigo T. | Daigo T. | Engi 21 | 921 |
| 14 | *Enshi Naishinnō* 婉子, 7th daughter of Daigo T. | Suzaku T. | Shōhei 1 | 931 or 932 |
| 15 | *Takako Naishinnō* 尊子, 2nd daughter of Reizei-In. | Reizei T. | Anwa 1 | 968 |
| 16 | *Senshi Naishinnō* 選子, also called *Dai* | En'yū T. | Ten'en 3 | 975 |

---

[1] Based on *Gunsho ruijū*, III, *Kamo Saiin-ki*; and Takamure Itsue, *Dai Nihon josei jimmei jisho*.

*Sai-In* 大齋院, 10th daughter of
Murakami T.

| | | | | |
|---|---|---|---|---|
| 17 *Keishi Naishinnō* 馨子, 2nd daughter of Go-Ichijō T. | Go-Ichijō | Chōgan 4 | 1031 |
| 18 *Kenshi Naishinnō* 娟子, 3rd daughter of Go-Suzaku-In. | Go-Suzaku-In | Chōgan 9 | 1036 |
| 19 *Baishi Naishinnō* 禖子, 4th daughter of Go-Suzaku-In. | Go-Suzaku-In | Kantoku 3 | 1046 |
| 20 *Masako Naishinnō* 正子, 5th or 6th daughter of Go-Suzaku-In. | Go-Reizei | Tenki 6 | 1058 |
| 21 *Yoshiko Naishinnō* 佳子, 6th daughter of Go-Sanjō-In. | Go-Sanjō-In | Enkyū 1 | 1069 |
| 22 *Atsuko Naishinnō* 篤子, 4th or 7th daughter of Go-Sanjō-In. | Shirakawa T. | Enkyū 5 | 1073 |
| 23 *Saishi Naishinnō* 齊子, 5th daughter of Ko-Ichijō-In, granddaughter of Sanjō-In. | Shirakawa T. | Shōhō 1 | 1074 |
| 24 *Reishi Naishinnō* 令子, 8th daughter of Shirakawa-In, also called *Nijō Daigū* 二條大宮. | Horikawa T. | Kanji 2 | 1088 |
| 25 *Teishi Naishinnō* 禎子, 9th daughter of Shirakawa-In, also called *Tsuchimikado Sai-In.* | Horikawa T. | Kōwa 1 | 1099 |
| 26 *Kanshi Naishinnō* 官子, daughter of Shirakawa-In (or Toba-In), also known as *Seiwa-In Sai-In.* | Toba T. | Tennin 1 | 1108 |
| 27 *Sōshi Naishinnō* 悰子, 3rd daughter of Horikawa-In. | Toba T. | Hoan 4 | 1123 |
| 28 *Junshi Naishinnō* 恂子, daughter of Toba-In, also known as *Jōsai-mon'in.* | Sutoku T. | Taiji 3 | 1128 |
| 29 *Kishi Naishinnō* 禧子, 1st daughter of Toba-In. | Sutoku T. | Chōshō 1 | 1132 |
| 30 *Ishi Nyoō* 怡子女王, daughter of Prince Sukehito, granddaughter of Go-Sanjō-In, also known as *Kita-koji Sai-In.* | Sutoku T. | Chōshō 2 | 1133 |
| 31 *Shikishi Naishinnō* 式子, daughter of Go-Shirakawa-In. | Nijō T. | Heiji 1 | 1159 |
| 32 *Zenshi Naishinnō* 繕子, 2nd daughter of Nijō-In. | Takakura T. | Kaō 1 | 1169 |
| 33 *Noriko Naishinnō* 範子, daughter of Takakura-In, also known as *Bōmon'in.* | Takakura T. | Jishō 2 | 1178 |
| *34 *Reishi Naishinnō* 禮子, 11th daughter of Go-Toba-In; given name of *Kayō-mon'in.* | Tsuchimi-kado T. | Genkyū 1 | 1204 |
| * The *Kamo chūshin zakki* here included *Koshi*, daughter of Toba-In. | Takakura T. | Shōan 1 | 1171 |

# APPENDIX II

# TABLE OF CONTENTS OF BOOKS IX AND X

## CONTENTS OF BOOK IX

## CONTENTS OF BOOK X

| | | |
|---|---|---|
| Shinano | 48 | 144 |
| Kōzuke (Kamitsuke) | 12 | 145 |
| Shimotsuke | 11 | 145 |
| Mutsu (Michinoku) | 100 | 145 |
| Dewa | 9 | 148 |
| Total Tōsandō | 382 | |
| **Hokurikudō** | | |
| Wakasa | 42 | 148 |
| Echizen | 126 | 149 |
| Kaga | 42 | 150 |
| Noto | 43 | 151 |
| Etchū | 34 | 151 |
| Echigo | 56 | 152 |
| Sado | 9 | 153 |
| Total Hokurikudō | 352 | |
| **San'indō** | | |
| Tamba | 71 | 153 |
| Tango | 65 | 154 |
| Tajima | 131 | 155 |
| Inaba | 50 | 157 |
| Hōki (Hahaki) | 6 | 157 |
| Izumo | 187 | 157 |
| Iwami | 34 | 160 |
| Oki | 16 | 161 |
| Total San'indō | 560 | |
| **San'yōdō** | | |
| Harima | 50 | 161 |
| Mimasaka | 11 | 162 |
| Bizen | 26 | 162 |
| Bitchū | 18 | 163 |
| Bingo | 17 | 163 |
| Aki | 3 | 164 |
| Suō (Suhō) | 10 | 164 |
| Nagato | 5 | 164 |
| Total San'yōdō | 140 | |
| **Nankaidō** | | |
| Kii | 31 | 165 |
| Awaji | 13 | 165 |
| Awa (阿波) | 50 | 165 |
| Sanuki | 24 | 166 |
| Iyo | 24 | 167 |
| Tosa | 21 | 167 |
| Total Nankaidō | 163 | |
| **Saikaidō** | | |
| Chikuzen | 19 | 168 |

| | | |
|---|---|---|
| Chikugo | 4 | 168 |
| Buzen | 6 | 169 |
| Bungo | 6 | 169 |
| Hizen | 4 | 169 |
| Higo | 4 | 169 |
| Hyūga (Himuka) | 4 | 169 |
| Oosumi | 5 | 169 |
| Satsuma | 2 | 170 |
| Iki I. | 24 | 170 |
| Tsushima I. | 29 | 170 |
| Total Saikaidō | 107 | |

# BIBLIOGRAPHY

A. EDITIONS OF THE *Engi-shiki*

(All published in Tokyo, unless otherwise stated.)

Kōten-kōkyūsho 皇典講究所. *Kōtei Engi-shiki* 校訂延喜式, 3 vols., 1929.

Kuroita Katsumi 黑板勝美, ed. *Shintei-zōho kokushi-taikei* (2) 新訂增補國史大系, VIII, IX, X, *Engi-shiki*, 1955.

Mozume Takami 物集高見, ed. *Kōgaku-sōsho* 皇學叢書, III, *Engi-shiki*, 1927.

Ookura Kunihiko 大倉邦彥, ed. *Shinten* 神典, Yokohama, 1936.

B. REFERENCE WORKS

(All published in Tokyo, unless otherwise stated.)

*Daigenkai* 大言海. Ootsuki Fumihiko 大槻文彥, comp., 4 vols. and index, 1937.

*Daikanwa jiten* 大漢和辭典. Morohashi Tetsuji 諸橋轍次, comp., 13 vols., 1955–60.

*Dai Nihon josei jimmei jisho* 大日本女性人名辭典. Takamure Itsue 高群逸枝, 1939.

*Dai Nihon kokugo jiten* 大日本國語辭典. Ueda Kazutoshi 上田萬年 and Matsui Kanji 松井簡治, comp., 4 vols. and index, 1915–28.

*Fūzoku jiten* 風俗辭典. Sakamoto Tarō 坂本太郎, comp., 3rd ed., 1958.

*Jimmei jisho* 神名辭書. Meiji jinja shiryō henshūjo 明治神社資料編輯所, 1921.

*Kogo jiten* 古語辭典. Kindaichi Kyōsuke 金田一京助 and Kindaichi Haruhiko 金田一春彥, comp., 1963.

*Kotoba no izumi* 言泉. Ochiai Naobumi 落合直文, ed., 5 vols. and index, 1921–9.

*Nihon rekishi daijiten* 日本歷史大辭典. 24 vols. Kawade Shobō, 1956–61.

*Nihon shakai minzoku jiten* 日本社會民俗辭典. Nihon shakai minzoku-gaku kyōkai 日本社會民俗學協會, comp., 4 vols., 1952–60.

*Nihon shokubutsu zukan* 日本植物圖鑑. Makino Tomitarō 牧野富太郎, 1929.

*Norito jiten* 祝詞辭典. Uda Toshihiko 菟田俊彥, 1963.

*Shikimei daijiten* 色名大辭典. Wada Mitsuzō 和田三造, comp., 1954.

*Shintō daijiten* 神道大辭典. Shimonaka Yasaburō 下中彌三郎, comp., 3 vols., 1937–40.

*Shintō jiten* 神道辭典. Anzu Motohiko 安津素彥 and Umeda Yoshihiko 梅田義彥, 1969.

*Shōsōin hōmotsu* 正倉院寶物. *Senshoku* 染織. Shōsōin Office, 1963–4.

*Tokusen jimmyō-chō* 特選神名牒. Naimushō 內務省, 1925.

*Wamyō ruijūshō* 倭名類聚鈔. Minamoto Shitagau 源順, comp., Enchō era (923–30). '*Wa-myōshō*' 和名抄.

C. BOOKS AND ARTICLES IN JAPANESE

(Published in Tokyo, unless otherwise stated.)

Abe Takehiko 阿部武彥. 'Engi-shiki jimmyō-chō no jinkakujin' 延喜式神名帳の人格神 *The Annual Reports on Cultural Science*. Fac. of Lit., Hokkaido Univ., 4 (March 1955), pp. 77–94.

Aida Hanji 會田範治. *Chūkai yōrō-ryō* 註解養老令, 1964.

Aoki Norimoto 靑木紀本. 'Norito-shiki no seikaku' 祝詞式の性格, *Geirin* 藝林, III, 4 (August 1951), pp. 19–35.

*Ban Nobutomo zenshū* 伴信友全集 (vol. 1) 第一. *Jimmyō-chō kōshō* 神名帳考證, 1907. (Comp. & ed., Ichijima Kaneyoshi.)

Ema Tsutomu 江馬務. *Shinshū yūsoku kojitsu* 新修有職故實, Kyoto, 1942.

Honda Masaji 本田正次. *Nihon shokubutsu meii* 日本植物名彙 *(Nomina plantarum japonicarum)*, 1963.

*Kamo Saiin-ki* 賀茂齋院記, in *Gunsho ruijū* 群書類從, III, pp. 3–9.

Kamo Wakeikazuchi Jinja 賀茂別雷神社. *Kamo chūshin zakki* 賀茂注進雜記, Kyoto, 1940.

Kaneko Takeo 金子武雄. *Engi-shiki norito-kō* 延喜式祝詞講, 1951.

*Kojiruien* 古事類苑. Articles: 'Daijō-sai', VII, in *Jingi-bu* II; 'Sai-in', IX, in *Jingi-bu* IV, pp. 1169–1240. 1935.

Komura Shōun 小村昭雲. *Man'yō shokubutsu zakan* 萬葉植物圖鑑, 1968.

Koyama Shūzō 小山修三. 'Kodai awabi sangyō no hattatsu' 古代アワビ産業の發達, *Koku-shigaku*, 81, March 1970, pp. 18–39.

——. 'Shintō ni okeru ikon hassei no genryū' 神道における偶像發生の源流, *Jimbungaku kenkyū*, 6, June 1971, pp. 107–24.

——. 'Shitsuoribe no kōkogakuteki kōsatsu' 倭文部の考古學的考察, *Jōdai bunka*, 38, Oct. 1969, pp. 14–25.

Kurita Hiroshi 栗田寬. *Kofudoki itsubun* 古風土記逸文, 1934.

Kusaka Tōsaku 日下東作 and Yamaguchi Nobuo 山口信雄, eds. *Gotairei kiroku* 御大禮記錄, Asahi shimbun gōshi gaisha, Osaka, 1916.

Matsuoka Shizuo 松岡靜雄. *Nihon kozoku-shi* 日本古俗誌, 1927.

Miyagi Eishō 宮城榮昌. *Engi-shiki no kenkyū*, 2 vols., 1955–7.

Miyaji Naokazu 宮地直一. *Jingi-shi taikei* 神祇史大系, 1942.

Miyaji Naokazu, Yamamoto Nobunari 山本信哉, and Kōno Shōzō 河野省三, eds. *Ooharae no kotoba chūshaku taisei* 大祓詞註釋大成, 1941.

Nishitsunoi Masayoshi 西角井正慶. *Kodai saishi to bungaku* 古代祭祀と文學, 1966.

Numabe Harutomo 沼部春友. 'Jinja saishi ni okeru kyōzen' 神社祭祀における饗膳, *Shintō shūkyō*, 20th anniv. ed., 1970, pp. 111–22.

Oobayashi, Taryō 大林太良. *Nihon shinwa no kigen* 日本神話の起源, 1965.

Oota Akira 太田亮 *Nihon jōdai shakai soshiki no kenkyū* 日本上代社會組織の研究, 1955.

——. *Nihon kodai-shi shin-kenkyū* 日本古代史新研究, 1928.

Origuchi Shinobu 折口信夫. *Kodai kenkyū* (II) 古代研究, *Kokubungaku-hen*, 1929.

Rikkokushi sakuin henshūbu, comp. *Rikkokushi sakuin* 六國史索引, 4 vols.: (1) *Nihon-shoki*; (2) *Shoku-nihongi*; (3) *Nihon-kōki, Shoku-nihon-kōki, Montoku-jitsuroku*; (4) *Sandai-jitsuroku*, 1967.

Saeki Ariyoshi 佐伯有義. 'Daijō-sai no enkaku oyobi igi' 大嘗祭の沿革及び意義, *Kokugakuin zasshi* 34: 7, pp. 27–38.

*Saiin-ki.* See *Kamo Saiin-ki.*

Sakamoto Tarō 坂本太郎. *Taika kaishin no kenkyū* 大化改新の研究, 1938.

Sakurai Katsunoshin 櫻井勝之進. *Ise jingū*, 1969.

Shiga Gō 志賀剛. *Shikinai-sha no kenkyū* (1) 式內社の研究, Kyoto, 1960.

Shiraishi Mitsukuni 白石光邦. *Norito no kenkyū*, 1960.

Takeda Yūkichi 武田祐吉. *Kami to kami wo matsuru mono to no bungaku* 神と神を祭る者との文學 (上代文學の研究第一篇), 1943.

——. *Kokubungaku kenkyū: jingi bungaku-hen.* 國文學研究；神祇文學篇, 1937.

Takikawa Masajirō 瀧川政次郎. *Ritsuryō no kenkyū* 律令の研究, 1966.

Torao Toshiya 虎尾俊哉. *Engi-shiki*, 1964.

Tsuda Sōkichi 津田左右吉. *Jōdai Nihon no shakai oyobi shisō* 上代日本の社會及び思想, 1933.

Tsugita Jun 次田潤. *Norito shinkō* 祝詞新講, 1927.

Tsukushi Nobuzane 筑紫申眞. *Amaterasu no tanjō* アマテラスの誕生, 1965.

Umeda Yoshihiko 梅田義彦. *Jingiseido-shi no kisoteki kenkyū* 神祇制度史の基礎的研究, 1964.

Wada Eishō 和田英松. 'Go-sokui-rei daijō-sai no enkaku', *Kokugakuin zasshi*, 21:9 (1915), pp. 1–79.

Yamada Yoshio 山田孝雄. *Nara-chō bumpō-shi* 奈良朝文法史, 1961.

### D. BOOKS AND ARTICLES IN WESTERN LANGUAGES

Abbreviations:

BSOAS     *Bulletin of the School of Oriental and African Studies*
MN     *Monumenta Nipponica*
TASJ     *Transactions of the Asiatic Society of Japan*

Aoki, Michiko Yamaguchi. *Izumo fudoki*, Sophia University, Tokyo, 1971.

Aston, William G. *Nihongi, Chronicles of Japan; from the earliest times to A.D. 697*, I, II, London, 1896.

Bachofen, Johann Jakob. *Mutterrecht und Urreligion*, Leipzig, 1927.

Brinkley, Frank. *An Unabridged Japanese-English Dictionary*, Tokyo, 1896.

Casal, U. A. 'Some Notes on the *Sakazuki* and on the Role of *Sake* Drinking in Japan', *TASJ* (2), XIX (1940), pp. 1–186.

Dumoulin, Heinrich, tr. 'Kamo Mabuchi's Erklärung des norito zum Toshigoi-no-matsuri', *MN*, XIX (1956), pp. 101–30.

Florenz, Karl Adolph. *Die historischen Quellen der Shinto-Religion aus dem Altjapanischen und Chinesischen übersetzt und erklärt*. . . . . [contains *Kojiki, Nihongi, Kogoshūi*], Göttingen, 1919.

Gundert, Wilhelm. *Japanische Religionsgeschichte*, Tokyo, Stuttgart, 1935.

Holtom, Daniel Clarence. *The Japanese Enthronement Ceremonies*, Kyōbunkwan, Tokyo 1928; reprinted by Sophia University, Tokyo, 1972.

——. *The National Faith of Japan*, New York, 1938.

——. 'The Storm God Theme in Japanese Mythology', *Sociologus*, VI, 1 (1956), pp. 44–56.

Katō, Genchi and Hoshino, Hikoshirō. *Kogoshūi: Gleanings from Ancient Stories*, 3rd ed., Tokyo, 1925.

Kōno, Shōzō. 'The Hitachi-Fudoki, or Records of Customs and Land of Hitachi', tr. Sakai Atsuharu, *Cultural Nippon*, VIII, 2 (1940), pp. 145–81; 3, pp. 109–56; 4, pp. 137–86.

Lewin, Bruno. *Aya und Hata: Bevölkerungsgruppen Altjapans kontinentaler Herkunft*, Wiesbaden, 1962.

Miller, Richard James. *A Study of the Development of a Centralized Japanese Government Prior to the Taika Reform (A.D. 645)*, Ph.D. Thesis, Berkeley, California, 1953.

Mills, Douglas Edward. 'The Takahasi uzibumi', repr. fr. *BSOAS*, XVI, 1 (1954), pp. 113–33.

Philippi, Donald L. *Kojiki, Translated with an Introduction and Notes*, Tokyo, 1968.

——. *Norito, a New Translation of the Ancient Japanese Ritual Prayers*, Tokyo, 1959.

Ponsonby-Fane, Richard A. B. *Divine Spirits of Shinto and Hirota Jinja*, Kyoto, 1934.

——. *Kamo Mioya Shrine*, Kyoto, London, 1934.

Rabbitt, James A. Rice in the Cultural Life of the Japanese People', *TASJ* (2), XIX (1940), pp. 187–257.

Reischauer, Robert Karl. *Early Japanese History*, A and B, Princeton, 1937.

Sansom, George Bailey. 'Early Japanese Law and Administration', Pt. I, *TASJ* (2), IX (1932), pp. 67–109; Pt. II, XI (1934), pp. 117–49.

Satow, Ernest. 'Ancient Japanese Rituals', Pt. I, *TASJ* (1), VII, pp. 97–132; Pt. 2, VII, pp. 393–434; Pt. III, IX, pp. 183–211.

——. *The Revival of Pure Shintau*, *TASJ*, Tokyo, 1879.

Snellen, J. B. 'Shoku-Nihongi, Chronicles of Japan, Continued from 697–391 A.D.', Pt. I, *TASJ* (2), XI (1934), pp. 151–239; Pt. II, XIV (1937), pp. 209–78.

Tange, Kenzō and Kawazoe, Noboru. *Ise, Prototype of Japanese Architecture*, Cambridge, Mass., 1965.

Thunberg, C. P. *Miscellaneous Papers Regarding Japanese Plants,* Tokyo, 1935.

Yamane, Tokutarō. *The Naniwa Courts and the Sumiyoshi Shrine (Naniwa no chōtei to Sumiyoshi Taisha)*. Historical Research Association for the Site of the Forbidden City of Naniwa. Osaka City University, Osaka, 1969 (in Japanese and English).

Zachert, Herbert. *Semmyō, die kaiserlichen Erlasse des Shoku-Nihongi*, Berlin, 1950.

# KEY

References given indicate passages where the entries are explained, defined, analyzed, or treated for some length.

## A

Abstinence, 13, 33 *and* n.141, n.166, n.280
Accession, n.12, 27
*Aidono*, 110
*Ainame* Festival, n.67
Amaterasu-ō-mikami, 1 *and* n.2, n.307, n.316, 94, n.427, 109
*Amatsu-kami, kunitsu-kami*, n.301
*Amatsu kami no yogoto*, n.418
*Ame-no-hina-dori*, 103
Ame-no-ho-hi, n.465, 103, 104

Ame-no-koyane, 65, n.292
Ame-no-waka-hiko, n.451
*Aoi* Festival, 6
Aramatsuri Shrine, n.430
*Arame*, n.150
*Ason/asomi*, n.1, n.120
Asuha, n.157
August districts, n.320, n.334, n.336
*Awabi*, n.28

## B

Bell, post-station, n.175
Blue print *(aozuri)*, n.221
Boundaries, deities of, n.294, n.415

Brewers, n.194, n.195
Buraku-in, n.263

## C

Caretakers, Palace, n.55
Carriage, n.62
Ceremonial, Ministry of, n.265
Chieftain, n.257, n.336, n.458
*Chinka-sai*, 89–90, n.410
*Chinkon-sai*, 4, n.164, 45, 93–4
Chōdō-in, n.196
Cinnabar, n.472, 109
Circuits, seven, n.130
Cloth, *aratae no miso*, n.241; bark-cloth, n.19; *corvée*/tax, n.31, n.70; for ceremonial dress, 16; hemp, n.19, n.52, n.91; *hosonuno*, n.91; medium of exchange, n.167; Mōda, n.210;

*nigitae no miso*, n.234; pongee, n.27; *sayomi*, n.70; *shizu/shidori*, n.52; silk (stiff, flossy), n.51, n.53, n.71; silk damask of Wu, n.77; tribute, n.93; *ungen*, n.107; *usuginu*, n.79
Cloth items, lists of, 11, 12, 15, 16, 17, 18, 20–1, 22–3, 25, 32, 33, 35, 36, 39, 40, 41, 42, 44, 45, 47, 49, 53, 56
Clothing. *See* Garments *and* Raiment
Controller, n.35, n.243, n.447
Cooking compound, 36; preparations, 43–4, 49, 52
Counselor, n.271
Curtain, wall, n.108

## D

Daijō-gū, construction of, 41–2
*Daijō-sai*, 27–56 (esp. 50–6), n.418
*Dajō-kan*, n.59, n.142
Dances, n.255, n.274, n.275, n.277, n.278, n.279, n.280
Defilement, n.163, n.377, n.380, n.383, n.384, n.396, n.398

Deities of Heaven and Earth, n.132
Deity, Great, n.133
Deity households, n.7, n.176, n.435, n.436; raiment, 37–8, n.234, n.241; seat, 5, n.245
Divers *(katsukime)*, n.186
Divination, n.15, n.341, n.398
Diviner, assistants, n.140; chief, n.49; of rice-